Luminos is the Open Access monograph publishing program from UC Press. Luminos provides a framework for preserving and reinvigorating monograph publishing for the future and increases the reach and visibility of important scholarly work. Titles published in the UC Press Luminos model are published with the same high standards for selection, peer review, production, and marketing as those in our traditional program. www.luminosoa.org

A Burdensome Experiment

A Burdensome Experiment

*Race, Labor, and Schools
in New Orleans after Katrina*

Christien Philmarc Tompkins

UNIVERSITY OF CALIFORNIA PRESS

University of California Press
Oakland, California

Suggested citation: Tompkins, C. P. *A Burdensome Experiment: Race, Labor, and Schools in New Orleans after Katrina*. Oakland: University of California Press, 2024. DOI: https://doi.org/10.1525/luminos.204

Cataloging-in-Publication Data is on file at the Library of Congress.

ISBN 978-0-520-40094-8 (pbk.)
ISBN 978-0-520-40096-2

33 32 31 30 29 28 27 26 25 24
10 9 8 7 6 5 4 3 2 1

CONTENTS

ACKNOWLEDGMENTS

I would first like to thank the educators, activists, and families in New Orleans whose generosity and dedication to students have sustained this project from its inception. I can't name you all here, but I continue to be overwhelmingly grateful for the time and space you gave to harbor my inquiries. Across the polarized landscape of education reform, I found great conviction but also a willingness to be vulnerable and reflective about the promise and failures of charter schools. I want to single out Black educators in particular for taking me under their wing. When I was still figuring out what questions to ask or who to talk to, you all lifted me up with your dedication to your calling but also your certainty that your story and my telling of it was important.

I settled on a committee early on in graduate school and their guidance has proven invaluable. In spite of the rumors that Chicago Anthropology can be a cruel and competitive environment, Joe Masco worked to make sure that, from the first days of Systems, my cohort and I felt confident and secure enough to see each other not as rivals but as each other's greatest allies. As a teacher,

I know this is no easy task. As chair of my committee, Joe was more responsive and supportive than I could have hoped for. Beyond his intellectual shaping of the project, he helped me to step into a fractious ethnographic landscape and regard everyone I encountered as a potential teacher, an orientation that opened up many opportunities to learn. I could not have asked for a better guide to New Orleans than Shannon Dawdy. There are many ways that Hurricane Katrina has been positioned as a kind of radical break for the city, and it is easy to be seduced into this perspective while doing ethnography there. Shannon has always encouraged me to root my inquiry in the deep history of this place and to not recreate in my own work the kind of tabula rasa that certain kinds of reformers imagined they were working with after the storm and levee failures. No one asks questions like Kaushik Sunder Rajan. Whether in class or at Monday seminar, Kaushik has a way of asking a five-part question that challenges you in ways that you had not anticipated but also reflects a deep engagement with and enthusiasm for your work. Kaushik has always affirmed and nurtured the political urgency of this project while he illuminated the larger philosophical stakes.

This project would not have been possible without the generosity and support of a number of organizations and agencies. The Mellon Mays Undergraduate Fellowship and the Ford Foundation Predoctoral Fellowship gave me not only the security to pursue my work but a community of diverse scholars and mentors to sustain it. In particular, MMUF has provided invaluable guidance on a career in academia since I was a junior in college. The Center for the Study of Race, Politics, and Culture at the University of Chicago provided a timely summer research grant that allowed to me to broaden my perspective on education reform with visits to London and Philadelphia. The Hymen Milgrom Supporting

Organization and the University of Chicago Committee on Education provided a very generous field research grant, allowing a deeper ethnographic engagement than might have otherwise been possible. None of this would have been doable without the logistical support of the Anthropology Department administrator, Anne Ch'ien. I don't know how she did it all, but I appreciate every timely response to a request for recommendation letters or a panicked email! Kevin O'Neill and Kate Marshall saw enough promise in this work, which was accepted when I was only a postdoctoral scholar, to include it in the Atelier series at the University of California Press and have been incredibly generous and patient through the ups and downs of life and the writing process. The final completion of the manuscript was greatly assisted by the Early Career Faculty Fellowship at the Rutgers University Institute for The Study of Global Racial Justice and, ultimately, by a much-appreciated sabbatical facilitated by the Hunt Postdoctoral Writing Fellowship from the Wenner-Gren Foundation.

Components of chapter 1 appeared in "There's No Such Thing as a Bad Teacher: Reconfiguring Race and Talent in Post-Katrina Charter Schools," *Souls* 17, no. 3–4 (2015). A truncated version of chapter 4 was published as "Pitch Black: How Design Entrepreneurs Are Rethinking Race in Post-Katrina Schools," *American Anthropologist* 126, no. 2 (2024). I am grateful for the editorial guidance of both journals and for permission to include the material in this work.

I have benefitted tremendously from an extended network of mentors. A group of alumni of color from the Anthropology Department have supported me since my early days in graduate school, taking me under their wing when I know that the demands of the tenure track must have been strenuous. Michael Ralph, Laurence Ralph, Jonathan Rosa, and Yarimar Bonilla have lit the way forward, and I am happy to follow. Cathy Cohen provided a model of engaged and intersectional scholarship that has inspired me along the way. I will always remember immediately buying every book she recommended after our first office hours appointment. Adolph Reed was kind enough to sit with me at the Wilder House on campus for three hours when I was just a first-year grad student with a glimmer of a project and facilitated many of my early connections in New Orleans. His strident and withering critiques of the ruling classes, Black and white, remind me that the generosity of the ethnographic encounter must be adequate to the urgent political stakes of the moment. A number of other scholars have been very kind in their responses to requests big and small over the years—too many to list.

I have such deep love and admiration for my cohort and fellow graduate students at the University of Chicago. I look back fondly at the potluck dinners that extended late into the night early in grad school. Meghan Morris, Karma Frierson, Eric Hirsch, Andrea Ford, Azara Golston, Jeremy Siegman, and Jay Schutte—you have all been such good friends and amazing colleagues. Beyond my cohort, I want to thank the US Locations workshop family, Kaya Williams, Molly Cunningham, Alex Blanchette, and Joey Weiss. You managed to create an invigorating intellectual community for an area of study once considered marginal in the discipline. I'm also grateful for the friends and colleagues I've grown with and learned from in the broader discipline through conferences and workshops—Savannah Shange, Ryan Jobson, Vivian Lu, Aisha Ghani, Samar Al-Bulushi, Christopher Loperena, Shreya Subramani, Sarah Besky, Orisanmi Burton, Cassie Fennell. My colleagues at Rutgers Anthropology have been incredibly kind and supportive in a tumultuous time—I was only on campus for a brief period before the pandemic upended our lives. The socio-cultural faculty, Angelique Haugerud, Louisa Schein, David Hughes, Parvis Ghassem-Fachandi, Ulla Berg, Zeynep Gursel, Omar Dewachi, and Becky Schulties have modeled generous scholarship and mentorship, and the Rutgers faculty union has inspired me with its willingness to fight for a profession rooted in principles of solidarity and social justice.

While I may have a doctorate in Anthropology, my intellectual heart will always be in African American and Ethnic Studies, and Columbia University was the perfect place to build a foundation in these fields. When I was a freshman in college and still thought I might want to be a politician who loved history and philosophy, Robin D. G. Kelley's "Black Movements" class taught me that the divide between political practice and rigorous intellectual inquiry is a false binary. In moments of political despair, I think back to how Robin would inspire us by guiding our attention to the work happening outside of the spotlight in the grassroots. I was overjoyed to work with him again as a postdoc at UCLA and I continue to heed his reminder to do the work not because it's a career but because it's important. I benefitted from many other mentors at the Institute for Research in African American Studies and the Center for the Study of Ethnicity and Race. Nick De Genova introduced me to Anthropology with a critical lens and has always shown me the importance of maintaining the courage of your convictions. Steven Gregory taught me how to do urban ethnography and playfully reminded me to not "become an asshole" when I left for graduate school at Chicago. Manning Marable provided a model of public and collective scholarship that I deeply admire. Going forward, I will carry his commitment to mentoring as a sacred responsibility.

Above all, I have been supported and sustained in this endeavor by my family. They have invested so much in me over the years, and I could never begin to convey the depth of my gratitude. In particular, my mother, Angelique Tompkins, tirelessly pursued every opportunity for me to receive an education and better myself, whether it was using "alternate addresses" to get me into a better elementary school across town, convincing my high school to pay for a philosophy summer camp at Stanford, or facilitating connections with potential colleagues and research subjects to this day. She did all this even when it meant letting me go out into the world for good. Although she did have to call me back for ten minutes of picture taking after she and my father dropped me off at college.

Jennifer Oki, you are my joy, my inspiration, and my partner in all things. You are my first and most important interlocutor, from those days at Columbia in the IRAAS seminar room, the Malcolm X Lounge, and the Intercultural Resource Center to Chicago, London, New Orleans, Ghana, Brooklyn, Tokyo, and Los Angeles. You opened up the world to me and have always pushed me to be my best self. I've never met anyone more dedicated, loyal, loving, and courageous. I could not ask for a better companion as we raise our son Hani to be a kind and brave citizen of the world. He humbles and inspires us every day and brings us together in ways I never anticipated.

My father, Irving Frank Tompkins, passed away suddenly during the final year of writing the dissertation that led to this book. In his eulogy, I reflected upon the ways that he nurtured my intellectual curiosity from a young age, in part by being a supportive listener. My father thought everyone's stories, aspirations, hopes, fears, and dreams were important and worthy of careful attention, no matter their station in life. I took this sensibility with me into the field. In 2015, on the last Father's Day we shared together, I wrote, "When I'm out doing field research and get nervous, I think about the ease with which my father can talk to anyone on the street, and I draw on his charisma for strength. Even when we're on separate coasts, we're still walking together." He used to address me as "Mr. Christien!" in a playful allusion to *Mutiny on the Bounty*. I had anticipated a playful change of title, but that will remain in my imagination.

Introduction

Great floods beget dreams of rebirth.[1] In the years following Hurricane Katrina, swarms of volunteers, entrepreneurs, and philanthropists descended upon New Orleans not only to help the city's residents recuperate and mourn but also to realize the dream of a revitalized urban landscape. Many of them sought a world unburdened by the practical and moral weight of entrenched racialized poverty, which had been compounded by decades of "aggressive neglect"—the abandonment of post-industrial urban centers by an attenuated welfare state (Ladson-Billings 2006). These newcomers and key local allies set upon their works—selectively rebuilding homes, businesses, and schools while shuttering or privatizing others—with religious fervor.[2] The most dramatic of these efforts—"education reform"—resulted in the first urban public school system in the United States of America entirely contracted out to private management.

What conditions enabled this stunning transformation? Months after Hurricane Katrina, under the aegis of a relatively new agency called the Recovery School District (RSD),[3] the state of Louisiana took control of the 90 percent of schools it deemed failing according to testing metrics mandated by state law. Promising a radical break with a past of bureaucratized incompetence and corruption and a model for the rapid improvement of test scores, graduation rates, and school safety, the state started on a path of converting nearly all public schools into charter schools. Then governor Kathleen Blanco claimed that this step was necessary for the recovery of the city since "families won't come back without good public schools."[4] At the same time, education reformers claimed that charter schools could "break the cycle of poverty" afflicting Black and brown low-income communities around the country. They sought to demonstrate that urban schools could be the key lever in improving the life chances of students in these communities (Chait 2015). In January of 2006 the Orleans Parish School Board mailed letters of termination to nearly eight thousand teachers and school employees of the New Orleans Public Schools, many of whom were still displaced and whose homes were yet uninhabitable. Working under the belief that an injection of fresh "talent" and "human capital" was necessary, charter school networks partnered with nonprofits, philanthropists, entrepreneurs, and politicians to recruit thousands of college seniors and "young professionals" from all over the United States to become teachers. At the beginning of this experiment, 94 percent of public school children in New Orleans were African American, 77 percent were under the poverty line, and over 80 percent of school employees were Black and often referred to by my informants as "the backbone of the Black middle class."[5] Over the next decade, the district teaching force became almost 50 percent white and largely without prior ties to New Orleans. By 2019, the RSD had closed, converted, or reopened every school under its supervision such that only privately managed charter schools remained.[6] This shift in the racial composition of school administration and conversion to a private management model on a district level is unprecedented.

New Orleans public schools became a crucible for a neoliberal takeover of education—a takeover that transformed not just schools but the labor that sustained them. Under the banners of private sector "innovation," "design thinking," "diversity," and "professionalism," education reformers dramatically altered expectations of who teachers should be and what kind of work they should do. Whereas in traditional public schools, teachers were evaluated by school and district administrators based on experience, work hours were clearly delimited, and connections to local communities were valued, in charter school networks, private nonprofit managers hired and retained teachers based on their perceived "fit" with the team culture of charter school brands. They favored young and inexperienced recruits with elite pedigrees whom school leaders judged to have the abstract talent and capacity to be coached on technical skills in the classroom. These new teachers were expected by their school leaders to work longer and harder hours than their predecessors and were subject to more frequent and intense forms of surveillance and evaluation. Charter school advocates valorized these new educators for their work ethic, yet, as at-will employees without a union contract, they had no formal recourse to challenge their working conditions. While these discourses of fit, talent, and work ethic were used to justify the recruitment of young, mostly white, elite teachers in the day-to-day workplace, they also functioned as techniques of selective inclusion and outright exclusion of veteran Black educators with local ties—despite the stated desires of school leaders to recruit faculty with experience and connections to students' communities.

The conversion to charter schools also profoundly altered the relationship between schools and the communities they served. In firing veteran teachers, getting rid of neighborhood school zones, and shifting from an ideal of community schools as civic institutions to a market-oriented, portfolio model of education as service provision, charter school advocates disrupted patterns of racialized leadership that had developed over the decades since the civil rights movement. While the mostly white reformers have gotten the lion's share of attention for remaking the New Orleans education system, under the radar, Black educators, nonprofit workers, and community activists have worked within charter schools and the expanded array of education nonprofits to compromise with and contest the privatization model. Black participation in reform efforts should be regarded as an expert and technical intervention rather than as a mystical power based on racial identity. White reformers were not able to unilaterally impose their will; Black participants in reform helped to re-articulate the charter school movement to a recomposed multicultural professional leadership class—one created by processes of selective inclusion and dependent on racialized expertise to sustain the legitimacy of the project. These expert interventions are themselves experiments in racialization whereby Black reformers not only reconfigured the terms of racial recognition in schooling but, as Black transplants intersected with local racial orders marked by creolism, they also partially reshaped the Black professional and leadership classes in New Orleans.

As the charter school project moved from the emergency footing of the first few years after Katrina to an enduring engagement with the city, segments of the reform community became dissatisfied with the strict discipline and conservative pedagogies of most charter schools and looked to Silicon Valley–influenced entrepreneurialism and "design thinking" for models for how to create more innovative schools and education products fit for a reconstituted constituency in public schools. In so doing, they also looked to incorporate the racial politics and fractures opened by the reform movement into ethnographically informed information economies as a way of recentering educators, students, and families as "users" of school services. By investigating education reform as a site of multiple kinds of work, I demonstrate the means by which charters not only changed labor practices but also transformed "racial regimes" rent asunder by the disruptions of Katrina and the plans of reformers and newcomers to the city.[7] New Orleans's charter school–based reform has been criticized for ignoring racial politics and the democratic will of the majority Black population of the city's public schools. A decade plus into the reform project, charter schools and education-reform organizations responded to these criticisms by developing increasingly sophisticated forms of racialized recognition and expertise. While the undemocratic foundations of these expert interventions may resonate with prior formations of white supremacy, charter school reforms are emblematic of a twenty-first century regime of multiracial technocratic governance.

This multiracial order evokes visions of liberty that flatter both neoliberal and American nationalist pretensions, but ultimately (though differentially) it bestows upon us the legacy of *a burdensome experiment*. The title of this book is inspired by Saidiya Hartman's theorization of "the burdened individuality of freedom" (1997). Charter schools were figured as "freedom schools" by proponents like RSD superintendent Paul Vallas. Parents were free to choose schools regardless of neighborhood. School leaders were free to hire and fire teachers at will. Teachers were freed of the strictures of unionization. Regarding Reconstruction,

Hartman asked, "How does one tell the story of an elusive emancipation and a travestied freedom?" (1997). She showed us how, in the aftermath of the Civil War, Black people were held accountable to notions of individual freedom that imposed more responsibility than they afforded liberty and that questioned their moral standing rather than honored their dignity. The neoliberal freedoms attributed to charter schools place upon educators and Black communities in New Orleans undeserved burdens and onerous debts. While experiment often implies novelty, here once again, Black people are called on to service obligations for which they are entirely unresponsible. This time around the collectors come in a range of hues.

DOING THE WORK

Sitting in the main office of a recently opened charter school in the Treme in the summer of 2011, I asked the founding principal, Pablo, "What kind of teachers are you looking for?" Pablo responded to my question without hesitation, with the pace of a man used to the almost impossibly urgent tempo of running a no excuses–style charter school. "We want people who can hit the ground running."[8] I pressed Pablo on where he got his teachers. I wanted to know what their backgrounds were. Pablo unapologetically replied, "We try to stay local, but it's hard to get quality. The teachers we have now, to be blunt, are smarter than they were ten years ago . . . I'm just focused on getting the best. I used to think it was about getting teachers who were mission driven and had cultural competency, but now *it's about doing the work*." The phrase "doing the work" is common in nonprofit circles more broadly and here represents one side of a tension within education-reform movements between narrowly technical definitions of schooling focused on quantitative measures and broader ideological projects. Education-reform organizations like Teach for America (TFA) have gone back and forth between focusing on quantitative results and hiring teachers who are "mission driven"—that is, teachers who believe and are invested in the big-picture goal of ending racialized and class-based educational inequity rather than being merely interested in affecting a specific classroom, school, or community. Over the course of the 2010s, insurgents within the organization pushed their selection models to increasingly focus on candidates' "mindsets" and perceptions of low-income communities of color, assessing whether they view these communities with "deficit mentalities" or express curiosity and empathy. Within TFA and related education nonprofits, others believed that the best teachers were those with records of achievement in elite colleges as well as with work ethics and organizational capacities that would accommodate the long hours demanded by charter schools. Given the focus of some wings of education reform on core beliefs and cultural attitudes and the focus on work ethic by others, I'm left wondering what Pablo had in mind with a phrase like "doing the work." What kind of "work" is this new charter school teacher doing? And what kind of institutions and subject positions are being produced to enable such work? Pablo's circumscription indexes for us the fact that work in education is not as straightforward as it may seem. What counts as "the work" is determined in fields of struggle that are informed by history, culture, and politics—a field that is a key site for understanding the "racial formations" (Omi and Winant [1986] 2014) emerging from education reform.

Teachers and school administrators aren't the only ones doing the work of education reform. In the decade since the takeover of the New Orleans public school system by the state government, the city saw the proliferation of institutions and organizations that contributed to an agenda of reforming and improving schools, part of a larger trend expanding civil society organizations in the years after the storm (Flaherty 2010). Most directly, there was the establishment of over forty charter school–management organizations in the city, many with national footprints. But the expansion of charter schools was also directed and supported by dozens of education nonprofits with various agendas and of various scales, from alternative certification organizations like Teach for America and Teach Nola, which provide the human capital that charter school leaders claimed they needed to function, to New Schools for New Orleans, which provided resources and expertise for charter school networks. I was intimately familiar with the workings of such organizations; I was a Teach for America corps member and science teacher at a charter school in New York City between undergraduate and graduate school and received direct training and support before and during my time in the classroom.[9] After Katrina, there was exponential growth in the number of entrepreneurs and education-related businesses providing services and products for charter schools. This is not a matter just of the multiplication of institutional structures but of a diversification of the kinds of labor and expertise that support school systems. Whereas public schools in the United States were originally envisioned as organic community institutions and the governance structures of public schools are therefore highly decentralized compared to other wealthy nations, charter schools relied on a growing institutional ecology of foundations, nonprofits, think tanks, and businesses. These ecologies don't centralize educational authority and regulation per se, yet they do subject schools to regimes of expertise dispersed over a greater array of institutional locations and influenced by a smaller number of key actors like the Gates, Broad, and Walton Foundations. Teachers and school staff may have been the ones most dramatically affected by post-Katrina reforms, but in order for them to "do the work," reformers have constructed a broader web of education labor.

How did charter schools come to be seen as the solution to educational inequality, and why did Louisiana and New Orleans come to embrace this model? Originally proposed in 1974 by Dr. Ray Budde, charter schools were framed as a progressive reform of American school districts. Rather than have school operations dictated by a centralized administration, Budde proposed that groups of educators contract with the district to run individual schools. Ideally these schools would use their greater autonomy from district mandates and their localized expertise to develop innovative methods of schooling. The concept did not gain much traction until the late 1980s, when American Federation of Teachers president Al Shanker advocated the model, arguing, "in charter schools, teachers would be given the opportunity to draw upon their expertise to create high-performing educational laboratories from which the traditional public schools could learn" (Kahlenberg and Potter 2014). Embracing the idea of a pedagogical experiment, Minnesota became the first state to authorize a charter school law in 1991, and in 1994 two Teach for America alums founded the Knowledge is Power Program (KIPP) schools (the most recognizable charter school network in the country, with schools in Texas, California, Louisiana, and New York) and pioneered the "no excuses" school model. No excuses schools adopt exacting behavioral and academic expectations focused on test scores, strict disciplinary codes, extended school days, college preparatory curriculum and cultures, and an intense focus on building branded school culture and community values. The model is the most popular style of charter school in New Orleans, and its influence can be seen in charter schools across the United States. Charter schools in New Orleans not only transformed the governance and management structures of schools, they also promised new disciplinary and pedagogical models for schools. Each one of the schools discussed in this book could fairly be described as a no excuses school.

Given the discourses of failure that surrounded urban public schools after the 1983 publication of *A Nation at Risk: The Imperative for Educational Reform* by President Ronald Reagan's National Commission on Excellence in Education, charter schools came to be seen as a promising means of fixing educational inequality absent broader transformations in racial segregation, capitalism, and the welfare state. While charter schools were originally proposed as a pedagogical experiment for teachers, they came to be valued by other constituencies as a means of organizational and managerial reform. The idea that teachers' unions were primarily responsible for impeding school reform became a kind of commonsense among education reformers. You can find versions of the line in films like *Waiting for Superman* or David Brooks columns in the *New York Times*. Critics of teachers' unions believed that charter schools (as independent contractors) would improve education because they could circumvent collective bargaining agreements with teachers' unions. This agenda dovetailed with the movement to impose punitive accountability structures on schools who failed to meet testing goals, a movement entrenched by the 2002 passing of the No Child Left Behind Act. In 2003, Louisiana board of elementary and secondary education (BESE) member Leslie Jacobs (one of the primary architects of New Orleans charter school reforms) shepherded the passing of Act 9, a bill that gave the state authority to temporarily take over "failing schools" and operate them directly or contract them to charter schools. This act was opposed by the New Orleans teachers' union, the United Teachers of New Orleans (UTNO), as well as by members of the Orleans Parish School Board, who saw these measures as targeting New Orleans specifically and as allowing a red state to usurp control of the largest public institution in a Black and blue city. The legal architecture for a takeover of New Orleans schools was therefore already in place years before Hurricane Katrina, and Jacobs and her supporters used the dislocations of the storm's aftermath to enact a sweeping agenda to convert nearly all the city's schools to charters.

NEW ORLEANS: A MODEL EXCEPTION

New Orleans is one of a small number of major metropolitan areas in the United States in which a majority (though internally stratified) Black population was able to realize institutional political power throughout government and civil society after the civil rights movement, an achievement exemplified by the election of Ernest "Dutch" Morial to the mayor's office in 1978 (Hirsch and Logsdon 1992, Germany 2007). During the fight for school desegregation, Black teachers themselves served as the foundation of for further Black political organization in New Orleans (Fairclough 2008). The "Black urban regime" (Reed 1999) of Black mayors, civil servants, and political and community groups that arose from the forms of organization catalyzed by school politics represented a level of Black participation in municipal governance across the United States unseen since the Reconstruction Era. Black politicians and community organizations were empowered to combat inequality through the formation of "the soft state" (Germany 2007) in the wake of President Johnson's Great Society agenda.

Black teachers and their unions, which made up an increasing proportion of the system, were key factors in enabling and executing this agenda (Fairclough 2008). The shift to charter schools in New Orleans thus represents not an innocuous change in institutional form but a massive shift in racial politics. Whereas previous waves of education reform engaged schools as community and collective institutions, charter school–based reforms see individualized parents exercising choice as the key political mechanism for the functioning of school systems.

The promises of racial justice and equality through Black governance were seen to have disappointed, if not outright failed, by the turn of the twenty-first century after decades of urban disinvestment and neglect (Reed 1999, Summers 2021). The devastation and reforms following Hurricane Katrina compelled many to reflect on the legacy of Black politics; some decried the relative weakness of Black "counterpublics" (Dawson 2006), or noted the millenarian desires of using the flood as a new beginning for Black politics (Ralph 2006), while others warned of white revanchism (Lipsitz 2006). New Orleans was widely viewed as an experimental space after Katrina, with some eager to use the disruptions of the storms to rebuild the school system and public housing, while others cautioned that experimentation would subject the city to the ideological desires of neoliberalism, education privatization, and the reestablishment of white governance (Giroux 2006, Klein 2007, Saltman 2007).

I came to this project having taught at a charter school in Harlem as a Teach for America corps member for two years after graduating college and before starting grad school. I had multiple years of experience teaching and tutoring Black and brown students from low-income communities prior to that through Summerbridge San Francisco and the Double Discovery Center at Columbia University. I was well aware of the contentious politics of charter schools and had many reservations when I was assigned to teach at one by TFA. We weren't allowed to pick our school assignments and I entered the program at a time when TFA began increasingly placing corps members in charter schools, a marked shift from previous practices. I was happy to be placed in Harlem both because I was familiar with the neighborhood and because of its symbolic importance as a center of the Black world. I had spent much time in the community as an undergraduate at Columbia. Having otherwise only ever lived in Black communities in San Francisco and Los Angeles and having family ties to the neighborhood through my grandfather, it was a particularly meaningful place for me to serve as an educator. I was not naive about charter schools going in and in fact was quite critical of the labor and disciplinary conditions, though as many young people are, I was naive enough to imagine that I would be able to transcend the circumstances and maintain a liberated classroom in a harsh environment.

The school I worked in was a no excuses–style school, with strict disciplinary codes and high academic expectations attuned to test scores above all. I was told during my interview for the position that working at this charter school would be "more like working at a high-powered law firm than a traditional public school." Once we were hired, we were told that we were more effective team members because we didn't have a "thousand-page" union contract getting in between teachers and management. These experiences inspired me to focus my subsequent research on how the education-reform movement transformed the racialization of teaching labor. As a newly opened school, we only had two grade levels, and we were placed on the third level of a building housing a traditional public elementary school, where there were conflicts over space the whole time. Our school network attempted to take over an entire school building down the street from a "failing school" during my first year, but they were thwarted after consistent protest by community members supportive of this other traditional public school. I remember hearing picket lines outside my window as I attempted to teach my kindergarten science class and later the passions on display as John White, then deputy chancellor for the New York City Department of Education and subsequently the state superintendent of Louisiana Public Schools from 2012 to 2020, attempted to facilitate a public hearing on whether or not my charter school network would be able to take over the new school building. My principal was a white man who was an early TFA corps member in 1990s New York and an experienced educator. He was an effective and inspiring mentor who seemed to have turned to the charter model out of frustration with his experience in traditional public schools. He constantly reminded us that we were doing some of the most important work in the world and that we were putting the lie to the notion that low-income children of color couldn't be served by public schools. For my principal and many of my colleagues at the charter school, it was self-evident that we were offering better options for Harlem families. Based on my knowledge of Black history and my experience as a Black public school student who had to travel across the city to go to "better" schools I knew better. I knew schools meant more to families and students than test scores and discipline and that a community school, something I never had, was not given up lightly. Watching Harlem parents, politicians, and activists defend their "failing school" outside my classroom window and at public hearings, I knew that charter schools were about more than pedagogy—they were changing the racial politics of urban education, surfacing conflicts and visions about the purpose of schooling.

Determined to research these phenomena, I began graduate school during the fifth anniversary of Hurricane Katrina. Reflections on the transformation of the city and its schools drew my focus to New Orleans. At first glance, New Orleans may seem an odd place to make claims about race and difference on a national level. The city is often characterized as culturally exceptional within the United States. Racial, class, and gender differences have been encoded in the city (and state) through particular policies, laws, and lawsuits, which have drawn and constantly reinvented strict boundaries between white, Black, and Creole and declared white ownership of property more sacred than Black kinship (Dominguez 1986). Within the United States, the city also has a unique spatialization of difference. Until the late twentieth century, unlike in Chicago, in New Orleans racial groups had not lived within homogeneous and separate residential homelands but within "superblocks" (Lewis 2003) in which grand, wealthy boulevards owned by white residents were interspersed by an inner core of smaller streets containing middle- and working-class housing that was often occupied by African Americans (though the city has become more segregated along "traditional lines" over the past few decades and particularly after Katrina). Thus, racial difference developed with a peculiar proximity in New Orleans, whereby even seemingly innocuous cultural practices such as the parades of Mardi-Gras Indians laid a claim to space and caused frictions that sparked police brutality and community reckoning (Lipsitz 1988). Nevertheless, there is precedent for looking to New Orleans to work out national issues of race and difference, from the movements that brought Homer Plessy to challenge segregation to the beginning of segregation's transformation (though not destruction) by the likes of Ruby Bridges, the first Black child to integrate an all-white elementary school in the Southern

United States. We can again see New Orleans as a racial problem space in the contemporary reconfigurations of its school system through the charter school experiment.

Education and public schools have been some of the primary fields of contestation over the constitution and maintenance of racial difference and inequality in the United States, from literacy among the enslaved to the fight for equal resources for segregated public schools to efforts to use busing to integrate schools in the face of residential segregation. Racial segregation has been a flashpoint since the establishment of public schools, and while it was formally abolished by the Supreme Court in 1954, public schools remain racially segregated to the present day.[10] In civil rights–era New Orleans, the struggle to integrate schools united Black communities and not only created novel political alliances between Black, Creole, and white city residents but served as a catalyst for reconfigured notions of racial difference between Black and Creole communities; it also created a new geography of race in the city as whites withdrew to the suburbs (Lassiter 2007). Mere weeks before the 1954 *Brown v. Board of Education* decision, which declared segregation unconstitutional, a boycott of an annual parade in celebration of the philanthropic contributions of John McDonough to New Orleans public schools served to unite Black and Creole communities and spurred further political organization (Hirsch and Logsdon 1992). Nevertheless, most white New Orleanians were slow to accept their Black and Creole neighbors as legitimate constituents of the public schools. Many whites believed that the school system was their "property," anticipating the language of the tax revolt and neoliberal ideals of entitlement through taxpayer identity. After a judge outlined a process for the desegregation of New Orleans schools in 1960 and the school board received survey results indicating majority support for integration, the school board president decided to disregard the survey because most of the parents voting for integration were Black and "whites are the people who support the system" (Vaughn et al. 2012).

Charter schools, which, unlike the neighborhood allotments of the previous system, have city-wide enrollment pools, have re-territorialized the school as a site of this boundary making and marking. Some have characterized this as part of a class conquest of cities in which schools lure middle- and upper-class families (Lipman 2011) and participate in gentrification at large (Smith 1996, Flaherty 2010). New Orleans locals often joke that one of the unique qualities of their city is that when people ask, "What school did you go to?" they mean high school, indexing the important local overlaps between school, place, and identity. Takeovers of neighborhood schools, such as the conversion of Frederick Douglass High School to the city-wide-enrollment KIPP Renaissance High School in 2010, sparked fierce conflicts over the nature of the connection between school and community. Where once students attended neighborhood schools with strong community bonds and teachers would "run into parents and students at their local Wal-Mart," families now became "free" to choose to apply to any school in the city, resulting in a system where the more than forty charter operators drew on student populations distributed across the map. The neighborhood school is no more in New Orleans. Both critics and supporters of charter school–based reforms wish it were not so. Principals wished they could draw on students from the neighborhood, and policymakers held out the promise that once all schools became high quality, families would no longer have to choose schools that were across the city. I suspect it will not be so easy or possible to resurrect the neighborhood school because the neighborhood itself has been unsettled.

As researchers, activists, and journalists have shown, a combination of massive disinvestment in and destruction of public housing and sharp rent increases have redistributed the population of New Orleans. While the city "only" went from 67 to 60 percent Black after Katrina, this obscures the redistribution of the Black population within the city towards East New Orleans, and the fact that the youth population dropped from anywhere between a third and a half of its pre-Katrina levels. Whereas school buildings were anchored within neighborhoods in the previous system, school buildings became islands in a charter archipelago that extended across the city in a system of choice. I'm sure something could be worked out to create some vision of community schools in the future, but the kinds of communities that my informants discuss and revere don't exist in the same way anymore; they have been profoundly altered and dispersed as a result of the destruction of public housing, an ongoing rent crisis, and the casualization of work represented in part by gig labor.

THE VIEW FROM NEW ORLEANS

The world of work in charter schools and education reform organizations is, in many ways, an incredibly thin slice of New Orleans. Many of the educators, nonprofit workers, and entrepreneurs I encountered went to work in schools no longer intimately connected to their surrounding neighborhoods; they commuted home to gentrifying strips of Mid-City, the Bywater, or the Irish Channel, often stopping at bars and restaurants with aesthetics and clientele not unlike similar neighborhoods in New York City, Chicago, or San Francisco. Readers may be curious about the social vision and community life of Black New Orleanians in the decade after Katrina—that was not a world my research subjects inhabited. That's not to say they weren't interested. But the hours they worked, the firing of veteran teachers, the system of choice, and the residential segregation of a rapidly gentrifying city militated against such intimacy.

My field research was grounded in sixteen months of participant observation and interviews at six charter schools in New Orleans as well as several educational nonprofits, community organizations, education start-ups and incubators, and education-policy think tanks. The main fieldwork was conducted while living full time in New Orleans for thirteen months from 2013 to 2014, but I also conducted preliminary interviews and observations in the summer of 2011 and follow-up interviews in the years after. I entered New Orleans as the charter school movement shifted from an emergency footing to a long-term presence in the city. Over the course of writing this book and in the decade hence charter schools have gone from an audacious novelty to the status quo. Rather than focus on a particular slice of time or school building, I've taken a long-term multisited view of the charter experiment. Charter schools claim to create a competitive environment in which schools develop and share best practices, which take many different forms, from test prep curricula and disciplinary systems to ideas for branding "school culture," making a comparative perspective useful. These distinct sites allowed me to explore the different approaches to education work that emerged at varying institutional scales and forms.

This research was primarily conducted at two different no excuses–style charter schools in two different charter school networks in New Orleans during the 2013–14 school year, as well as at several other no excuses charter schools, education nonprofits, and education businesses. In the following chapters, I do not present each school as a discrete entity as the goal of this research was not to characterize charter schools as bounded work places but to investigate work in charter schools as a site of racialization and subject formation. The first school was a K-8 charter school that was part of a network that managed between four and six schools. I spent all my time in this school with the middle-school grades, sitting in on classes, shadowing teachers and the principal for a whole workday, observing teacher interviews and sample lessons, and attending professional development sessions. This school network liked to emphasize that it had more local roots and a slightly more diverse teaching staff than other no excuses schools. The second school was also a K-8 charter school; it was located in a different part of the city and was part of a smaller charter school network. I spent most of my time in this school with one elementary grade team in particular, though I did observe and shadow teachers at every grade level as well as administrators. This school experienced a leadership transition during the school year and was facing decreasing test scores after being held up for years as one of the top examples of a New Orleans charter school.

Throughout the school year I also made targeted visits to several other charter schools to observe specific features. A school in a different network from the first two was reputed to have an "intense" or "exemplary" staff culture, an extreme version of a no excuses–ethic, and I visited them one day to see their morning staff meeting. At an arts-focused school in another network, I observed teachers over several meetings as they organized an ad hoc leadership council to attempt to have a collective voice in the running of the school. I visited Jay, an education entrepreneur and teacher, several times at a school in yet another network. Hayden, the human capital manager at the network of the first school, encouraged me to observe the school leadership meetings at another school in their network, and I did so a couple times. Finally, at several different charter schools, I shadowed substitute teachers employed through the company that is the focus of chapter 5.

Various nonprofits and education businesses were also key sites of research. At one education reform nonprofit, I interviewed and shadowed a community liaison and a teacher coach to observe the brokering of racialized expertise. I interviewed and shadowed the New Orleans director for an organization I call the Black Organization for Choice. I also attended several of their public events and their annual national conference, held that year in New Orleans. Most of the material for chapters 4 and 5 was gathered while conducting observations at an organization I call Incubator, which developed programming and support for budding education entrepreneurs. I interviewed and observed a summer-long cohort of entrepreneurs as they trained and competed for funding for their businesses and school models, the core of chapter 4. I also spent most of the school year shadowing and interviewing the management and teachers at a company that Incubator started. I call the company, which provides substitute teachers for charter schools, ConnectED.

EDUCATION AS WORK

This book interrogates the formation of education workers under charter school reforms as newly mobile and ostensibly universal agents of social and economic reproduction in New Orleans. It does so through an ethnographic consideration of privately managed yet publicly funded charter schools as workplaces. Furthermore, I focus on the charter school teacher, workers in education nonprofits, and education entrepreneurs as emergent forms of racialized labor. While schooling has been theorized as a contributor to socioeconomic reproduction, public education's status as a site of labor remains ambiguous and is often outright effaced—with teaching being seen variously as mission work, service work, or as a profession. Some have argued for the promise of schools in shaping students as citizen-subjects (Dewey 1923), and others have emphasized the roles schools play in reproducing racial and class domination in various forms by establishing arbitrary hierarchies of racialized cultural values, preparing working-class students solely for industrial labor, and molding students as disciplined subjects (Bourdieu and Passeron 1990, Bowles and Gintis 2011, Foley 1990, Foucault 2012, Willis 1981). However, these meditations have emphasized above all how schools shape students. Teaching itself has been characterized as a feminized form of labor that lies somewhere between a job, a calling, and parenting (Apple 1986). But an infusion of money and human capital has changed things. Given these extraordinary new investments from national foundations, the federal and state governments, and transplant education reformers in this new form of schooling and new institutional assemblages, what kind of work do these teachers, nonprofit employees, and entrepreneurs do exactly? Charter school reform affords us the opportunity to reconsider education as a site of work and to explore structural and ideological experiments in labor carried out under its banners. Anthropologists have long understood that workers are created, not found, at the point of production and that the workplace is a site of subject formation (Amrute 2016, Freeman 2000, Salzinger 2003). Furthermore, political theorists have emphasized that work is a site of political domination (Anderson 2017, Postone 1995, Weeks 2011). Following these threads, this project shows how the transformation of a school system from a site of unionized bureaucracy to a constellation of entrepreneurial and precarious contractors deeply changes the socio-technical production of racialization through the work educators do to shape and produce rising generations.

During the second Bush and Obama administrations there was a particular zeitgeist for transforming the basis of teaching labor and organization. In 2013, the federal Department of Education partnered with the National Education Association (NEA), American Federation of Teachers (AFT), and other education organizations to put out a call for "Transforming the Teaching Profession" (Duncan et al. 2013). The call emphasized that the global spatio-temporal orders of the twenty-first century have placed new demands on Americans as citizens *and* workers. According to this agenda, it is necessary to elevate the teaching profession so that every student will emerge from high school "well-informed as a citizen, and ready for the workplace" (ibid.). Thus, the neoliberal logics of stakeholders and consumers don't erase ideas of citizenship but subordinate them to its logics. In this document, teachers' unions were typologized as being industrial-, professional-, or social-justice-focused organizations. The constituents of the above call, including the largest teachers' unions in the country, believed that teachers were too tightly tied to an industrial model and that they had to become more professional, with attendant changes in forms of evaluation, compensation, and accountability. Thus, even though charter schools mostly do not employ unionized workforces,[11] these schools participate in a larger field of the reorganization of teaching work under the sign of professionalization.

As teaching in charter schools moves from unionized bureaucracy to affective entrepreneurialism, attending to the teacher as a worker opens up new understandings of transformations in American identity and social structure. Anthropologists and sociologists have long been engaged in ethnographic accounts of industrial labor and organization (Burawoy 1979) and these, along with accounts of service labor in the US, can critically inform an engagement with teachers as workers in a capitalist society. While there have been many accounts of reforms and contestation over education labor and organization (Apple 1986, Fairclough 2007), thinking of teaching as a form of labor akin to others is critical for thinking through the changes to teaching in charter schools. Ethnographic work has demonstrated how workers as subjects are made, not discovered, in a process mediated by race, class, and gender (Freeman 2000, Salzinger 2003) as well as in service work routines and scripts (Leidner 1993) and how the fetishization of hard work and flexibility structure the labor process and laboring subjects (Ho 2009). Urciuoli (2008) has argued that under neoliberalism we are seeing particular transformations in labor as a culturally and semiotically constructed form, including the reinterpretation of the concept of skill itself and a shift in emphasis from experience to expertise. Furthermore, the boundaries between life and work are being blurred as life becomes more like work under "emotional labor regimes" (Freeman 2014, Weeks 2011). Thus attending to education reform as a site of labor helps us understand transformations in American identity and social structure by shedding light not only on the way teachers shape students but also on how teaching work is subject to the same forces of de-skilling, affective demand, and precarity that workers in many other sectors are facing.

RACIAL CAPITALISM AND NEOLIBERALISM

New Orleans offers a privileged vantage point from which to rethink relations between race, labor, and neoliberalism. Studies of race too often fixate on questions of culture and biology or on enumerating inequality without accounting for its production. This book takes a "nonbiocentric" approach to the study of race and racialization whereby race is not a property inherent to bodies or even identitarian notions of cultural practice but is something that is produced, in part, through socially mediated expert activity (McKittrick 2020). How have the dramatic and unprecedented reforms of post-Katrina New Orleans public schools transformed education work as a socio-technical site of racialization? The privatization of the city's entire school system has been the key lever for moving the twentieth-century detente between a white "Bourbon bloc" (Woods 1998) and a "chocolate city" government (Hunter and Robinson 2018) managed by the Black professional middle classes to a twenty-first century regime of multiracial technocratic racialized governance. New Orleans's citywide experimentation with private management and education labor has led to the proliferation of novel topographies of racialized governance, where educators, policymakers, and entrepreneurs reconfigure and mobilize race under emergent expert cultures. Whether through diversity-focused hiring initiatives, community consultants, or "grassroots" intelligence gathering and digital media production informed by design thinking, education reformers' engagement with race should be characterized as a process of intensive and multiplying knowledge production with the power to name, recognize, and reshape the contours of racialized access to educational services—with uncertain ramifications for New Orleans and cities around the globe looking to emulate its model. Racialized and racializing forms of expertise, like design thinking, are not merely technical implements but ethnographically inflected and aesthetically sophisticated technologies that work to transform the exceptional violence and flat temporality of the immediate post-Katrina reconstruction into normalized infrastructures and enduring futures.

Scholars have depicted post-Katrina reconstruction as a defining example of neoliberalism run rampant (Johnson et al. 2017,

Klein 2007). While these accounts rightly underscore the manner in which factions of white elites used the dislocations of the storm to advance racist and ideologically charged agendas, they nevertheless foreground exploitation, profit, material interest, and market ideologies as primary motives. I am skeptical of such narrowly economistic frameworks. Adolph Reed has downplayed the distinctiveness of neoliberalism as a historical formation, claiming that it is "capitalism in the absence of credible opposition" (2014), highlighting the need to attend to recent decades' transformations in economy and society as above all the result of political struggle. Following Wendy Brown (2015), this project emphasizes the ways that the privatization of New Orleans schools has transformed educators and education workers as political subjects and furthermore argues that racialization is a fundamental part of this process.

Adrienne Dixson's long-term field research with Black educators and community organizations in New Orleans form the basis of her critique of the white supremacist foundations of the dominant reform model (Dixson 2011; Dixson, Buras, and Jeffers 2015; Jeffers and Dixson 2023). Her work argues that the dominant reform model disregarded not only the expertise and experience of veteran Black educators, but also disrupted public schools as incubators of Clyde Woods's "blues tradition" (1998).[12] Marc Perry's (2015, 2021) theorization of "contractual blackness" gives us another framework for thinking through the ways that the post-Katrina racial order provides new sites and scenes for the ways in which Black folks are deemed deserving of inclusion or vulnerable to dispossession and premature death. Black educators and professionals often sit at the crux of this malignant partitioning. Sometimes they do so unwittingly, but as Woods argues, Black middle-class and professional reformers have often done this sorting with great enthusiasm in the name of a politics of uplift. In her critique of the antiblack foundations of progressive coalitional politics in a progressive public high school in San Francisco, Savannah Shange (2019) shows that the bio-political imperatives to improve Black subjects exist in the "afterlife of slavery" and are premised on notions of "burdened individuality" (Hartman 1997) that prefigure many of the subject positions and moral quandaries often attributed to late twentieth-century neoliberalism. Forms of racialized expertise have intensified with the rapid expansion of dozens of education nonprofits in post-Katrina New Orleans and are also an exemplar of the ways that many of the key features of neoliberalism (both economic and political) can be conceived of as being modeled on the post-Reconstruction South.[13] If neoliberalism can be conceived of as a counteroffensive of capital against the democratic aspirations of the global masses and formerly colonized subjects (Slobodian 2018), then the ongoing and haltingly successful suppression of the freedom dreams of Black Southerners post-emancipation provide a chilling template, if not an outright antecedent, for such authoritarian market ideologies.

Rather than view neoliberalism as a prescribed set of transcendent ideological projects, I see the varied components of neoliberalism (freedom of choice and contract, individualized notions of human capital, hostility to democracy, rule of economic experts, and privatization of public goods) as "repertoires" (Von Schnitzler 2016) that are assimilated and articulated to long-standing and emergent political projects at multiple localized scales and registers. Like Adams's (2013) ethnography of privatized recovery efforts, this work shows how ethics of atomized and ascetic labor come to be internalized by voluntarist subjects in emerging forms of education labor; it further argues that these fetishized commitments form the justification for the continued exclusion of certain kinds of Black educators and the selective inclusion of others. While it is true that the initial wave of privatization in New Orleans favored white outsiders, this book demonstrates how school leaders, nonprofits, and entrepreneurs came to value and valuate diversity and inclusion after years of community critique and activism. However, as anthropological studies of recognition have shown (Povinelli 2002), these multicultural turns are also an occasion for dominant groups to consolidate authority over the terms of inclusion. As in Summers's (2019) study of gentrifying Washington D.C., blackness eventually came to be formulated in charter schools as an aestheticized asset, whose terms were controlled by white reformers and select factions of Black professional agents, a form of "unequal" (Getachew 2019) or "predatory" (Taylor 2019) inclusion. The concept of "racial capitalism" theorized by Cedric Robinson and others (Robinson 2000, Johnson and Lubin 2017) ameliorates many of the shortcomings of economistic analyses of neoliberalism. Theorists of racial capitalism posit that classes and workers under capitalist societies are always already racialized in the context of colonial exploitation and racialized expropriation (Dawson 2016, Fraser 2016). While the early stages of education reform after the storm were rightly characterized by racially naive power plays by white-dominated interests, ethnographic elaboration of the diversity and inclusion efforts of reformers shows that the continuing endurance of the charter school project can be attributed to the ways in which a multiracial cohort of educators and allies have embraced racialized expertise. It is mastery, rather than ignorance, of racial codes that consolidates their class power.

DESIGNING RACE

The final two chapters of this work meditate in particular on the ways Silicon Valley–inspired "design thinking" became a technique of stratified inclusion (see also Benjamin 2019, Irani 2019, and Sims 2017) through ostensibly democratic design protocols, creating the terms by which some but inevitably not all Black New Orleanians could be recuperated as charter school educators. This elevation of design thinking and entrepreneurialism assimilates racialized political conflict into ostensibly frictionless design processes. How did design become such an appealing method for social, political, and institutional transformation? Anthropologists and theorists of design have provided us with robust tools and evidence for understanding how design works to simultaneously know and remake the world, how it has anchored and materialized political will, and how design subjects and subjectifies the willing and unwilling into new forms of citizenship (Dilnot 1984, Escobar 2018, Irani 2019, Murphy 2015, Suchman 2011). In some of these conversations, design has been posed as a fundamental part of what makes "us" human, as a shared capacity that can facilitate equality and be rescued from the predations of markets. But there are also many critical design studies that recognize design as a site upon which the designing human is constituted through foundational violence and exclusions steeped in racialized and gendered hierarchies and capitalist logics. These studies are particularly critical of the universalist assumptions of dominant design frameworks (Agid and Chin 2019, Ansari 2019, Costanza-Chock 2020). The provincial perspective of the designer is too often the model for the user or the human at the center of the design process. Users and designers are frequently assumed to be operating as individual units on a level playing field rather than as members of communities with histories that must be accounted for within design protocols (Akama and Light 2012, Rosner 2018). Critical design scholars emphasize that design methodology has been fetishized, centering products and processes over the ostensible human relations and needs designers intend to serve

(Hargraves and Jafarinaimi 2012). Crucially, by standardizing protocols, universalizing participants, and discarding history, design processes can facilitate interventions whereby all designers are innocent and unaccountable to foundational violence and structural inequality (Williams 2019). These moves privatize and individuate efforts to address inequality and privilege particular forms of Western racialized agencies as the central characteristic of the human.

Design thinking assumes a common humanity. But what of those of "us" whose humanity has never been fully recognized despite noble and relentless efforts to at some times insist on and at others to move beyond such easy universals? Many of the critical design scholars above recognize the colonial frameworks and legacies that dominant forms of design operate within; in particular, they reckon with the ways that indigenous epistemologies call into question design methods. In New Orleans, our understanding of false universals and the racialization of design must be specifically attentive to blackness as a racial formation. Antiblackness theory asks us to reckon with the fact that post-Enlightenment humanity has never been a genre fully available to Black subjects. Indeed, this humanity is not incidentally exclusionary but is constituted through the subjection of blackness by both earnest oppressors and so-called allies (Shange 2019; Weheliye 2014). The "over-representation" of Western white humanity (Wynter 2003) is no free-floating symbolic phenomena. As McKittrick (2021) reminds us, overrepresentation is a genre-making activity, a social and symbolic process that makes and occurs within space, which entails architecture, production, circulation, and all manner of material consequence. She underscores that the critique of this form of humanity is a critique of a system of knowing and making the world, one that produces multiple historical constructions of the human. The fabrication of this genre of the human occurs in major part through design and technological development and is refracted through Western attempts at creating nonhuman intelligence that is ultimately neither intelligent nor reflective of any broader humanity (Suchman 2007).

Scholars of antiblackness emphasize that the genre-making activity of the Western and white human takes place in necessary contrast to Black people and blackness. While design's embrace of humanity attempts to create solidarities, we should subject its optimistic claims of world-building and species making to careful scrutiny lest we lose sight of the fundamental subjections entailed by its premises. Contrary to the biocentrism of American folk theories of race (Fields and Fields 2014, McKittrick 2021), the line between the human, the not-quite-human, and the inhuman (Weheliye 2014) is no mere discursive boundary; instead, it materializes in an astounding array of designs, from the hold (Sharpe 2016) to debt-financed municipal bonds (Jenkins 2021) to the algorithm (Benjamin 2019, Noble 2018). It is on this other side of the Janus face (Trouillot 2003) where Black studies can help attune us to the ways that design molds inhumanity as well as humanity, to the ways it goes beyond merely participating in inequality or resulting in discrimination and actively works to continuously reconstruct race. Crucially, these studies don't seek to recuperate humanity for Black people, nor do they long for inclusion. As Rinaldo Walcott asks, "Who wants to be human anyway?" (Walcott 2021, 71).

The historical and material nature of blackness necessitates that we reckon with its ultimate "plasticity;" blackness can take whatever form or connotation is needed to stabilize a particular white supremacist social and political order (Jackson 2020). More than creating any innovative products or institutions, the mobilization of blackness as affect and narrative in the design thinking turn in New Orleans education reform shows how blackness is not only plastic but can be rendered fungible through design thinking. It is this element of conversion within design thinking protocols that is problematic—not just whether or not design outcomes can be judged to have humanizing or dehumanizing or positive or negative effects. Whereas the earliest phase of privatization in New Orleans schools treated Black populations as objects of salvation and administration, the design thinking turn became a key component in a broader pivot towards incorporation, participation, and inclusion among reformers. The forms of design thinking and human-centered design being used in post-Katrina New Orleans are both compelling foundations for building liberal multicultural institutions and at the same time mechanisms for further exploitation through the rendering of Black marginalization and subjection into "behavioral surplus" (Zuboff 2019). What limits do design communities come up against when they move from managing to "centering" Black humanity?

WHAT ARE SCHOOLS FOR?

While this research seeks to advance debates on racialization, labor, and neoliberalism, it has stakes in the politics of public education as well. As an anthropological project, this research is uniquely capable of charting how education stakeholders are negotiating work, accountability, and difference in New Orleans charter schools; it helps to move the terms of the debate over charters beyond scorekeeping and opposition and to articulate the new relations emerging through charter schools. By redefining the stakes and contours of this conflict, by refusing to take received categories for granted, and by showing how seemingly dominant projects are doubted, insecure, and full of contradictions, anthropology can open new possibilities for collaboration and communication. There is no shortage of local and national debate on the merits and consequences of the proliferation of charter schools, particularly in urban districts in the United States. New Orleans has seen the most dramatic turn to charter schools as a means of redefining the school as a socioeconomic institution and teaching as a form of labor, but the spread of private management of public schools is a national and international matter. The media and academy are saturated with claims about charters, which are depicted as emblematic of the decline of the civic virtues of the public school and as tools of wealthy oligarchs (Ravitch 2010, 2014), as the key to national security (Klein and Rice 2014), as a piece of a plot to take back New Orleans from Black control (Lee 2010), or as necessary to do away with the malfeasance of teachers unions (Guggenheim 2010). Charters in New Orleans are posed as a potential model for solving the problem of education inequality for the nation and also as a key touchstone in reflections on the state of Black politics after Hurricane Katrina (Ralph 2009). For many in the public, the stakes are high, and they are clear in no small part due to the way that discussions of combating racial and class inequality in the US have come to focus ever more myopically on schools as the sole institution responsible for or capable of making a difference. New Orleans charters are the site of a battle between the public and the private, white educators and Black families, rich and poor, adult interests and child interests, and much more. While these antagonisms are real, my engagement with educators, entrepreneurs, and education nonprofits in New Orleans suggests that it is necessary to take a step back from reified polarizations and show how the actual lived relations between teachers and students, administrators, families, and other stakeholders demonstrate that the terms of the charter school debate are continually shifting under the feet of even its most ardent belligerents.

Educators in charter schools, as well as most Americans and New Orleanians, believe that their students need them, that for many students their teachers are "all they've got."[14] As citizens, educators, activists, community members, stakeholders, users, and in almost any other way in which we interface with public schools, we tend to hold the bedrock belief that teachers are the most important tool and institution in combating systemic race and class inequality. There are differences of opinion and politics as to what constitutes this need historically, but there is broad agreement about its existence. The American public school first took form with the "common school" in nineteenth century New England. These schools were seen as community-supported institutions that would provide a combination of moral, spiritual, and academic instruction for youth. Schools were posed as necessary for the moral formation of young people and the communities they hailed from. Over the course of the early twentieth century, regional and professional authorities wrested control of public schools away from local and religious figures, attempting to standardize curricula and craft public schools as universal institutions. Progressive reformers believed that schools should be the training grounds of democracy and develop youth above all as intelligent and engaged citizens. This vision of schooling has remained dominant through to the present but is being challenged by the proliferation of charter schools. Charter schools in New Orleans as well as across the nation disproportionately serve low-income students of color and broadly express the belief that they are the best mechanism for saving their students from entrenched racialized poverty. In this model, schools are needed and indeed are the only politically plausible remedy for pervasive social and economic inequalities. Teachers and administrators at charter schools as well as policymakers often refer to the need to prepare American students to be competitive in a "global marketplace." The idea that low-income students of color are in need of the tutelage of schooling is as much a moral and spiritual project as that of the common school, and the idea that they must be prepared to be competitive on the global marketplace is as much a reconfiguration and recommitment to citizenship as a rejection of it in favor of cosmopolitan economic subjectivities. On the other hand, the way charter schools intensified commitment to schools as economic preparation is perhaps as much a reflection of the prevailing insecurities and precarity wrought by deindustrialization and the evisceration of the social safety net as any kind of philosophical project.

One of the distinguishing beliefs of charter proponents is that schools alone can combat racial and class inequality. This belief persists despite decades of evidence that broader socioeconomic factors have a far greater impact on education and life outcomes than the efforts of schools themselves. Pedro Noguera, for example, suggests that schools cannot improve the lives of low-income students and students of color without a focus on equity both within public education and in our broader society (Noguera 2016). I agree with Noguera that too much weight is placed on schools as a lever for ameliorating the effects of racial capitalism. At best, schooling can help a limited number of individuals in marginalized communities better strategically navigate the challenges of the day. This is not insignificant. I'm sitting here writing these words in no small part due to investments in education programs for "at-risk youth" that facilitated my entry into elite educational institutions. Indeed, more than ensuring my relative privileges as a Black professional academic, educational interventions literally change and save lives, and I would not besmirch or denigrate the work that millions of educators do around the United States to impact the lives of these students. But this work alone is not a systemic or transformative response to structural violence. What if we rejected the notion that schools should serve a strategic meritocratic function at all? What kinds of theory and politics might emerge from this kind of utopian refusal? This is not a rejection of the idea that schools can serve some kind of beneficial social or political purpose. What I want to reject is the idea that public schools have any bearing on "solving" the question of racialized class inequality. Indeed, education has much to recommend it for its own sake. By relieving schools of the responsibility to fix this broader problem, we might discover more of their benefits.

Who is this book for? The students, families, and communities affected by charter school reforms don't need someone to tell their story to them. I don't presume to speak for their experience, as much love as I have for them as a brother whose political consciousness was in part shaped by witnessing the horrors of Katrina from a New York City dorm with my fellow Black students. I hope, among other readers, to reach the professionals who have taken it upon themselves to intervene through this burdensome experiment as well as those of us who can imagine ourselves in similar positions in other places and times. I hope they feel humbled by reading this book. Teaching is humbling. As grand as the designs of charter school advocates may seem on the surface, all you have to do is spend five minutes in a classroom to see how even the most sophisticated plans are remade by determined students.[15] Ethnography too is humbling. Living communities hold you to account in ways you can't imagine prior to fieldwork. This experiment, neoliberalism, meritocracy—they all seduce us into investing ourselves with undeserved mandates and to enjoy the cheap satisfaction of our overestimated and overesteemed talents. I hope to inspire a particular kind of humility among Black professional readers. This book depicts a moment in which many Black folks entered the reform experiment with ardor and reservation, hope and compromise. While liberal multiculturalism often celebrates this integration, we should recognize the unsustainable weight of these efforts. I do not write this in a celebratory or self-congratulatory mood. I wish to catalyze a sense of release from a specific kind of responsibility, to encourage us to divest ourselves of the meritocratic impulse to overcome racism through achievement and of the belief that our ability to navigate white dominant structures entitles us to leadership of the race. This burdensome delusion may produce short term results, but it undermines enduring solidarities and collective dreams of freedom.

CHAPTER ONE

Human Capital

Nearly a decade after Hurricane Katrina and the mass firing of New Orleans public school teachers, charter school leaders had been given plenty of time to reflect on their hiring practices and consider the long-term standing of their schools in their communities. Whereas policymakers focused on talent in the abstract, principals and school-level staff were confronted with the living and breathing presence of a transformed teaching corps. Across the schools I observed in my research, there were a number of principals and school leaders who had recently been appointed and were eager to correct for the shortcomings of the early human capital strategies of charter schools and desired to hire teachers and staff that reflected the communities they served. Nearly all of them confronted a troubling dilemma—despite their desire to hire Black teachers from New Orleans they were failing to do so in significant numbers. Their frustrated desires are symptomatic of the racialized nature of the notions both of the human and of capital driving their recruitment strategies.

Rachel was a white local of New Orleans and a first-year principal who wanted her school to become more integrated with the local community. Facing the pressure of recruiting staff and meeting testing goals, she reflected on the challenge of realizing this intention: "My number one goal is to have the best teacher, but that doesn't feel good when you have ten people show up for the job and they're all white. So the big question is: why aren't local Black people applying to work at this school?" Rachel claimed that she wanted to recruit teachers with a long-term commitment to her school and her city: "If I had diversity in my applicants I could build a diverse staff, because I don't just want Teach for America people. Not all of them stay." Echoing the befuddlement of hiring committees and HR departments in white-dominant institutions across the land, this mode of questioning and puzzlement stakes out a kind of innocence for the second wave reformer. People like Rachel didn't fire all the Black teachers. They didn't even hire all the white ones. They said that they wanted Black teachers back in the schools. They nevertheless perpetuated systems of hiring in which Black teachers were rendered invisible.

Even when local Black teachers were hired in no excuses–style schools, it was difficult to retain them. Vanessa was a talent recruiter for a high-scoring charter school and spoke to me about one such case. Like Rachel, she emphasized the difficulty of finding teachers that "fit" at all, let alone Black teachers that were compatible with her school network's work culture. Vanessa hired a Black upper-level math teacher who she wasn't sure was a "culture fit" but thought could be coached on the norms and values of the school team. Ultimately, this teacher did not "fit in" and was asked to leave. Vanessa told me that they replaced him with a first-year Teach for America recruit; but, she explained, despite his lack of experience, "We think we can coach him" because "we are such a culture driven organization." The CEO of Vanessa's network expressed similar confidence in the culture of his school, claiming, "We don't make huge mistakes in cultural alignment" and that, when things don't work out, " We just fix it with dismissal." Charter schools were empowered to hire and fire their at-will employees as teachers and staff were without a union or contract. While the charter school leaders I encountered emphasized culture and fit above technical competency as the reason to wield this power, their commitment to dismissal as a tool reflects a long-standing transformation in teacher quality discourses in both policy and popular culture. While these leaders might try to distinguish themselves through a focus on culture, they have much in common with those who seek to center school success on the difference between good and bad teachers.

"After lots of studies, we've come down to just what most parents believe, and that is a good teacher is what's working, and a bad teacher is what's not working," states Eric Hanushek, fellow at Stanford University's Hoover Institute and a specialist on economic and education policy (Guggenheim 2010). Davis Guggenheim, the director and narrator of the 2010 film *Waiting for Superman*, tells us that Dr. Hanushek "has tracked the effect of individual teachers on groups of kids." Dr. Hanushek tells us that "the difference between a really good teacher and a really bad teacher is one year of learning per academic year." The film cuts to cartoons of good and bad teachers as Guggenheim narrates, "Students with high performing teachers progress three times as fast as those with low performing teachers, and yet they cost the same to the school. A bad teacher covers only 50 percent of the required curriculum in a school year. A good teacher can cover 150 percent." Ten minutes later, after Guggenheim and various educators and reformers discuss the inability to get rid of bad teachers, he returns to Dr. Hanushek who claims that "if in fact we could just eliminate the bottom 6–10 percent of our teachers, and replace them with an average teacher, we could bring the average US student up to the level of Finland, which is at the top of the world today."

According to this film, in order for schools to *work*, we need to cultivate and retain *good* teachers and get rid of fiscally and pedagogically costly *bad* teachers. Working is both the function of broader social mechanisms and of the labor of teachers as embodied practitioners. The film claims that charter schools can identify and calibrate the proper talent because they have the flexibility to hire and fire teachers at will without the impediments of collective bargaining.[1] This approach to education atomizes teachers as a class and places them under the individual administrative control of school leadership, which assumes a kind of audit culture whereby results can be quantified and fixed to individual teachers as somatic units. This idea that good and bad teachers can be identified with quantifiable evidence and reasonable certainty is a powerful fantasy and one of the key persuasive fictions of education reform discourses.[2] The film was enthusiastically received by charter school proponents; reform-oriented nonprofits organized trips to showings with colleagues and set up screenings at colleges and universities across the country to encourage undergraduates to apply to alternative certification organizations.

By firing nearly 8,000 school teachers and employees of a "failed" school system in one fell swoop and shifting towards recruitment from alternative certification organizations like Teach for America and Teach Nola, policymakers in New Orleans embraced the fantasy of good and bad teachers at a scale and pace far greater than any other city in the United States.[3]

Charles Payne, examining the "persistence of failure in urban schools," claims that the question of "what works," despite its enduring place in education reform discourses, is woefully inadequate (Payne 2008). For Payne, the question of "what" works usually ignores the question of "who" works and how they work together. The danger of the "what works" question is that it radically decontextualizes the practice of education, ignoring singularities and situations, flattening actors and history, by suggesting that pedagogical and institutional knowledge can be easily translated from one context to another. Following Payne, we must pay attention, in a social and historical context, not simply to what bad teachers, *as fact and fantasy,* do and to what values they produce but to who they are and how they work. New Orleans is a city that embraces its history and uniqueness with greater flair, intensity, and industry than perhaps any other in the country (Dawdy 2016, Sakakeeny 2013). That this city, which cultivates a sense of its distinctiveness so boldly, would become ground zero for a project that seeks to model, scale, and replicate the institutional units and discourses of charter schools is one of the great contradictions of charter-based reform.

At the no excuses charter schools in which I conducted my field research, Black teachers (especially ones from New Orleans) were either absent, present in limited numbers, or were not retained because of issues of fit. Whereas it was rare to hear school leaders and charter boosters categorically claim that local and Black teachers were "bad teachers," it was very common to hear that they were a poor fit for the culture of charter schools. While "fit" and "talent" may seem to be more innocent criteria than making claims about good and bad teachers, they are in truth an evolution of the justificatory apparatus of racialized exclusion among New Orleans teaching corps. Dominique, a Black Teach for

America recruit who had worked in one of the few schools run by Black veteran teachers after the storm, was highly critical of the discourse of fit and the perceived lack of interest from Black teachers: "Veteran teachers tried to come back and get hired. But they couldn't get hired anywhere, because we didn't fit. It was like, 'Fuck you, this is a freeze out.'" She claimed that fit was used to exclude Black teachers even when they were technically competent: "I've seen good and great teachers who hit all the goals, but they do not embody the values and vision of the school, they don't fit, then they get called a bad teacher." Dominique reveals how seemingly incompetent teachers are really teachers who don't fit often despite performance. Dominique didn't even necessarily think that the culture of these schools themselves were "wack;" the problem was that schools "define it for a group of people, rather than bring people together." Fit and culture sound organic but reflect a continued commitment to diminishing the power and authority of Black teachers in New Orleans charter schools.

New Orleans has a long and rich history of teacher organizing and political involvement. Black teachers were critical leaders in the civil rights movement and organized the first interracial teachers' union in the Southern United States (Devore and Logsdon 1991, Fairclough [1995] 2008). A wide array of my informants and other stakeholders have referred to Black teachers in New Orleans as "the backbone of the Black middle class." With such a strong cultural and institutional base, how did Black teachers become vulnerable to being fired en masse and slotted into the role of the bad teacher? How did young, alternatively certified, predominately white transplants become the ideal vision of "talent" in the eyes of policymakers, education nonprofits, and charter management organization (CMO) leaders? Others have documented the policy changes and imperatives that incentivized the shift to hiring these teachers, who were more flexible and inexpensive than veteran teachers, who had prior expectations for work discipline and benefits (Buras 2015, Dixson 2011). I focus on the ideological deployment of teacher quality discourses that became embodied in the figures of "bad" or ineffective teachers and of the "talent" that came to replace them. What kind of work does the figure of the "bad teacher" do and how is the "good teacher" or "talent" constructed in response to these narratives? How do these figures articulate and reproduce entangled race, class, and gender ideologies? Surely, before and after Act 35, which authorized the takeover of New Orleans public schools by the state government, there have been both deficient teachers and excellent teachers who have had great impact on their students' and community's lives. But the figures of the "bad teacher" and of "talent" are tethered to these actors in only a partial fashion, and their purposes and deployments exceed pedagogical imperatives. They are heterogeneous fantasies with lives of their own, and it is important to engage them as such in order to break out of a debate framework that is often constricted to either defending or critiquing the performance of traditional public or charter schools and the people that work in them.

These figures are effective in part because, rooted in the common experience of attending schools, they seem self-evident. However, they also draw much of their potency from their flexible and experimental character. Like many other kinds of myths, they are adapted to the circumstances at hand and change over time. Indeed, as charter schools have become the dominant institutional form in New Orleans, the "bad teacher" has receded as a figure and teacher quality discourse has become more oriented around discussion of fit and "talent pipelines." Rather than try to figure out who is "really" a bad or a talented teacher,

I ask us to consider the relationships of these conceptions to each other, and how the ideological character of the boundary making between the two is mediated by notions of fit and culture. By doing so we can begin to reconsider our investments in the discourse of teacher quality itself and the baggage this discourse carries with it.

The twinned fantasies of bad teachers and talent focus conceptions and critiques of education and reform on individuals, shifting responsibility for failure and success on atomized educators at the same time that power and authority in charter schools have shifted towards administration, CMOs, and the state government.[4] This restructuring of accountability is at the heart of the charter school model as adopted in New Orleans. Individual CMOs contract with the state government or another public oversight body to run one or several schools and are responsible for hitting targets heavily weighted with quantitative metrics such as test scores, yearly progress rates, and graduation rates. The responsibility spirals downward, and individual teachers are held accountable to these metrics at the level of the classroom and individual students. Furthermore, notions of fit shift accountability from the community and civic ideals to the school model, network, and market and human capital ethics. These shifts desocialize educators, encouraging strategies of self-care and entrepreneurialism of the self rather than of collective action; they also encourage a relationship to data, which social scientists have cautioned corrupts its pedagogical validity (Palko and Gelman 2016). While dataphilic reformers and researchers see great promise in the ability to track and hold accountable teachers and students on an individual level, there are unintended consequences for the labor process, incentive structures, and social coordination of educators that may impede teaching and learning. Chapter 2, which focuses on the working lives of teachers in New Orleans charter schools, will address these strategies more directly.

The ideological distinctions between bad teachers and talent are not only formed in ways that that have racially discriminating outcomes; they are themselves racializing processes. Race is not an objective and a priori factor that can be analytically applied to discourses of teacher quality. Rather, race and racism have been crafted and reproduced within regimes of human capital from enslavement to the present. Charter school leaders' ideas of fit and culture are an example of the everyday naturalization of ideologies of race and racism.[5] The distinctions made between bad teachers and talent not only involved intergroup competition, prejudice, or discrimination. They are the culmination of day-to-day practices and institutional imperatives that form a crucial part of the terrain upon which race and racism are reconstructed in post-Katrina New Orleans.

PUBLIC DISINVESTMENT

While Hurricane Katrina is often conceived of as marking a sharp break in the history of New Orleans and its schools and while tens of thousands of newcomers arrived in the city in the years following the storm, there were still many educators who worked in the schools in years prior living in the city and up to a third of those who were fired after Katrina ended up working in charter schools (not to mention families and community members). Their memories and reflections on the way the schools were before Katrina helped drive and justify the notion that something had to be done to the schools in the aftermath of the storms. New Orleans Public Schools (NOPS) and Black teachers were vulnerable to takeover and exclusions because the people who knew the school system best already felt wounded by their experiences. Before the storm, educators and families were frustrated with the schools, and while they had many intimate attachments to schools, they did not love the status quo. It was not uncommon for educators I spoke with to reflect on it as a "nightmare." While these narratives were often used to reinforce teacher quality discourses, these wounded attachments were not driven by bad teachers but by broken systems and decades of disinvestment in the public sphere.

New Orleans public schools have been subject to national intervention and embroiled in battles over racial and class inequality since their inception. An alliance of local elites and New England transplants founded the system in the nineteenth century and African Americans and Creoles fought for most of the following century for equitable access and participation within the institution (Devore and Logsdon 1991). Black educators organized into a union that would become the United Teachers of New Orleans, which was instrumental in fighting for civil rights and school integration and served as a model of social justice unionism (Buras 2015, Fairclough [1995] 2008). These gains were compromised and provisional, like most political accomplishments. White families began a dramatic exit from the public school system and the city in the late '60s and early '70s.[6] From that point forward until 2005, New Orleans schools were subject to "aggressive neglect" (Ladson-Billings 2006), and the gains of decades of organizing and agitation were eroded—as were other aspects of the welfare state, including public benefits and public housing, which was converted into mixed-use private developments (Arena 2011, Germany 2007).

Before the impact of Hurricane Katrina and subsequent levee failures in 2005, New Orleans public schools were regarded by many as some of the worst in the United States. People both pointed to quantitative performance indicators and invoked qualitative descriptions of the corruption, ineffectiveness, and neglect of the system—issues that characterize many "inner-city" or "urban" school districts. "What were the schools like before Hurricane Katrina?" was one of the first questions I asked my informants, whether they had been living and working in the school system for decades or were fresh arrivals. The stories that followed from my query can help us better understand the registers within which systemic critiques are made and give us a better appreciation of the justificatory landscape produced by tales of "failure."

My informants, mostly educators and nonprofit employees (and a handful of community activists), painted a critical picture of New Orleans Public Schools before Act 35. Dr. Broadus, a Black nonlocal former charter school network executive, said the system was a "nightmare," a word that, as mentioned above, popped up for several others. Both Jessie and Val, novice white transplant teachers, claimed that their perceptions of prereform New Orleans public schools as a failure were shaped by popular media (e.g., *New York Times* 2011) and advisors in their ongoing training sessions. They were told that the schools were "completely dysfunctional" and that "teachers didn't care." According to these two young teachers these narratives were always coupled with proclamations about how much better things are now. Emile, a non-Black woman of color transplant and charter school principal who had taught in the city before Katrina, remembered her frustration at having to make extraordinary efforts to track down her paycheck and other administrative paperwork, a far cry from the efficiency and care of her current CMO. "Corruption" on the Orleans Parish School Board and among politicians was also cited as a problem by several interviewees.[7] These characterizations evoked an image of an institutional bureaucracy in chaos. The pre-Katrina school district cut checks inappropriately to "retired, fired, or even dead" recipients and came under federal indictment for contracting violations (Harris 2020). Rather than validate the notion of the entire school system as irredeemably corrupt, however, we should recognize the ways that public resources, including schools, have a long record of being subject to rent-seeking strategies from unscrupulous groups and individuals. There were many frustrating and unacceptable dimensions to the public schools before the storm. Rather than cast blame on them or see them as mere symptoms, we would do well to remember that veteran educators, students, and families were the ones offering some of the most potent and incisive critiques of these deficiencies.

Informants also keyed in on academic performance when assessing the pre-Katrina schools and, as they did so, often shifted between qualitative and quantitative registers. Aubrey, a transplant Black woman and director of an education nonprofit in the city, who noted that she had arrived to teach in New Orleans five years before Act 35, couched her critique of the old system in more quantitative terms. "Sixty-six percent of schools were unacceptable" and "not prepping kids on any major indicator." This reckoning was rooted in a familiarity with state accountability standards in which New Orleans had consistently ranked near the bottom.[8] Despite the widespread notion that schools were failing, Aubrey asserted that the "dominant narrative doesn't do justice to the inadequacy. . . . In 2004, the top student in NOPS couldn't pass a college entrance exam." This story was used frequently by education reformers to justify transforming the entire school system. I was able to find news stories from that year about a valedictorian at one high school who flunked the math portion of the high school exit exam five times. Terry, a transplant Black woman and community activist familiar with the student in the narrative, expressed frustration to me with the way their story was being used to drive notions of wholesale academic deficiency. At the end of her reflection, Aubrey shifted tack away from quantitative measures and emphasized that "there was a lot of belief that you couldn't solve the problem.... If you look around now, you can see excellent schools. Before Katrina, there was not one."[9] While the quantitatively measured challenges facing NOPS were daunting, for Aubrey, a foreclosed sense of possibility and lack of faith were the most debilitating. She indicated that something in these discursive shifts prompted by post-Katrina reforms reopened a sense of possibility. Aubrey's support for charter school–based reforms was rooted partly in her own experience of the pain of disinvestment and neglect; it did not simply represent an abstract ideological commitment to the privatization of public institutions.

Other interlocutors emphasized the structural constraints facing public schools in the post–civil rights era. Brett, a local white self-described radical and veteran teacher with over twenty years of experience, emphasized how severely underresourced NOPS was before the influx of reformers after Act 35. Framing failure narratives in terms of class and race struggle, he cautioned me, "Most narratives about the schools before Katrina are deliberately simplistic and ill informed. They're narratives of people in power.... The narrative of abject failure is wrong.... This city doesn't care about educating poor people." Ryan, a Black local, former teacher, and graduate student, noted that after official school desegregation white people carved out their own private sphere.[10] Reverend Douglass, a Black local from the Ninth Ward, conceded that there was an "academic crisis" but that it was "exaggerated by metrics."[11] The real problem was that we had a "culture which neglected the education of children and a disintegration of the family and school system." For Rev. Douglass, an excessive focus on test scores obscures other more salient issues in Black communities that should also be within the purview of the education system. For all of these informants, public schools were beset by external structural and cultural forces that impeded their ability to serve students and communities.

Salim, a Black transplant but longtime resident, activist, and teacher, asserted that schools were functioning properly before the storm, but within political economic imperatives "appropriate for a tourist-based economy. . . . The schools are like this [not preparing students for college] to staff hotels. . . . You have the ingredients of an apartheid school system." Furthermore, Salim insisted that in evaluating education reform after Act 35, "I wouldn't fall into the trap of the schools being better or worse." Salim asks us to think what economic purpose charter schools' new orientation to schooling may represent.[12] Despite the broad consensus that NOPS faced significant barriers to educating children, many informants insisted that there were spaces in which positive efforts were made to improve education. These spaces were most often described as "pockets of excellence," and the people who carried out these efforts were called "reformers"— or informants would point out that "there were some good teachers." Aubrey felt that these efforts were isolated and ineffective. Brett, on the other hand, felt that the efforts of veteran teachers were ignored because they didn't link up with the ideologies of education foundations on the question of charter schools and unionization. Nathaniel Lacour, a Black local and former leader of the United Teachers of New Orleans, stated in an interview with *Democracy Now!*, "Let me simply say this: I don't think there's anybody in New Orleans who would say that they were satisfied with the school system prior to Katrina, because there's an effort to say that there are people here who want the status quo. That is not true" (*Democracy Now!* 2007). One of the effects of an individualistic focus on teacher quality is that it obscures the complex histories of contestation over schools in New Orleans, categorizing anyone who wants to paint anything more than a uniformly bleak picture of the public schools before Katrina as a defender of the "status quo." The new system versus the old system debate became a kind of identity politics, and there was no room to recognize the variety of agendas, perspectives, and alliances involved.

A crucial aspect of these assessments about good teachers before the storm was the feeling that while veteran teachers were not measuring up according to certain testing metrics,[13] other contributions were not valued or even accounted for. Dr. Sullivan, a white local and school administrator before Act 35, thought that "teachers before Katrina were outstanding." She particularly esteemed their presence in NOPS after white flight: "Some people wouldn't venture into the neighborhoods that we served. These were violent places, but we did our job because we cared deeply about educating these children." George, a Black local and former teacher, stated, "those who would paint a broad picture of failure are not seeing the big picture. . . . Success is lowering the dropout rate, lowering violence, increasing the possibility for kids to succeed and go to college." The audit cultures favored by charter schools cannot capture these dimensions of success with their quantifiable metrics.[14]

Familial connection and the ties between school and community emerged as a critical theme among positive accounts of teachers before Act 35. Harper, a Black local and veteran teacher of twenty-nine years, told me that "at my school, everyone was a family member." She stressed that she "went into homes . . . sometimes in dangerous areas." Ryan, a Black local and recent graduate of Douglass High School, claimed that he chose Douglass over high schools with better academic reputations because of his family history. It was important to him that the teachers there knew his family. Ryan was one of the informants who told me that "in New Orleans, people don't ask you where you went to college like other cities. 'What school you went to?' means high school . . . That makes you who you are." Ryan loved that his civics teacher lived close by and that he would run into them on the way to and from school saying, "there is just something to having teachers that live close." Johnny Bridges, a local and veteran teacher, recounted his feelings on the radio program *The New Orleans Imperative* after Act 35: "I was on the job for twenty-nine years, so I got into generations and when you get into generations you have the support of those families because I taught your mother, son. So all I have to do is make a phone call. So it was our relationship with those children that a lot of folks didn't understand" (*The New Orleans Imperative* 2011). After the conversion to charter schools, transplant teachers would often tell stories about venturing into homes and neighborhoods of their students and the value of the communal relations they built during their teaching experiences.[15] In 2014, I observed teachers at a charter school and new Teach for America corps members on separate occasions as they prepared to canvass the communities of their students, a sign of growing cultural sophistication and racialized expertise.

The media, academia, and popular culture have all produced countless accounts of inner-city public schools as pathologically dysfunctional in the post–*A Nation at Risk* era. These narratives, in their sober and sensationalist forms, certainly formed a discursive background for education stakeholders. However, what I found, particularly among veteran educators, both pro- and antireform was a kind of wounded reflection on "what the schools were like" before Katrina. Charter advocates and operators included many like Emile and Aubrey, who worked in public schools before the storm as self-conscious reformers and felt stymied by the traditional public school system. The principal at the charter elementary school in which I taught in Harlem was one of these people. Their support for charter-based reform was rooted in an intimate frustration with the bureaucratic dysfunctions of traditional school systems. On the other hand, many veterans critical of reform articulated feeling unappreciated despite undertaking the difficult task of teaching in such an environment and feeling that they were unfairly blamed for outcomes beyond their control. While many accounts of post-Katrina reform have asserted that the storm "destroyed" the school system, which allowed reformers to "start over," there was no particular reason the system had to be reconstructed as primarily composed of charter schools. A storm can destroy physical capital and harm and displace "human capital," but that does not necessarily mean that it also destroys institutional and political structures. The traditional public school system in New Orleans was vulnerable to destruction, in part, because even those who knew it best were deeply wounded by it and either unable or unwilling to defend it.

TERMINATED

In the aftermath of executing Act 35, letters of termination were sent to all of the nearly 8,000 New Orleans Public school employees in schools taken over by the state-run Recovery School District. As noted in the introduction, more than 70 percent of these employees were Black and they represented 4 percent of the working-age Black population of the city at that time (Harris et al. 2015). In the subsequent reorganization, terminated employees were not given preferential hiring status, a right typically bargained for by unionized teachers. Technically, all the schools under the RSD were considered new institutional entities. According to a United Teachers of New Orleans (UTNO) report (United Teachers of New Orleans 2007), only 46 percent of the dismissed teachers returned to NOPS by August 2006, and my interviews with union members indicate that attrition and retirement rates were high in the following years. Furthermore, charter management organizations (CMOs) opted or were discouraged from participating in the teacher retirement system, hampering their ability to hire and attract veteran teachers.

Johnny Bridges recounted the moment he was notified: "And then the school board sent a letter saying that we were all terminated. And it was devastating because, working at a place for so long and then being sent a letter of termination with no reason. Now it's OK to fire somebody, I imagine, but you have to have a reason and there was no reason, you know, no reason given in that letter" (*The New Orleans Imperative* 2011). Mr. Bridges seemed to be disconcerted less with the termination itself than with the impersonal way in which it was communicated. Given the enduring dislocations after the storm and levee failures, many teachers did not even receive the letters and found out about the mass firing secondhand (Buras 2015). Mr. Bridges further explained the betrayal of his termination, "In order for you to be a teacher, it's a special gift. It's not about the money, number one. You spend a lot of years trying to train kids to be productive citizens in society and what you do is for the love of children, it's not for the love of money. The loyalty that the teachers of Orleans Parish had, it's unbelievable, I mean we're educated people, we could all find something else to do, but we decided to make this our life's work."

The emphasis on a calling here draws a sharp contrast with the perception of charter school teachers as transient, inexperienced outsiders. For Mr. Bridges, who fired him and how they did it is as important as the fact of dismissal itself. He knew and accepted that regimes of evaluation were part of the game, so to speak, but the standards seemed to have changed. He claimed that he and other teachers sacrificed for their love of children and that their efforts and expertise were not respected: "To be terminated by people who sit on a board, never walked in a classroom, don't understand the art of teaching and they decide they want to change course and leave you out of the equation . . . that's not fair . . . it's not fair. If I can be loyal to you for twenty-nine years and accept all the foolishness that the board should have been doing to improve test scores . . . because this is a partnership . . ." (*The New Orleans Imperative* 2011). Mr. Bridges was deeply hurt by the way in which people, *whom he did not know,* sat in judgment of him without the courtesy of presenting themselves.[16]

At the same time, Bridges romanticized the teaching profession and challenged the ability of outsiders to relate to the student population, implying that there were people, people with "the gift" who were proper stewards of the students of New Orleans. This narrative evoked long-term discourses of uplift in which middle-class African Americans had a moral calling to bring the lower classes up, or in the words of Mr. Bridges, to "train kids to be productive citizens in society." Dr. Spears, a white local educational researcher and longtime activist, laughed at those who imagined Black teachers as uniformly progressive, claiming that to do so ignored conservative tendencies many had and that it papered over class difference among Black communities.[17] The common sense that Black teachers were the "backbone of the Black middle class" shouldn't only evoke sympathy because an entire section of the New Orleans Black community was eviscerated. It should also remind us that these teachers lived and operated as a "professional managerial class" that was partially responsible for managing deviance and respectability among marginalized poor and Black students and families. Their dismissal should be sympathized with; but it should also provoke us to ask what their dissolution or diminution as a class can tell us about the realignment of class forces within the city at large.

To go from respected, secure, and relatively well-compensated employment to precarity, derision, and suspicion was quite jarring for many veteran educators. I sat with Harper at the United Teachers of New Orleans office, and we discussed her teaching career and her feelings about being fired as a result of Act 35. Rather than reenter the system and attempt to compete for a job at a new charter school, Harper decided to take an early retirement package.[18] She described her decision, "It's heartbreaking, going through Katrina and then finding out you don't have a job . . . I taught for twenty-nine years." In the face of claims of poor teacher quality, she reasserted her credentials, "I have a master's degree. I never got a U [unqualified rating]. Then you say you are looking for highly qualified teachers and I have to take a test! I was not going to do that! They don't respect your credentials." Pushing against the received notion that new talent was needed she claimed, "They could have brought us back . . . You can't do just anything to veteran teachers . . . I would still be teaching, but once they started talking about not hiring us back and doing all this testing, I said no. *I was good enough before and after.*" Harper indicated that for some period, it seemed possible, even likely that she and other veteran teachers would be able to easily transition back into the classroom, a possibility foreclosed by new regimes of accountability. But when I asked Aubrey about the exclusion of veteran teachers, she was puzzled by the notion that they might feel shut out, claiming that "there were plenty of jobs." Indeed, in the first years after Act 35, the district claimed to be facing a teacher shortage. However, this was not due to a lack of experienced teachers but to a lack of human capital—namely, teachers who met new standards of accountability, which Harper felt to be disrespectful and dehumanizing.

A group of teachers and lawyers filed a class-action lawsuit against the state and the Orleans Parish School Board and this became a site for the articulation of loss as well. Karran Royal, a parent activist, used her twitter account to live report the testimony of Cynthia Jordan, a fired teacher, writing on Twitter,

> #nolaed Ms. Jordan became very emotional as she talked about being given 2 hours to clear out 16 years of possessions at her school ... #nolaed, it never occurred to Ms. Jordan that she wouldn't have a job to come back to. She was ready to clean her school . . . #nolaed This kind of job instability compounds the stress of losing your job in the midst of the worst disaster in this country's history. (June 6, 2011)

On an intimate scale we see how the specific belongings and the space of Ms. Jordan's classroom possessed an irreducible and incommensurable value. The disruption and detachment experienced by teachers after the flooding are not merely experiences of emotional distress; they also mirrored the disintegration between subject and object and the space they occupy. This mirroring was articulated by Royal when she retweeted a tweet about the testimony of another teacher: "#nolaed breaks down as she describes the disrepair of the bldg in 2006. Cries as she describes bldg torn down ..." (June 7, 2011).

The destruction of old school buildings and the relative exclusion of veteran teachers from charter schools represented the forfeiture of a calling and an identity for the educators I spoke with. After proclaiming that she was "good enough," Harper continued to articulate her sense of loss: "I was a very dedicated teacher. I was the first in the door in the morning, and the last out at night. They took that away from me. That was a part of me, my livelihood ... I'm sorry. I have to stop. I might cry and mess up my makeup. [*Smiles*] Once you're a teacher, if it's in your blood, it's there until you die ... What else can I do?" What exactly was taken away from Harper or Johnny Bridges or Ms. Jordan or Ms. Lockett? More than a job, these teachers seem distraught at the rending of a profoundly meaningful social and professional relationship, one deepened by its duration. The mass firing of mostly Black veteran teachers in New Orleans after Hurricane Katrina is but the most dramatic instantiation of a nationwide trend.[19] The firing of New Orleans public school employees was not only a profoundly painful experience for those educators; it also realigned class forces in the city.[20] The firing of Black teachers and their framing within a discourse as insufficient talent atomizes their class power and places them within a framework of individualistic evaluation. Even sympathetic renderings of veteran teachers as victims of pernicious reforms trap them within the atomizing framework of victimhood without articulating the significance of their dismissal as a class.

Superintendent Paul Vallas, brought in to run the RSD in 2007 after serving similar roles in Philadelphia and Chicago, argued that veteran teachers were not pushed out but that CMOs were expressing their autonomous preferences by hiring a "mixed selection of teachers." National philanthropies, such as the Bill and Melinda Gates and Eli and Edythe Broad foundations, who agreed that there was a need for a "new influx of talent" in order to improve New Orleans schools, provided injections of funding for alternative certification organizations (Teach for America,

Teach Nola) and human capital incubators (New Schools for New Orleans), turning to new sources for their teaching staffs. As a result, the overall New Orleans teaching corps became "younger, whiter, less indigenous, and more likely to come from an alternative certification program" (Vaughn et al. 2012). This trend was also reflected in the composition of decision-makers at the administrative and policy levels (Buras 2015). By the time I moved to New Orleans in 2013, there had been a significant increase in racial diversity and teachers of local origin provided by Teach for America and increases in partnerships with local universities to build talent pipelines and in locals taking policy leadership roles (such as RSD superintendent Patrick Dobard who occupied the position from 2012 to 2017). These trends demonstrated that though the dominant "color of reform" (Dixson, Buras, and Jeffers 2015) may have initially been white, it was possible for pro-charter organizations to embrace and generate new racial politics of recognition and selective inclusion.

Charter schools and private management of schools in particular not only became a favored method of reconstructing public education but also served as a symbol of the rebirth of the city of New Orleans as a broader political, economic, and cultural entity. Proponents of charter-based reforms have argued that charter schools benefit students through increased autonomy, flexibility, choice, and accountability while critics have responded that charter schools are unaccountable to the public, undermine teachers through labor precarity, impose false or asymmetric choices, and narrowly focus on testing (Buras 2015, Ravitch 2013). While charter-oriented critiques of traditional public schools have a basis in the "common sense" of educator and community dissatisfaction with neglect and disinvestment, they also encourage the erosion of communal solidarity in favor of atomized and individual responses to school reform (Lipman 2011). This creates a contradiction insofar as parents and communities are supposed to be empowered through exercising choice in their consumption of education services at the same time as they are reduced to "objects of administration" at the level of policy and politics (Reed and Steinberg 2006).[21] Teachers, meanwhile, are generally discouraged or barred from unionizing in charter schools, with some exceptions. Self-cultivation and entrepreneurial development of individual human capital became the alternative to collective bargaining. It is important to place the figures of the bad teacher and talent in this historical context. The bad teacher became the bête noire of charter school–based education reform at the precise moment when decades of racialized disinvestment in public institutions dovetailed with ideological investments in the individual as the font of political action, responsibility, and blame.

REPLACING BAD TEACHERS WITH TALENT

While the dismissal and attrition of the veteran teacher corps was a part of a classed realignment of power in post-Katrina New Orleans, it is essential to probe the racialization of educators to understand how public schools came to be pathologized in ways that are similar to the pathologization of other facets of Black life in the postwar era. Dr. Spears claimed that in New Orleans before Act 35, "public school teacher meant Black teacher" and thought that the "bad teacher talk" helps to "assuage the guilt of Teach for America people" for taking jobs away from Black teachers. Inveighing against "school reform liberalism," he claimed that "people who are self-consciously antiracist construct self-justification through demonization." For Dr. Spears, "privatization" was not something perpetrated by neoconservatives or Republicans alone. Rather he believed that white conservatives and liberals both support charter schools because of their shared images of bad teachers and a failed school system. Dr. Spears believed that the logic of the bad teacher myth in New Orleans was inherently racialized, a product of "white supremacy," and said that according to the ideology of school reformers, "the worst thing that ever happened to Black children was Black adults." The failure of these teachers was not just about pedagogy; it was also the result of the failure of a racialized stewardship on the part of Black parents and perhaps unions and politicians as well. The "bad teacher" can be read as a metonym for a failed Black public sphere post Jim Crow.

There were also more technocratic and ostensibly race-neutral takes on teachers' working capacities before Act 35. Ash, a white transplant and, at the time, a researcher at a New Orleans–based education think tank, expressed sympathy for the teachers who were fired, claiming that they were "products of the system." But Ash explained that they were not willing to work the hours or display the flexibility that new teachers, like Teach for America corps members, were. The new "talent" in the city was on a "different level professionally," and, "bottom line, scores are up." Dee, a Black local, RSD employee, and community organizer, claimed that bad teachers were "like a virus infecting others," which perhaps acts as a justification for the replacement or quarantining of the "bad teacher" from kids. While conservative and neoliberal ideologues have used the morally charged term "bad teacher" directly, those working in nonprofits and at the school level preferred the more technocratic and sympathetic language of skill gaps and talent insufficiencies, referring to the inability of veteran teachers to pass skills exams, turn in resumes without typos, or respond to digital correspondence in a timely fashion. These accounts render veteran teachers as victims of their own system; they are sympathetic but incapable subjects. While this language may seem more objective and value neutral, it too is subject to ideology. Some have contested that there is no solid research basis for judging school performance pre-Katrina that controls for demographic factors and the changes in funding and population that have occurred after the storm (Harris 2013).

These conceptions of veteran teachers before the storm were challenged by Dr. Freeman, a Black local and former principal, who claimed that there was "no evidence" for lazy teachers and who furthermore challenged the basis of using work ethic as a critique. He questioned both the equation of working hard with progress and the ability of charter school advocates to claim that their teachers somehow worked harder than veteran teachers from before Act 35.[22] The subject of work hours will be analyzed in depth in chapter 2, but for now, we should note that one of the primary markers used to differentiate bad veteran teachers from talent was working hours, or more specifically the willingness to work long hours without restriction from family or community commitments; even expressing of the desire to limit one's working week to a reasonable amount was looked upon as disqualifying. In explaining the efficacy of the bad teacher myth, both Dr. Spears and Dr. Styles, Black transplants who had never met each other, independently claimed that the myth drew power from "white people's biggest fear": that white tax dollars might go to a Black person who "hadn't earned" the money. In the political economy of New Orleans the bad teacher could index profound fears that the state, which was properly owned by white people, had been infected by undeserving Black subjects. Unlike the welfare mother or their criminalized children however, the figure of the bad teacher suggested that the state was not just being leeched by spooks; rather the state itself had become the succubus.[23] Rather than simply defend the position that veteran teachers were "really" good or bad, effective or ineffective, we should refuse the trap of deviance (Cohen 2004) and become suspicious of the framework of evaluation itself.

What kind of teachers did CMOs, the RSD, and education nonprofits imagine they needed when they began reopening and expanding schools in the years after Hurricane Katrina? While the dominant image may be the young white female transplants from elite colleges provided by alternative certification organizations, the picture on the ground was a bit more complicated a decade and more after the storm. According to Buras (2015), by 2011, Black teachers comprised 50 percent of teachers in charters, down from 75 percent, and white teachers were 46 percent of the workforce, up from 24 percent. Forty percent of teachers had three years or less experience. However, the hiring profiles at New Orleans charter schools were highly stratified, with some no excuses–style charters relying heavily on the stereotypical transplant recruit, and other networks having more mixed faculty. Furthermore, TFA began to recruit significantly more Black and local corps members, shifting the racial contours of how talent gets defined. Every network and nonprofit had particular interests and processes that shaped their conceptions of who they wanted in their school building and how to find them. In the following, I highlight some of the dynamics that shaped this process, focusing in particular on the themes of mindsets, fit, and selective inclusion.

In recent decades firms across diverse industries have begun to value "talent" over experience when making hiring and retention decisions (Urciuoli 2008) and this shift can be seen in the hiring practices of several New Orleans CMOs. Kerry, a white transplant and the CEO of a no excuses–like CMO, told me, when hiring, "we are flexible on technical skills." Kerry believed that technical skills could be coached and developed but that "mindsets" were fundamental indicators of a potential hire's success on the team. Kerry brought in potential hires to conduct sample lessons with students and then gave the applicants what he conceived of as withering and honest feedback. The applicant was then invited to reflect on the feedback and incorporate it into a subsequent sample lesson, being tested on the changes they made. Showing "grit" and receptiveness to feedback throughout this rigorous interview process was more important than accumulated qualifications. During the hiring process, Kerry and the team gave all the info they could, positive and critical, to applicants and left it up to them to decide whether their school was the kind of place they could envision working at. The school leaders sometimes took the time to see how the applicant interacted with their potential colleagues by taking them to dinner. Jamie, a transplant of color and principal at another school, wanted people who were going to "do the work."

Talent manifested on multiple registers in the hiring process: pedigree, perseverance, potential, and the performance of recognizable social cues. One of the ironies of the human capital regimes of charter networks is that while they aspired to create a system for the universalizable, scalable, and portable judgment of talent, their actual practices are highly ritualized, particular, and provincial. Walker, a white transplant and human capital manager at a charter management organization, described some of the ways that veteran educators were disqualified during the hiring process: "Like anyone, we want to hire locally. Unfortunately we see the legacy of a bad education system, where sometimes the applicant pool from local educators that are older, over forty . . .

If I were to pull up their resumes, there's going to be more than one spelling error, there would be a lack of urgency or responsiveness to requests, or trouble uploading resumes." Walker claimed that technological skills were particularly deficient among experienced applicants: "We moved to an online video platform. I have seen a lot of older applicants that continually say they struggle with that. We need people to be technologically savvy in order to work well and be efficient . . . Unfortunately, I think that's a legacy of a bad education system." White-dominant professional cultures recognized these norms as standard indications of professionalism, even though the expectations around technology are ultimately arbitrary. These standards and rituals made it difficult for Black educators who were recognized interpersonally as being quality staff to secure positions and promotions.

The evocation of older educators as themselves victims of a failed education system facilitates the idea that human capital processes are technical and neutral and that racially disparate outcomes are unfortunate and unintended byproducts—another move to claim innocence from making racially discriminatory decisions on the part of reformers. Hayden, a white transplant and a hiring manager at another CMO, discussed this in terms of promoting career pathways for support staff who are disproportionately Black and local: "I don't think schools have thought about it [using support staff as a diversity pipeline] deliberately. It's just how it falls out." When Black and local candidates aren't able to meet the expectations of hiring rituals, their deficiencies are naturalized: "One of our best teachers . . . was a para [paraprofessional assisting teacher] though, and she didn't get into Teach Nola twice. I worked part-time at Teach Nola, and one of our principals called me and asked how I could help her get in. . . . I work with her, but she's just a terrible interviewer, it's just not something she's good at." While the bad teacher myth helps to justify the mass firing of Act 35, it was this kind of sympathetic and pathologizing essentialism of cultural difference that vexed reformers and perpetuated the exclusion of many Black and veteran educators.

The cultural performances involved in tests of mindsets invited racialized arbitrariness into the hiring process in ways that collectively bargained contracts were designed to mitigate, and some reformers recognized this as an ongoing problem in the prevailing human capital sector. Toni, a white local and an education-nonprofit executive, portrayed this as a difficulty endemic to human nature:

> If you're a person who is not from New Orleans, who has come here and knows the schools were terrible and you're starting a charter school and you have someone from OPSB [Orleans Parish School Board] who is a former OPSB teacher who comes to you and didn't go to a prestigious university and comes and applies to you for a job and you have someone who went to Princeton and taught for two years in St. Bernard Parish and all over their resume are the performance gains that they had with their kids and you yourself went to Penn or something, it becomes hard to make that decision. Just as if you worked in the old system and you know the nuances of what schools were good and what weren't, and you have people you can ask for reference checks on folks who come to apply for you, you look at the resume of the guy who's not from New Orleans, and you're like why would I hire that person when I have this person who has been teacher for fifteen years, and that exacerbates the segregation issue.

Toni asserted that both traditional and charter school models were imbricated within social norms that privileged culturally arbitrary connections. Their concern about the persistence of network effects in charter school hiring demonstrated the illusory nature of the tabula rasa of reform.

Mindsets were one of the primary ways school leaders decided if someone was a "culture fit" at a school. Many principals didn't necessarily have the resources to conduct as extensive an interview process as Kerry could. Nevertheless, fit was one of the primary attributes they looked for as they recruited and retained teachers. Casey, a white local and principal at another no excuses school, told me that "even excellent teachers" have had to leave their school because they did not fit in on the team. While fit was often characterized in terms of positive attitude, work ethic, and team orientation by school leaders I spoke to, teachers also expressed frustrations that indicate that it also meant adherence to management imperatives, group rituals, and a willingness to prioritize work time above other commitments. Being willing to spend time at school was perhaps the single most apparent indicator of fit. Hayden said that they would "love to hire more veteran teachers" but that veterans often asked very direct questions about when school was dismissed. Hayden continued,

> I don't believe there's a teacher shortage in the area. One of the reasons some of the veteran teachers aren't choosing to stay here is that mindset as well. . . . The charter schools ask a lot more. . . . Connecting back to that veteran school base of staff that's available out there. . . . When I've had conversations, a lot of them will ask, "Well, what's the school day?" And I tell them, and they say, "Oh, yeah, yeah, sure . . . I'll be interested or apply," and I know that's a big factor, that previous way of operating in the school system. The biggest challenge is just having that mindset. It's more common among the TFA world because we got six weeks of teacher training with a constant sense of urgency. Those of us who got placed into charter schools, it was like a continuation, where it's not uncommon to put in ten to twelve hours a day. Someone who was like, Yeah my day used to be 8:30 to 2:30, 3:30, depending on when the kids would leave. It's tough to say,

"Hey we need you to come in earlier, we need you to stay later. In addition to that, we need you to cover lunch and do advisory."

Here we see that fit was more than just a metric for management. It also involved additional affective labor and was a burden placed on teachers as workers, demonstrating vividly the ways that, like other service workers in neoliberal economies (Leidner 1993), teachers were compelled not only to get results but also to cultivate their own capacities as "human capital."

While this focus on mindsets and fit might seem to lend itself to excluding all but young transplants who, without connections to their communities or families, can work seemingly unlimited hours, I found that the school leaders I observed were trying to move away from a sole reliance on that kind of recruit. School leaders I interviewed at charter schools with higher test scores and reputations shied away from hiring first-year alternatively certified teachers if they could even though most of them started their own careers with Teach for America. They preferred to hire TFA alumni who had been seasoned already at other more "dysfunctional" schools. Kerry in particular spoke of one TFA-alum hire who was so glad to be starting at a school that wasn't a "shitshow" that they were very enthusiastic participants in team culture the following year. As mentioned earlier, TFA itself began recruiting significantly more Black and local corps members. I attended the orientation for a local program designed to train school leaders of color for charter schools. Participants spoke freely and honestly about the ways in which they felt they and their Black colleagues had experienced glass ceilings within the charter landscape, exchanging knowing nods and exclamations at the mention of the "dean of discipline," a role they were often filtered into and one that limited their aspirations for leadership. These teachers nevertheless remained committed to navigating leadership pathways within charter schools, if only out of necessity. Contemporary school leaders uniformly proclaimed their commitment to diversity though their mechanisms for pursuing it were more constrained than those that TFA and other nonprofits used. Hayden told me, "Look, the perfect candidate is going to be a young Black male from New Orleans who teaches math" before lamenting about the rarity of such a subject.

Hayden continued to define the problem of teacher diversity in terms of scarcity: "Our biggest source for (diversity) is TFA and Teach Nola. Leaders tell me all the time, 'I need teachers like this [i.e., a Black person].' But I can't send an email to TFA saying, 'I need to see all your Black corps members.' We can say, 'We want to grow the diversity of our school, please help us with that with your candidates.'" This sense of scarcity requires discounting locally trained educators by claiming that they lack fit. Here Hayden stated, "I know Xavier has a school of Ed, but our challenge is we don't hire first-year teachers out of traditional-ed schools. We feel that TFA and Teach Nola prep better for our type of classroom and our settings. Dillard doesn't have an ed program. It's a tough talent pool coming in. I've watched teachers from ed programs making lateral moves get declined by our schools for not meeting what they're looking for as far as the deliverables in the classroom. They met what they were looking for in terms of: this is a Black male in front of the classroom, discipline seems to be fine . . . but not that great of a teacher." Whereas twenty-two-year-old Ivy league grads have great potential to be molded, Hayden indicated that locally trained educators were not seen to be as pliable: "Usually they decide to not go with that person because we don't have the capacity to support or develop them the way we'd like, or we do have pretty good teacher development, but we're determining that we're not going to help this person become the kind of teacher we need them to be."

The hiring practices of charter schools in New Orleans should be thought of as selectively inclusive rather than absolutely exclusive. The process of selective inclusion created a site of contestation over the racialized character of the educator class in New Orleans. Black and other educators of color who were engaging with charter schools in various capacities weren't merely secondary accomplices to reform agendas; instead, they had their own pedagogical and political visions that were constrained and compromised by the contemporary environment. In the early years of reform after Katrina, young, predominately white transplants were more able to do affective and cultural signaling of fit, flexibility, and talent, but there is no reason to think that Black and local teachers could not learn these skills and that education reform could not have developed a more sophisticated politics of recognition. While transplant teachers were at times criticized for being less experienced and less expensive than veteran teachers and were accused of being less effective, we must recognize them not as "deskilled" labor but as "reskilled" labor. This reskilling of the teacher around new demands for affect, self-cultivation, and work discipline is another force of atomization—but one that is not taken up by new teachers in straightforwardly predictable or enthusiastic ways.

AMBIVALENT TEACHERS, AMBIVALENT TALENT

Transplanted white educators were not passive wearers of the mantle of talent. They engaged in their own ambivalent and racialized interpretations about the ways they were positioned as different kinds of both laboring and ethical subjects.[24] In order to get a better sense of who these newer "good" teachers were in contrast to the figurations of bad teachers and veteran teachers, I interviewed many young Teach for America corps members, exploring the ways they articulated their own relationships to the politics and ethics of race, labor, and care in post-Katrina school reform. I sat with Val on a hot but rainy day at a café uptown near Tulane University. I met her at a UTNO racial healing-circle meeting and was intrigued to find out more about her perspectives on coming in after Act 35 as a new teacher who was part of a small number of hires who actively sought out relationships with veteran teachers and the teachers' union. Before coming to New Orleans, Val was excited to find out more about the education scene in the city although she had heard criticisms. Val exchanged emails with a professor of education about her potential to help and recounted the correspondence to me, "He told me that I shouldn't come, that I was doing harm and taking a job away from a Black teacher. I still came, but I was really freaked out by that email. How could someone think that about me? I had good intentions! I didn't know about the firings until I actually moved here." Val understood that she was entering an ethically fraught arena by taking a teaching job in New Orleans though she was not aware of many of the details until sometime after arriving. She nevertheless felt sufficiently committed (in both the active and passive sense) to helping that she took the position anyway.

Despite the concerns raised by the email exchange, Val claimed that she actually found her greatest network of support with veteran teachers at the teachers' union offices. Val was unsure whether she was going to continue in New Orleans after the two-year commitment: "I think about going back to my hometown. I'm not sure if New Orleans is where I belong . . . Sometimes I want to teach at my neighborhood school." Val was deeply conflicted about her place in the reform landscape, uncertain of her effectiveness, claiming that the way she had been told to teach contradicted the way she learned growing up going to "good schools." Her experience both with the ethical dilemmas of being a young white teacher who had "replaced" veteran Black teachers and the relationships she had built with some of those very same teachers had led her to question the very meaning of racialized belonging—should she go back to where she "belongs" or stay and find a new way to be in community?

Jessie, another young transplant teacher, also asked the question "Whose job am I replacing?" However, our discussion focused more on the conditions of labor she experienced as a first-year teacher at a charter school. Jessie admitted that, like many first-year teachers, she had a difficult time adjusting to the rigors of the profession. Jessie "thought about quitting all the time," even going so far as to rehearse the speech she would give to the principal. After learning more about the history of teachers in New Orleans from engagements with veteran teachers, Jessie admitted to being "angry" because she was "cheaper." For Jessie, being a good teacher was not just defined along the metrics of learning outcomes but also upon the character of her labor, "I was discouraged by my principal and by TFA from associating with the teachers' union and advocating for labor rights. . . . My principal was patronizing to me; he claimed that I was too busy to go to board meetings. I always felt belittled and disempowered. . . . It goes into this martyrdom complex of serving disadvantaged communities." Jessie felt that what made her a good teacher was the willingness to work hard and comply with the administration. While Jessie and other talent were valorized for being the "best and the brightest," she questioned whether she was really a good or even better teacher, asking, "Who am I to say I know better?" Longtime teacher union leader Nathaniel Lacour criticized this "self-sacrificing" ethic of new teachers in New Orleans, claiming that it individualized teachers in a way that undermines labor solidarity (*Democracy Now!* 2007). Here, talent is a rubric for both exalting and undermining teachers as laboring subjects, inviting both ambivalence and paranoia.

Listening to the reflections of Val and Jessie, we can see that the role of talent itself is subject to marginalization and ethical dilemmas in the way it serves as a vehicle for the transformation of the teaching profession.[25] In contrast to the caring labors and communal connections discussed earlier in the chapter, the good teacher comes to be increasingly defined not by the quality of their relationships but by the quantity of their labor and outputs. The quantification and fungibility of such a status as human capital perhaps accounts for the ambivalence teachers like Jessie and Val felt towards their role in school reform efforts. The changing character of teaching as labor in a charter school and the material and institutional dislocations of reform after Act 35 seemed to hamper their ability to form the quality of relationships that would have enable them to continue in a caring and ethical manner.

So where does the ambivalence of new teachers lead? While Jessie and Val were clearer about their discomfort with the political contradictions of reform, even pro-charter organizations increasingly recognized the fraught terrain they operated in. There is not yet any organized mass movement of transplant educators in alliance with veterans. Knowledge of contradictions doesn't necessarily lead to resistance, and there are many teachers who continue to work in schools despite their critical attitudes. This is because even critical educators often work within frameworks of individual responsibility and responsibilization. As with the immediate reconstruction efforts (Adams 2013), help and care are matters of private ethics and voluntarism and, in the face of the inadequacies and contradictions of reconstruction and reform, teachers looked to individual self-mastery and cultivation of human capital in progressive and neoliberal modes, and the capacity for collective action was eroded.

Like the "underclass" that formed a discursive weapon for decades of neglect and disinvestment in the welfare state, the "bad teacher" doesn't really exist in identifiable somatic units. Yes, before and after Katrina, there were, and are, teachers that did not serve students adequately, and they should be of concern to us all. However, the process of making distinctions between bad or ineffective teachers and good or talented teachers is ideological and includes terms of evaluation that far exceed measures of classroom effectiveness. Ultimately these distinctions better serve us as maps for values and politics than as guides to effective school practice. Discourses of teacher quality present us with a framework of debate with two concerning restrictions. First, they locate judgments of educators within individualizing frameworks. This atomization is significant insofar as it aligns with broader political and economic shifts from social responsibility to individual responsibility, and it encourages educators, progressive and neoliberal, to respond to the dilemmas of schooling with individualistic strategies of self-cultivation. Second, teacher quality discourses don't merely affect racial groups in unequal ways, they are themselves vehicles of racialization. The danger of responding to bad-teacher myths only in terms of quality, either by defending veteran teachers or questioning the quality of transplants, is that of a flat-footed identity politics that accepts the framework of reformer's depiction of a failed school system.

Debates over teacher quality, talent pipelines, diversity, and recognition are all crucibles within which new configurations of racial and local identity can be forged—and different relationships to the projects of charter schools and their reconfigurations of teaching labor created.

CHAPTER TWO

Professionalism

Teachers are workers. Indeed, despite all the ways that public school teachers have been devalued and undercompensated, they are some of the most effectively organized workers in the United States. But what does it mean to take them seriously as such? This is one of the key stakes in the transformation of New Orleans schools to a privatized and mostly nonunion system. Charter schools emphasize and are lauded for their focus on professionalism and the work ethic of their teachers and school leaders. At the same time, critics of the charter school model decry the teachers' relative youth, inexperience, and lack of traditional credentials. It's clear that charter schools have sought to recruit a different kind of person to teach, but what is it exactly that they do every day? How have charter schools transformed teaching practice in addition to teacher subjectivities? Attending to the working days and work ethics of teachers in charter schools underscores the mechanisms and forms of expertise through which charter school teachers came to be exalted as valuable talent and "human capital"; it also exposes the rituals and practices through which veteran Black educators were excluded and discouraged from belonging in new school work cultures. While charter school leaders often expressed the desire to hire and retain local Black and veteran teachers (as covered in the previous chapter), the ideals of professionalism, work ethic, timeliness, the willingness to collaborate and be surveilled, positivity, and fit reinforced new labor regimes, which excluded these same educators. Despite the friction between Black and veteran teachers and the work norms of charter schools, a commitment to hard work as necessary for eradicating educational inequality was shared between them. This commitment itself must be questioned if schools are to regain their promise as sites of empowerment and laboratories for modes of democratic living. In order to highlight these dimensions of the transformation of education work in New Orleans, I approached several school sites as if I were conducting a shop-floor ethnography. Worker identities are made and remade at the point of production and relations between and among workers and management are laden with contests over power and authority. The privatization of schools in New Orleans not only transformed the contract status and economic standing of educators, it also served as grounds for reconstructing the workplace as a site of racialized governance, authority, and selective inclusion.

Over the course of thirteen months of fieldwork I observed teachers at six K–12 schools in four different charter school networks, all of which could be fairly characterized as following a no excuses approach to school discipline, testing accountability, and implementing human capital strategies. Most days I popped in and out of individual teacher's classrooms at various points during the school day, sitting in an unobtrusive corner of the classroom quietly taking notes, sometimes working with students during individual and group work sessions, and once a week listening in on professional development sessions where teachers worked on lesson plans, reflected on collective goals, and prepared for upcoming standardized tests. Every couple of weeks, on average, I shadowed a teacher or administrator for an entire working day, arriving at school when they did and staying with them until they walked to their cars to leave the building. These full day observations were grueling marathons, almost always starting before 7:00 a.m. and ending after 5:00 or 6:00 p.m. Teachers would typically arrive thirty minutes to an hour before students, using the calm before the storm to make copies, organize the classroom, or attend brief daily morning staff meetings, which school leaders used to check in with staff and build morale. Teachers would then spend most of the rest of the day with their students, with brief breaks for lunch, recess, or elective classes where students would be handed off to another teacher. School leaders spent much of the day observing teachers in classrooms, meeting with teachers and other administrators individually and collectively, or attending to students who had been sent out from classrooms for disciplinary infractions. Teachers and school leaders would both typically stay after school (which ended somewhere between 3:00 and 5:00 p.m.) to finish planning for the coming days and weeks. Almost every teacher or administrator I spoke with claimed to work a half day or more every weekend lesson planning, grading, or speaking with parents, amongst other tasks.

All of these are activities that teachers at any kind of school would be familiar with. However, teachers and school leaders at charter schools narrated their working day as though they shouldered more of these burdens than educators at other kinds of schools. As noted in the prior chapter, one of the ways that school leaders, human capital managers, and teachers at charter schools distinguished the talent they sought for their organizations from veteran teachers at traditional public schools was by the hours they put in. *Talent* at charter schools did not ask hiring committees when school let out because they were willing to work as long as the working day went. I was intimately familiar with this emphasis on an extended working day, having previously worked as a teacher at a charter school in New York City where, although the official school day ended at 5:00 p.m., my principal reminded us that we worked at a place where people weren't supposed to be rushing to clock out at 5:01. Every day I wondered, "How long before I can leave the premises without causing gossip or disapproval? Is 5:15 too early? Maybe I should wait until 5:32?" You should never leave on a nice round number, lest it appear that your egress was planned with malicious forethought.

This anxious preoccupation with time was not limited to my own experience or solely concerned with clocking out. Marion, a young white transplant, described to me his disgust at the kinds of status games teachers would play to be seen as the hardest working. "People will park their cars in strategic spots where they'll be seen. You can be in the building twiddling your thumbs, but as long as your car is there, you're a hard worker. When you're leaving and you pass someone's car who is still there it's like, 'Fuck, I'm not as good a teacher as they are.'" Of course, school faculty in all kinds of places are subject to status games, but in New Orleans, the focus on intense and exclusive commitment was notable. Youthful transplants often had no other local social ties to command their attention, and thus the approval of their colleagues took on even greater importance. This commitment to long hours as an ethic and status-elevating behavior is itself a recent historical development among the relatively elite strata that charter schools recruited their teachers from. Whereas privileged elites earlier in the twentieth century often prided themselves on not working and on the pursuit of leisure, a rise in working hours among the salaried professional classes in the later twentieth and earlier twenty-first century combined with the development of ethics exalting a grinding commitment to long hours in professional class work roles.

Employees at charter schools were under intense pressure to perform (both to achieve and to perform the cues that indicated excellence), and school leaders were constantly strategizing about how to best support teachers to execute under these conditions. In 2014, during the August following my year of fieldwork, I observed professional development for the start of the school term at two charter school networks that both turned to the same solution for helping their teachers to negotiate the demands of the working day. These professional development sessions were mostly comprised of programming facilitated by school leaders and veteran teachers to help the staff plan for upcoming lessons, strategize about classroom management and discipline, or discuss human resources issues like changing health care plans. However, sometimes schools would bring in outside consultants. That summer, two of the networks I had followed over the course of the previous year brought in a consultant with a program designed to provide teachers with an organizational system and philosophy for working efficiently and saving time.

This program, which I am calling The Disciplined Teacher, was founded by a former teacher and executive in education nonprofits. I was able to sit in on one of these sessions during which the founder introduced the program and set forth an enticing aspiration for the room full of over 150 teachers from across the charter school network. Early in the session, the facilitator, equipped with a microphone headset and a no-nonsense tone, asked the room, "Why is being disciplined important?" The teachers in the room ventured various responses, sharing a theme of being able to handle all the responsibilities of teaching in a high-stakes charter school environment. The facilitator underscored the importance of proper planning for sustaining the efforts and energies of the teachers in the room, saying she is "really, really worried about burnout, and planning is probably about fifty percent of that." The official literature for the program stated, "The cost of not having a plan is enormous: Your students and colleagues suffer, you sleep too little, and you all feel overwhelmed. Thankfully, with some intentionality, routines, and habits, it is possible to be an effective professional—and *have a life!* [emphasis mine]" The vision of the teacher that was disciplined promised much. It reminded the educators collected in the room that time was a scarce resource and that the stakes of inefficient laborers were not only lessened capacities and availabilities for life-sustaining and replenishing activities but also diminished value for students and colleagues.

This aspiration differed from Taylorist designs on increasing worker efficiency through intense supervision and subdivision of labor insofar as it emphasized the personal nature of teaching work. The facilitator reminded the audience that "you love your work." In an official testimonial, a school leader wrote, "[The facilitator's] personal management systems and her work with our senior and middle leaders to customize these systems to their own personal styles has significantly improved the quality of their lives."

The facilitator encouraged the audience to eschew the dichotomy of "work-life balance" and consider "blending . . . personal and professional together," noting that "about 10 percent of you will refuse to blend." This articulation of the personal and the professional took the emotional labor that service industries have developed over the past thirty years (Leidner 1993) a step further and posed that the organization systems of a "disciplined teacher" could be a desirable way to structure one's life off-hours, which were no longer strictly "outside" the working day. While this blending might sound oppressive in the abstract, The Disciplined Teacher website quoted teacher testimonials that described it in an alluring way as a model that could provide relief; for example:

> The principles I have learned this year from [The Disciplined Teacher] have helped me keep it all together in a really busy time. Since February, I have sold a condo, bought a house, moved, and started construction on the new house, all while working full time as a teacher/coordinator and teaching 2 nights a week in addition to my day job. . . . [The Disciplined Teacher] principles can be applied to many areas of life. I am so grateful that [The Disciplined Teacher] came into my life!

While the facilitator surmised that 10 percent of teachers would reject these aspirations, they had a hunch that the other 90 percent would find the idea of being disciplined not only an attractive option for working *but also for living.* Charter schools and education reformers liked to emphasize the ways they were trying to elevate teaching as a profession, often using examples of collaboration, pay, and expertise as justifications for increasing demands and the dissolution of teachers' unions. These attempts to make teaching more like a "profession" than a "job" certainly entailed a great deal of recalibrating of the workday and organizational structures and cultures. However, in the neoliberal era professions and professionalism have been marked by discourses of "loving your job" and the rise of the "creative class" (Jaffe 2021, Tokumistsu 2015). As much as these affective orientations to work represent desires to counter alienation in the labor process, they also invite the colonization of the working person's inner life and subjectivity by work. In addition to the aforementioned means, the synchronization and blurring of work and life is one of the primary ways that charter school reform "professionalized" teaching.

Across many interviews, teachers and administrators at the schools I observed both celebrated the long working hours as proof of the commitment to students and expressed concern about being able to retain teachers in the face of burnout. However, the Disciplined Teacher model should alert us to the possibility that the organization of the working day is about more than quantities of time or expenditures of energy. Indeed, teachers at all kinds of schools have always worked long hours, if not in ways that are recognizable or rewarded in charter school environments.[1] Members of the American Federation of Teachers Local 527, the New Orleans Teachers Union, would argue that they worked for many years to raise the professional standards of teachers and that their members were just as hard working and committed as teachers working in charter schools. What is distinctive about working in a charter school if it is not the number of hours worked, the professional standards of the workplace, or the intensity with which teachers and school leaders pursue their labors? It is charter schools' commitment to a particular vision of work as professionalism that distinguishes them from other types of schooling. It is this vision of professionalism and the affective labor of fitting in and positivity at no excuses charter schools that is responsible on a day-to-day level for the relative exclusion of Black teachers from their working environments.[2] By blending the personal and the professional, these labor regimes not only intensify the working day but introduce racialized norms of fitting in that work to exclude teachers who don't conform to recognized practices of collaboration, organization, and positivity. Charter schools should be distinguished not by the fact that their teachers and school leaders might work more but by the fact that they are more committed to a culturally particular ideal of work.

THE WORKING DAY

The length of any given working day can seem self-evident and mundane. School days in particular are familiar to the vast majority of Americans who have attended public schools, but the schedule and shape of a teacher's working day is the outcome of decades of struggle (Apple 1986, Spring 2018). At traditional public schools operating under union contracts, teachers' working hours are strictly delimited. The "Know Your Rights" section of the United Federation of Teachers (UFT) website, for example, states that the school day is to be no longer than six hours and twenty minutes. The length of professional development sessions and sessions for parent engagement in addition to these instructional hours are likewise explicitly enumerated. The duties that teachers can be asked to perform during lunch or before or after school are listed, as well as protocols around the compensation of overtime work. The key difference between charter schools in New Orleans and the traditional public schools that preceded them was that, save a few schools that have voted to unionize over the past ten years, teachers at charters were at-will employees whose working day was undefined. Charter school teachers were not just asked to work more hours than teachers at traditional public schools, they were compelled to be flexible in ways their counterparts were not, taking on duties and responsibilities without extra compensation.

Yet, charter school teachers did not work simply at the whim of school leaders. They too shaped and contested the working day, if in highly individualized forms distinct from collective bargaining. By changing the shape of the working day, charter schools not only transformed work time, they altered the temporal landscape within which the everyday politics of the workplace occurred.[3] Work under capitalism is a provincial assemblage of forms of organization, labor, value, belief, ideology, ethics, and more, and the history of public schooling in the United States clearly shows a tendency towards organizing teachers ever more intensely as workers and professionals. Insofar as teachers are workers and because charter school teachers in particular are subject to intensifying professionalization and precarity, they are engaged in struggles over the working day.

The working day can be quantified in time or expenditure of labor or reckoned in terms of the value produced in a given term, but it cannot be reduced to these measurements.[4] The working day is a fault line between the needs of the worker to labor in sufficient quantity to reproduce themselves and their labor power and the compulsion of the employer to extract surplus value from labor over and above the value of their efforts. These imperatives form a core contradiction within the working day and remind us that its terms are the outcome of histories of struggle.[5] Through decades of organizing, the United Teachers of New Orleans, AFT Local 527, had won the right to certain limits on hours, amongst other concessions (Fairclough [1995] 2008). The force of Hurricane Katrina, the levee failures, and above all the organizing of pro–charter school policymakers wiped away this detente and instituted a new set of norms around an extended and indeterminate working day. Charter schools have expanded in many other districts across the country but nowhere on the scale that they have in New Orleans. In part the scale of expansion was made possible by the coercive actions of the state, which dissolved the traditional public school system and the teachers' union base, a kind of primitive accumulation and taking of hard-won economic rights by force.[6] It would be hard to imagine such a widespread change to the working day without the coercive force of the post-Katrina maneuvering of education reformers.

Among teachers in my field sites, it was commonplace to regard a ten-plus-hour workday as normal. Nora, a white transplant and elementary school teacher, told me she arrived at school "around 6:45 a.m." and stayed "until 5:00 p.m. most days." Nora also typically worked one day on the weekend, and if she didn't "do enough on the weekend," she explained, she would "then . . . work until 7:00 p.m. on Monday and Tuesday." Rob, a white Louisiana local and teacher at Nora's school, arrived at school around 6:30 a.m., an hour before students, in order to prepare and worked all day on Sundays to submit lesson plans to school leaders due that evening. Rob recognized the strenuousness of this routine and reassured me (or himself?), "I try to get six hours of sleep every night." Jay, a Black transplant teacher at another elementary school, left the job at the end of the school year because it required "too much of my time," saying that if the job was a "nine to five, that would be one thing, but I'm working ten hours a day at least." When teachers complained of exhaustion from the long hours they either contemplated leaving for another position or turned towards strategies of self-care, such as treating themselves to a vacation or massage, going out for drinks, or simply watching a favorite television program before going to sleep. When teachers were let out early from a professional development session, or in the case of Nora and Rob's school, when the principal announced that the following year, the school term would end a week early, these concessions were framed as gifts of time to teachers rather than concessions or compromises.

Teachers may have been exhausted or displeased when they deemed particular activities a waste of time, but they mostly took for granted the extended and flexible nature of the working day.[7] As noted in chapter 1, while charter schools value "teamwork," "collaboration," and "fit," they did so under models of subjectivity that isolated and atomized teachers as a class of workers. In the face of the exacting demands of the charter school environment, teachers were mostly only capable of accommodation, escape, or self-mastery. What is it that drove the administration at typical New Orleans charter schools to push for such an extended working day and why did teachers at these schools seem willing to accept these working hours, even to the point of exhaustion? At each of the schools I observed as well as at various education non-profits, educators regularly used the expression "these kids" to index the profound social inequities that faced the predominately low-income Black students in New Orleans public schools. This linguistic marker was used in many different ways, each underscoring the ostensibly tremendous need this population had for education-based interventions. While the supposed deficits of "these kids" could be described using the language of "the achievement gap"—that is, the persistent test-score gaps Black students face compared with white children—"these kids" ultimately referred to an indeterminate source for valuing teachers' labor. However much "these kids" can be used to justify alternative approaches to schooling based on audit cultures, this discourse also bears the mark of culturally arbitrary impositions. Annalise, a Black local who worked to develop an alternative school model counter to a no excuses approach, felt that "these kids" served as a vector for white elitism: "The underlying thing is there are people who believe that white people are simply better role models, period. So these kids need to see how white people walk, talk, and interact with each other. 'You need to see how I act, because being like you is not the definition of success.'" However it was used in education reform, "these kids" and the work that was done for them was the coin of the realm, justifying severe audit cultures and the destruction of prior work regimes in the name of children.

The working day of the charter school wasn't extended because principals and network executives were domineering people who personally profited from the exertions of their teachers. Rather a combination of the discursive framing of the needs of "these kids," an audit and test-based accountability culture, and charter school contracts with districts worked to produce an impersonal drive for producing results, mostly in the form of higher test scores and school performance scores, which at times included measures like attendance, graduation, and year-to-year growth. Evidence of results could also include narratives of success, which emerged out of school visits, websites and promotional materials, and grant applications for foundation funding. It is easy to sympathize with this drive. The vast majority of teachers and administrators I encountered at these schools sincerely believed in doing all they could to help their students succeed, however they may have defined success. But, by structuring teaching as a kind of labor that satisfied the generation of a particular kind of value, teaching as work took on destructive qualities.[8]

Burnout was a high-priority concern for teachers and school leaders as well as upper management at charter school networks as they faced one of the core contradictions in capitalism—namely, that workers are needed at the same time that their working conditions rob them of the vitality needed to continue their labor.[9] At all points in the organizational chart, employees of charter school networks were well aware that the exacting demands of their positions were in conflict with whatever they may have conceived of as a healthy lifestyle. When Jay told me of her decision to leave the classroom at the end of the year, she said, "I just needed to take a break from killing myself." Rob reflected, "Work life is funny. I feel like work is my life. I talked to my mother about it, she said that's how it is at first [i.e., work takes over your life before you get experience]." This wasn't just a matter of the number of hours worked or the zeal with which employees pursued their tasks; this was a sacrificial ethic.

Donovan, a white transplant and the human capital director at one of the charter school networks I observed apologized to me for his illness before I sat down to interview him between his other meetings for the day, saying, "If I was a normal employee, I wouldn't be here today. The work is so urgent and important that I have to be here." Donovan suggested that the extensive working day was reinforced by the cultural orientations of both teachers and organizations: "Is it the drive of the employee or the organization or both? I suspect it's both. I think all orgs that are successful attract a certain kind of employee. Our organization attracts the kind of people that will power through walking pneumonia[10] and be present on the day before the Fourth of July. That's the nature of the beast." Note how this framing naturalizes the idea of teachers being a "culture fit" for specific kinds of charter schools.

Donovan knew that this relentless drive was unsustainable in the long run, telling me, "Work-life balance is the million-dollar question in this industry. We work very hard. As a human capital director, I should be advising myself to stay home. . . . How do we create a space where we say it's OK to call in sick? They [teachers] work just as hard or harder than I do, and they deserve it as much as I do." Donovan spent a greater part of the year strategizing for how to improve working conditions for teachers, and crucially, none of these strategies involved working less. Some of the strategies outlined included quality-of-life perks like "on-site car washing ... dog walking ... discounts with area gyms ... " in addition to more serious benefits like "more affordable child care that matches our teachers' schedules." Donovan wanted to save his teachers time, saying, "We're trying to remove those annoying tasks from your daily life. This past year, we had tax help for the first time. I got an email from a high-performing teacher asking for help managing her money." Donovan recognized that this could appear exploitative but claimed that his network's dedicated teachers would not be working less anyway: "People say it's because you want to keep people at the office. Yes, we do! But we know they're going to stay whether we offer this or not; how do we help them?" These programs all carried with them a concern for making teachers' working lives less difficult, but they also contained the logic of maximum extraction of value.

The remaining major factor in the extension of the workday was the charter schools' reliance on youth as a reservoir of energy. Besides race and place of origin, age and experience were the other defining differences between teachers before and after the post-Katrina expansion of charter schools.[11] While many considerations of youth perspectives in New Orleans schools focus on students (Michna 2009), we also have to consider teachers under the rubric of youth and youthfulness. More than a statistically significant feature of charter school teachers, youthfulness was part of a powerful ideological structure. Anthropologists have long understood youth to be a plastic cultural category (Bucholtz 2002). The dramatic shift in the demographics of the New Orleans educator workforce has shifted local understandings of the relationship between youth and teaching as a form of labor. While recognizing the coercive means through which veteran, local, and Black teachers were excluded, it is important to also reckon with the ways that new teaching demographics also transform teaching as a generational phenomenon. The turn to youth by charter schools allows them to mitigate some of the "life-destroying" aspects of their labor regime.

Youthfulness became a highly prized characteristic in the human capital practices of charter schools. There were several institutional incentives for charter management organizations to favor young teachers, including being able pay them lower salaries and offer fewer benefits. Free from satisfying a contract with the teachers' unions, charter schools were not required to take part in the Teacher Retirement System of Louisiana, meaning that veteran teachers' retirement benefits would not carry over to charter schools. This served as a disincentive for veteran teachers to look for positions in charter schools and shows how the demographic shift in educators was shaped by our privatized health care and retirement systems. However, youthfulness was also imbued with ideological powers and was associated with a "culture of smartness" (Ho 2009). This could make teachers feel "old" or veteran when they would not otherwise have recognized themselves as such. Nora told me that at her previous position at a traditional public school, "I was the youngest teacher by fifteen years. I'm one of the older teachers at (this school)!" Transplanted from other places, youthful teachers didn't have the kinds of local connections or family commitments that could compete with their work time. Teachers who stayed long enough to start to have children ran into difficulties negotiating their new families with the demands of school as a workplace. One teacher in particular, Kelly, a white transplant, recounted to me how she timed her pregnancy to have the baby at the beginning of summer break to avoid missing school time to be with the newborn. During the following school year, she struggled to get legally mandated accommodations such as a room for pumping breast milk and felt the school director to be unsympathetic to her burdens as a mother. Kelly told me, "I asked him what he would do if his wife were in the situation I am, and he would make ridiculous, stupid comments like, 'I would never let my wife be a teacher and have a baby!'"

While perceptions of the benefits of youthfulness played out in many complicated ways in the day-to-day operations of charter schools, they also structured hiring and retention processes in meaningful ways. In my time in New Orleans I interviewed administrators who explained that young teachers didn't ask when school got out at career fairs, that they worked longer hours, that they didn't question managerial authority, and that their lack of familial attachments tended to increase their investment in workplace status games as a source of social belonging. Kerry, a charter CEO, told me, when hiring, "we pretty much select for people that fit in culturally, and they know they fit in, and it makes them feel special." Youthfulness was a key element in the construction of teachers and educators as working subjects, endowing them with a pliability and sense of attachment that enabled new intensities of working culture in New Orleans charter schools.

The working day is a field of struggle in which value is generated, subjectivities are formed, and rights are contested. However, the extension of the working day isn't the only means by which charter schools attempted to distinguish themselves from traditional charter schools. Charter schools in New Orleans have also worked to "professionalize" teaching as a means of shaping their teachers as particular kinds of workers: professionals.

PROFESSIONALIZATION

When my informants working in schools were critical of the work regime of charters, it was mainly in terms of sustainability and capacity, a question of strategy and efficacy. The primary question was whether teachers worked too much or too little, too hard or not hard enough. Teachers, school leaders, nonprofit workers, and entrepreneurs were all uniformly committed to the idea that some species of "hard work" was necessary to serve "these kids." Zadie, a white local and an administrator at one of my field sites, was particularly enthusiastic when describing the unique work environment at her school,

> I would not go back to working at a traditional public school. . . . Everyone is here for a greater purpose, and everyone is aware of the sacrifices that must be made, and they take joy in that sacrifice, being together and feeling like we're working for something. In traditional schools, people stopped believing that what they did could make a difference. That's it: people are willing to make a sacrifice, and willing to improve themselves. I mean—have you hung out at a traditional public school?

No one, not Zadie nor any of the other employees at her school or others, ever questioned whether we should consider teaching "work" at all or raised the question of whether this particular form of "work" was the right way to organize the pedagogical development of our society's children—with understandable reason.

Americans have longstanding commitments to understanding the self as a worker and teachers in American public schools generally and in New Orleans in particular have organized for many decades to be recognized as workers and won many concessions in so doing. Since the nineteenth century, teachers in public schools have been caught between two poles—that of being an occupation of care, feminized and craft-like, and that of being professionalized and scientific, masculinized and industrial. While post-Katrina New Orleans is a dramatic example of moving from one pole to the other, there have been multiple waves of transition between the two in American history, typically resulting in the displacement of female and racially marginalized teachers in favor of professionalized educators. Embracing teaching as work has been used to exclude educators as unqualified and unfit, but it has also served as the basis for union organizing to protect these same teachers and build a power base among Black communities in New Orleans. Work is not uniformly oppressive in its effects, but it is nearly universally regarded as an appropriate and desirable framework for organizing school life.[12] By focusing so intently on how teachers should work, charter schools also end up changing what kind of people teachers should be. Therefore, professionalizing teaching is not a matter of colorless organization, it is the grounds for many layers of subject making, racialization, and class conflict.

It can be difficult to make a critique of work that is composed of more than a criticism of working conditions, one that does not valorize people who work for being workers as it decries their exploitation.[13] It is important to keep this antiproductivist and antiwork perspective in mind when analyzing the working lives and conditions of teachers in New Orleans charter schools. The point of analyzing the working day is not to sympathize with the benighted charter school teacher's exhaustion or exploitation, though such sympathy may have a place in both political advocacy in education and in ethnographic ethics. By scrutinizing the professionalizing discourses of charter schools, we can point out how they work to exclude certain kinds of racialized and class subjects from teaching positions while privileging others—important political and analytic work that has already been done by others (Buras et al. 2015). In taking antiproducerist stances, we can appreciate how these dynamics of exploitation and exclusion are both rooted in and productive of the relations structuring work itself, and we can understand how an embrace of work is one of the key factors in the changing shape of teachers in New Orleans schools as racialized, localized, and generational subjects.

One of the central criticisms of Teach for America and other alternative certification organizations as well as charter schools themselves has been that they "deprofessionalize" teaching by bringing in "talent" who have not been trained in schools of education or traditional teacher-preparation programs, who have fewer years of experience, and who stay in the classroom for less time—in classrooms that generally have not been unionized.[14]

While these critiques put valuable attention on the way that charter school–based reforms have circumvented the traditional hierarchies of teacher preparation, characterizing these agendas as "deprofessionalizing" can obscure as much as it reveals. Staking such a strong claim on the grounds of professionalism buys into the same productivist tendencies as charter proponents themselves have. I have no doubt that many of those deploying this kind of critique are sincere in their beliefs. However, such investments represent an analytical failure to see the productive effects of charter schools' attempts to reshape the teaching profession. It would be more accurate and effective to frame the human capital practices of charter schools and education-reform organizations as a case of "hyperprofessionalization." This dynamic should be analyzed in a way that is critical of attachments to the professional status of teachers and other education workers.

Advocates of charter schools recognize the kinds of demands that are placed upon teachers there but believe that ultimately charters are better places to work than traditional public schools that serve low-income Black and brown students. Eli, a white local and a director at an education nonprofit in New Orleans, had been a teacher at a traditional public school before working to expand charter schools, and, as he described reformers' efforts to raise professional standards in schools, he used his experience to draw the following contrast:

> The things that keep people in their jobs are the same in schools as elsewhere. A culture of high expectations where people feel supported, strong professional development, stretch opportunities, clear goals and feedback, incentives to stay, monetary and nonmonetary rewards. This is the same thing you would find in the private sector. There are opportunities for advancement. Schools that are better at retention do that. There wasn't a lot of turnover at [the traditional public school], but it was a terrible place to work and low performing.

Here, Eli exemplifies the ways that teaching can be conceived of as an arena within which to develop one's own human capital, a step in a career path rather than a simple calling or caring labor. Eli was adamant that teachers should be shaped as professionals rather than workers, explaining, "I would say it's problematic to think of teachers as labor. You don't think of doctors and lawyers as labor; you think of factory workers as labor. If you want teachers to be innovative, thoughtful, resourceful professionals, then making rules about how long they should work every day and exactly how they should be paid and fired and when is just sort of antithetical to that; you would never do that to what we think of as a profession." Whereas the AFT defines professionalism in terms of the rights of teachers, the concessions they are able to win from employers, and protections over their expert knowledge, Eli sees professionalism in terms of flexibility, career pathing, and information flow, using the private sector rather than the public sector (which is the largest source of union employment in the United States) as a model.

In embracing professionalism, both critics and proponents of charter schools spoke of "elevating" the teaching profession, indexing the kinds of demonization of teachers analyzed in chapter 1. One of the concrete ways this goal manifested was in discussions of how to give teachers recognition for increased mastery and progress. In unionized schools, such recognition, in the form of increased salary and rights according to tenure proceedings and seniority schedules, is often baked into the contract. However, at charter schools, no such progression was formalized, and methods of recognition were more fragmented and haphazard. Lisa, a white transplant and an entrepreneur who consulted on teacher professional development, told me about one effort to award teachers with digital badges like Xbox achievements to recognize their successes. But she was deeply skeptical of the effort: "I think it's a great idea for kids—but for teachers? . . . We're trying to elevate the profession, and I don't want to treat teachers like children. I want serious elevation of my professional growth, recognition that feels authentic. I don't think badges is the solution."[15] It was possible for both charter advocates and critics to claim the mantle of professionalism because they were both using this signifier to pursue different ends and maneuver in different discursive territories. On the one hand, unionized teachers use professionalism to protect teachers as a class and ensure certain rights whereas, on the other, charter advocates use professionalism in an atomized politics of recognition.

One of the ways that technology-focused reformers discussed teacher professionalism was under the rubric of "unbundling the teacher." Unbundling is a tool they used to take a complex problem and break it down into its component parts. They would talk about the teacher itself as a problem that needed to be unbundled. Lisa told me, "I think the role [of teacher] is unsustainable.

We need to rethink the role, and then we'll see greater retention. . . . We expect teachers to be everything, and we need to think about specialization and professionalization." Campbell explained to me her belief that teachers were asked to do too much in the current charter school environment, that a "one-size-fits-all" approach to teacher roles was not adequate to the challenge of education the New Orleans public school population, and that new technologies would enable the role of the teacher to be radically redesigned to better fit the individual talents of teachers themselves as well as the needs of students. Monica, a white transplant and a facilitator at Incubator, a startup I discuss further in chapter 4, was particularly excited about a school being developed by a former participant in Incubator programming, where the idea of unbundling was the foundation of the school model.

Technology is one of the primary mediums through which attempts at unbundling are executed. Many charter schools in New Orleans have expanded their use of "blended learning" programs, including some of my field sites as well as one of the new school experiments I discuss in chapter 4. In a blended learning environment, students used internet and digital media to navigate academic content at an individualized pace. There are various methods for implementing this basic structure, but the examples I observed usually involved students completing a selection of "learning modules" while the teacher used the time previously spent on facilitating the whole class to take data from these programs to target specific students for interventions, requiring a different skill set from educators. This model promised greater personalization for both teachers and students, but schools also used it to justify a higher teacher-student ratio. An informant familiar with the model expressed some skepticism as to district and network motivations before affirming their support, stating,

"The district is interested in cost savings, 'How can we leverage technology to reduce staff and lower the budget?' I felt ambivalent about that, but I no longer feel ambivalent, because we are dealing with a crisis, and we do not have enough quality teachers. We have a very real talent problem. If this helps us keep good teachers and reduce poor performing teachers, awesome. . . . Publicly, the plan is about personalized learning, privately, it's about budget." At the same time that "unbundling" could be a means of shaping the teacher's role according to personalized aptitudes and needs, it could also be a vector for austerity.

Techno-professionalism ultimately entailed a level of collaboration and surveillance that employees at charter schools felt distinguished their work environment from traditional public schools. Hayden, a hiring manager at a charter school network, used neighboring Jefferson Parish as a contrast:

> We lost a teacher at one school to Jefferson Parish because she wanted to be in a more traditional public school setting . . . where she can close her door and be an all-star and not have to worry about collaborating and sharing, and maybe that fits a little bit more to her lifestyle. We lost another teacher over requirements to teach and develop other teachers. She told me if we just left her alone to teach, she'd stay . . . Yes Orleans Parish and Jefferson Parish are separate districts, but now they're like two different worlds entirely.

The trope of "closing the door" was used by Kim, principal of a school in Hayden's network, when she discussed her experiences working in Orleans Parish before the storm. (Several other educators I spoke with who had become teachers through TFA and other alternative certification organizations before charter schools became prevalent also used this trope). Closing the door was a term they used to describe their isolation and abandonment in traditional public schools, whereas charter schools emphasized "open doors," constant collaboration, and frequent observations of classrooms by administrators and other teachers. As a novice ethnographer I was nervous about intruding upon classrooms and disrupting teachers and students, but teachers were so used to being observed by a number of different individuals that they were openly indifferent to my presence in the classroom. I was just another visitor passing through and, indeed, many of the classrooms I visited had dedicated desks for observers with folders including the day's lesson plans, forms for giving feedback, and lists of classroom rules and procedures. To be a professional in these settings meant to be open and collaborative.

There were times however, when techno-professionalism, collaboration, surveillance, and unbundling combined to turn teachers into a kind of prosthetic of the teaching process. Rob was a first-year teacher during my fieldwork and, like many first-year teachers, struggled with classroom management and lesson delivery. As such, Rob was frequently visited by his administrative coach for observation. About halfway through the school year, the coach decided to try out a new system called "real-time teacher coaching" whereby the teacher would wear an earpiece and the coach would give corrective instructions as the teacher delivered their lesson. Earlier in the year, Rob told me, "I don't really feel like myself in the classroom," and he talked about being nervous about the real-time coaching in his grade team meeting before the observation. I arranged with Rob to come observe during this session, but the coach asked that I not attend so that Rob would be more focused while trying out the new technology. In the grade team meeting following the observation, Rob spoke with the other teachers in his grade about the stresses of this kind of observation. Rob said, "I usually feel good after an observation, but I cried after the first session. . . . I didn't like it when [the consultant from the real-time coaching company] was telling [the coach] what to tell me . . . I don't like doing things that go against what I want to do." Apparently, the coach was being trained on how to use the real time coaching technology at the same time, adding another layer to the prosthetic professional rabbit hole.

I can imagine that some schools find the rapid feedback cycles of real-time coaching to be very useful in improving teacher performance. On the other hand, it's clear that Rob was profoundly stressed by the experience. The technological mediation of his observation can come off as a bit surreal. What is important to recognize here is the way that this technology accelerated an already existing vision of professionalism in charter schools and facilitated the employment of Rob and other teachers as a kind of prosthetic to experimental visions of "what works." I would argue that this techno-prosthetic professionalism is not a break with previous regimes of professionalism in traditional or charter schools but an intensification of it. Technology enables particular manifestations of "rendering someone prosthetic," but the core dynamic is social, political, and organizational.[16] Rob's distress however, isn't just because the technological mediation of feedback was unfamiliar or confusing. It can also be connected to his feelings of not "being like himself" in the classroom. At the same time that Rob was rendered prosthetic through devices like real-time coaching, charter schools also trafficked in discourses that personalized work and intensified the affective demands of being a teacher and a worker. These demands existed in tension with techno-professionalism and are the subject of the next section.

THE JOY OF FITTING IN

Despite the many attempts to professionalize and standardize teaching throughout American history, the job has persistently carried heavy connotations of care and femininity. The veteran teachers that were fired en masse after Katrina were overwhelmingly Black women. Critiques of their dismissal balked at the violations of their rights; they underscored that these women were not only the "backbone of the Black middle class" but were also the proper stewards of the mostly low-income Black children attending New Orleans Public Schools. In chapter 1, we found that veteran teachers spoke of special relationships with students and parents, intimate connections to the neighborhoods and communities that their schools served, and of their long-term investments in their schools. These emotional bonds existed alongside and in spite of the labor regime of public school teaching between the end of official segregation and Hurricane Katrina. Charter schools make affective demands of teachers as workers and professionals with greater intensity than do traditional public schools, and crucially these affective imperatives are racialized in such a way as to subtly exclude many of the veteran Black teachers that formed the majority of the teaching corps before the post-Katrina reforms. These changing demands on teachers aligned with broader transformations in neoliberal economies, service and professional labor, and entrepreneurial spirits and conflicted with the kinds of working subjectivities veteran teachers had been accustomed to.

It would be fair to say that even though teachers in charter schools were younger and more often white and not from New Orleans, they still formed powerful affective bonds with the students and communities they served. Teachers often referred to their students as "my kids," and even years after leaving the classroom, managers at education nonprofits would still affectionately reminisce about their favorite students. Walking around the offices of education nonprofits in New Orleans (where many employees were former teachers), you would see pictures of students on cubicle walls along with classroom paraphernalia. What was distinct about the charter school work environment was the way it made affective demands on teachers as an explicit and routine professional duty.[17] In the "closed doors" narrative of teaching, teachers were "left alone" so long as they satisfied certain requirements, but in charter schools, collaboration and fit in unique school cultures required affective self-management in new ways.[18] Recalling the example of The Disciplined Teacher, the idea that teachers should blend their personal and professional lives begins to make more sense. There is a way that this idea was packaged with the ideological notion of "loving what you do" to make it seem like work was an extension of personal preferences and fantasies of life trajectories, but these broader trends in service work point to the possibility that this blending was a way for work itself to colonize and shape these preferences and desires.[19] Teachers in charter schools don't just face increasing demands on their time, as discussed earlier in the chapter. The hyperprofessionalization they undergo also makes demands upon their affect and subjectivity in ways that repel teachers accustomed to previous labor regimes.

Many of the school administrators and human capital managers I spoke with at charter school networks expressed a genuine desire to increase teacher diversity in the schools and to hire more veteran teachers. They claimed that the problem wasn't that they were rejecting veteran Black teachers outright but that Black teachers "just don't apply" or that they "don't work out" when they are hired because they don't "fit" with school culture. This lack of fit was often framed in terms of veterans not wanting to work the kinds of hours and schedule that charter schools demanded or not wanting to participate in collaborative activities. Zadie recognized that they had a problem bringing on a diverse set of teachers to their staff, telling me, "I want a school full of people that want to be moms, that want to stay, and that doesn't happen if we just hire young transplants. But I'm not getting the people. I talk to Donovan, and I ask, 'Why aren't people applying here?' He says there is a stigma about our school—that it is temporary, that it is run by foreigners, that people don't understand our kids, so I don't want to work there." Rather than imagine these reactions to charter school work cultures as a kind of stubbornness or unwillingness to change old routines, we should consider that, in part, these veteran teachers didn't apply or "things didn't work out" because they resisted the affective demands of day-to-day work in charter schools.

Charter schools couldn't just make school culture and collaborative work appear through decree—they had to create rituals and practices to shape teacher enthusiasm and assent to these modes of professionalism. One of the rituals that staff at many charter schools across the city were asked to participate in was something that was often called "staff standup" or "morning meeting." Typically, at each school, all school staff would have a ten-to-fifteen-minute meeting in the cafeteria, gym, or theater. Staff would stand in a large circle facing each other and school leaders and teachers would share announcements and issues of concern. On Mondays during football season, there was often talk about the Saints. A crucial part of these meetings were affirmations, whereby staff would give "shout outs" to particular teachers or staff who exemplified school culture or were especially helpful. Often these affirmations were tied to specific values in the official school culture, such as "grit" (e.g., "Shout out to Rob for showing grit. He had an honest conversation with me before real-time teacher coaching"). Kerry's school had the most intense version of morning meeting I observed. Kerry and the leadership at their schools insist that "adult culture should be the same as kid culture," and thus when teachers broke up into small circles for part of the meeting, they addressed each other, clapped, used turn and talks, and other classroom techniques that they would use with children all with a relentlessly positive and energetic tone.

Zadie dealt with a staff that was less enthusiastic about these morning rituals. As a new school leader, Zadie was eager to make her imprint on school culture and was astounded by the lack of purpose teachers had in morning meetings, saying, "Some people thought we did staff standup in the morning so I can see who is on time. That's not why we do it! I could have you punch a card. People didn't understand. You have to communicate the purpose." When I interviewed Zadie, she had just finished hiring teachers for the new school year and was excited to bring in people who fit her vision for a positive work environment: "Hiring for next year is my first chance to shape exactly what I want this building to be next year. . . . I want people who are incredibly positive, incredibly resilient, and people who do not speak negatively about past jobs or students. . . . That means hiring for people who are able to stay emotionally constant when the work gets tough." Zadie told me that she was happy with the composition of the new staff and that they only lost people who were not asked to return or who were not good fits.

Zadie emphasized that even though some of the people that left were "good teachers," they were not a good fit for the school culture she was trying to build, telling me, "As a school leader you want to have a strong enough school culture that people can identify for themselves if they fit in or if they don't. And if you don't, no hard feelings. Go have fun somewhere else." One of the other teachers on Rob's grade team was a young Black transplant who was recognized among their peers to be the strongest teacher on that grade level, but this teacher clashed with administration because they did not adopt the classroom management techniques Rob and the other first-year teacher in the grade were advised to employ. This teacher felt that the standard classroom discipline techniques of the school were cold and oppressive. They left over the summer because they no longer fit with a school culture in which they felt they had to "flip a switch to teach and demand authority." One of the affective demands of teaching in charter schools like Zadie's is the desire to fit, the ability to express enthusiasm for a unique school culture, and crucially, to present oneself as the kind of person that aligns with the value and the mission of the school.

Hayden, the human capital manager at a different school network, agreed that school leaders were focused on positivity. I spoke to him about one of his network principals emphasizing the need for positive attitudes among teachers and Hayden responded, "When I heard you say the [other] principal said 'positive,' I knew exactly what that person meant, just with different words. It's team player, have a smile on their face, bringing a lot to the table, and things like that. It's great to have 100 percent compliance on that." Hayden admitted that discipline and authority underpinned this logic, continuing,

> But if you have someone who has great results, will you sacrifice that if someone is a little bit more of a prickly pear to deal with, for lack of a better description? . . . They're not always on board with everything at the school, the rah-rahs, the pep rallies the things like that—over the person that may be a first-year grad from TFA and will basically let you do and say whatever you want to them and they're going to do it because they're that type of person, but now they're getting 20 points less on their scores with their kids because they don't have that teaching experience. It's definitely one of the things my school leaders look for—are you going to bring something positive to school culture? They'll definitely place a higher value on

someone who is trying to get better and is positive than someone who may get the best test scores but doesn't play well with others. To use a sports analogy, we're not building an all-star team, but guys that work well together. Our schools are in that camp where we would take that positive person over someone who is draining the culture.

Zadie and Hayden show us that positivity was more than an externalized display of affectively legible gestures, expressions, or attitudes. Positivity connoted a kind of compliance and flexibility desired by school management, as well as a personalized enthusiasm for the particular school culture.

Annalise, a Black local and school founder who was in the process of designing a school model explicitly counter to the dominant trends in no excuses charter schools, was highly skeptical of fit, particularly as a tool of race and class reproduction. "Fit is just another word for 'You're not enough like me. I want to hire doppelgangers of myself.' Even when I do see Black people in some of these schools, many of them are, um, cognitive replications of the school leader or CMO leader. . . . Fit means I need to reduce the chance of being challenged out of fear it might spread." The idea that school leaders and hiring managers might want to hire people "like themselves" has a commonsense quality to it. When I asked Donovan, the human capital director at Zadie's network, about the ways that social network effects might be hampering efforts at increasing teacher diversity, he somewhat defensively assured me that this is something you see "in every industry." But as decades of research on racialization have shown, identification of likeness is a very complex and multilayered process mediated by cultural practices and instructional imperatives. There is no particular reason in the abstract that school leaders should want to hire people like themselves. It is the particular labor regime of charter schools in New Orleans as well as broader intensifications of affective demands in professional settings that drive this tendency.

These reflections should cause us to reframe our understanding of what it means for veteran teachers, local teachers, or Black teachers to not fit in at a charter school. School leaders at charter schools will insist that these are personalized misalignments with school culture, in other words, "this just wasn't the place for them." What these characterizations show us instead is that no excuses–style charter schools aren't explicitly excluding these kinds of teachers; instead, they have constructed a work culture in which the affective demands of the workplace exclude those who do not conform to particular modes of professional subjectivity. When veteran teachers refuse to apply or refuse to conform, they are resisting new kinds of demands of an encroaching work culture, even if only to hold up the expectations of the old one.

The work ethic at charter schools is not just a matter of working longer hours or with more intensity, it is also a vehicle for new professional subjectivities and affective demands in the school as a workplace. Critically, it is one of the means through which Black, local, and veteran teachers continue to be excluded from charter schools.[20] It is tempting to respond to attacks on the work ethic solely in a producerist vein and defend the record and capabilities of all of the kinds of teachers that have been excluded and maligned in the post-Katrina school system. This is important work, and scholars, educators, and activists have been doing it since the major wave of reforms began. But it shouldn't be the only critique of the work sensibilities and structures of charter schools.

When I began my fieldwork, I imagined that I would conduct a labor ethnography of teachers in charter schools in order to take teachers seriously as workers and that I could take the same kinds of analytics applied to factories, offices, and entrepreneurs to the school building. I believed that doing so would be an ethically appropriate way of illuminating how the work cultures of charter schools were racialized and would respect the efforts of both those excluded from and empowered by education reform. However, during the course of my fieldwork and post-field reflections, it became apparent to me that I, like many of the educators I observed, was too committed to work, too enthralled by its dignity and importance as a social form. I've come to think that the problem with teaching in charter schools is that it is too much like work: too professional and too regulated.

This isn't to argue that we should go back to some idyllic pastoral vision of community schooling but that it might be productive to question the place of work in schooling. I have no idea what a school that was less entangled in work and the work ethic might look like, but I think the utopian question has a provocative political utility. I've come to now think that taking teachers seriously as workers means taking work less seriously. A good starting point would be for teachers in charters to all become unionized and to demand fewer working hours and stricter boundaries between their professional and personal lives. Until that day in which labor is abolished and teaching is freed from its strictures, the very least we can do is limit its hold on our pedagogical and vital capacities.

CHAPTER THREE

Racial Arbitrage

"We have got to stop letting people tell a single story," Darryl said, thrusting his finger out towards me before planting it firmly on one of many stacks of documents strewn across his desk. Darryl's face twisted up and his head turned a bit sideways when getting ready to give the gift of revelation—a not too infrequent occurrence. I got the sense over our many rap sessions in the grey offices of one of numerous education nonprofits in New Orleans's Central Business District that I was not a privileged listener—this was Darryl's normal mode of address. Darryl leaned in a little closer, crossing into my informant-distancing force field. The door was open, as usual, and Darryl's voice dropped a bit as if the mostly white ears all around us were too delicate for the truth to come.

"There isn't a single story now—there are multiple stories." What was the dominating narrative that Darryl sought to disrupt? It is the story covered in chapter 1—namely, that the public schools were terrible failures before Katrina and that a set of reformers, who Darryl insisted were all ultimately controlled by a single wealthy and influential figure, had turned New

Orleans schools around after the storm by reorganizing school governance, which had been made possible by the conversion to charter schools and the influx of transplanted human capital. Darryl consistently defended the record of New Orleans educators before 2005 and questioned the progress made by leading charter networks. Darryl challenged the basic democratic legitimacy of the reform agenda while praising the fortitude of Black educators, saying that "without Katrina they [reformers] wouldn't have had the stamina" to push through such drastic changes against local resistance. Darryl believed this because Darryl had been around: "I was a veteran educator, I played every role, school leader, teacher, and knucklehead." Darryl constantly lauded the local Historically Black Colleges and Universities (HBCUs) and claimed that their efforts to prepare teachers and serve students were ignored in favor of arbitrary preferences for people from places like Harvard. Through all these pronouncements on the history of education and reform in New Orleans, Darryl was an unapologetic champion of the quality of the overwhelmingly Black veteran educator corps that served New Orleans students before the storm and, in a diminished capacity, afterwards. His unshakable confidence in the dedication and effectiveness of these teachers called into question the credentials and mythology of talent associated with the influx of human capital from elite colleges and national nonprofits.

Darryl's insistence on spreading his story was indicative of the changing winds of education reform in New Orleans. By the time we first spoke in 2014, reform organizations and charter schools had become more focused on diversifying their leadership and teaching cohorts. These moves were not merely the cunning adaptation of liberal multiculturalism but were one element in a shifting terrain of struggle over the racial governance of public schools. The singular narrative was losing steam. Nonprofit employees worried that donations from outside New Orleans had begun to diminish, and students and families increasingly bristled at the often harsh disciplinary cultures and fragmented bureaucracies of a system of privately managed charter schools. Scholars, activists, and community members vigorously challenged reform narratives and agendas, including during a walkout that year at a charter school that had been lauded as a success story. The school had students walk through a checkpoint every morning to ensure compliance with the dress codes (a process I witnessed myself on a visit). In the ten years since the levee failures and the seizure of 90 percent of the public schools by the state government of Louisiana, there was a vast proliferation of stories about the city and its schools in the media. The problem became not just challenging the dominant story about education reform but navigating the narrative deluge.

Darryl argued that the storm had so disrupted Black community political organization that powerful, mostly white interests were able to organize a reform agenda in its absence. Part of this was "our own fault" because "we lost the dynamics of politics and power."[1] Darryl lamented that "there was a split in the Black community where some wanted to be in the room" with charter school reformers rather than build their own power. Darryl wasn't convinced the coming return of schools to local control would change much as, in his estimation, reformers had won most of the school board seats.[2]

What I realized over my time getting to know Darryl was that his sense of grievance was not just about what kind of stories get told about the people outside of that literal and metaphorical room. It was not just about the way we talked about educators before Katrina. It was more about the Black and local folks who managed to stay in the room—the ones who had been working with reform organizations all along or who joined along the way. Darryl spoke this dissatisfaction from inside the room. Darryl worked at (and maybe sometimes for) one of the many white-dominated education nonprofits that had proliferated in New Orleans after Katrina.[3] The door was open because Darryl was constantly receiving reminders about meetings and functions to attend and updates from directors and assistants on the progress of current projects. Darryl never sat in that room for too long. Walking around the office, we passed by staff responsible for recruitment, placing teachers and talent in schools, and assisting teachers in those schools and development staff glued to headsets talking with donors or in conference room meetings. Darryl usually had a word or a handshake for each of them.

I was never exactly sure what Darryl did for this nonprofit, and he no longer works at the organization. I asked many times, both Darryl directly and colleagues and critics. "Nobody knows what Darryl does!" was a common response. Darryl told me that he was responsible for advising the organization on Black community engagement and political affairs and conversely connecting members of the community back with the nonprofit. Darryl helped broker a community governance agreement with a controversial charter school. Darryl also worked on a contract for unionized bus drivers at another. Darryl worked to build community support for reform-oriented candidates for the school board. Darryl worked with a program to build a pipeline of local Black educators who were trained to work in charter schools and break through the perceived glass ceiling of leadership in these organizations. When students at one charter school went on strike against the administration, Darryl came in to talk to them. When the state brought in new leadership at a newly merged charter high school, Darryl worked to represent community interests.

Unlike the age of "aggressive neglect" in the late twentieth century when public schools were abandoned and segregated, charter schools were part of a selectively integrative project in a gentrifying city. This called for new kinds of expertise and mediation of community interests, and people like Darryl were ready to step into the role. Darryl worked as a *racial arbitrageur*, a person responsible for connecting and translating between factions of communities whose relationships to each other were in flux as a result of the dislocations of the levee failures and the reform agendas that followed. In economics, arbitrage is a process in which traders take advantage of disconnections and inefficiencies between segments of the market in order to profit from privileged knowledge. Anthropologists of finance and markets have emphasized that arbitrage has a peculiar temporality (Miyazaki 2013, Peterson 2014). It is a speculative and future making activity while also inhabiting an ephemeral horizon. Arbitrageurs exploit knowledge gaps between markets, but their interventions also tend to stabilize the very breaches from which they benefit. Arbitrage is a particularly apt metaphor for thinking through a moment in the charter school reform project in which reformers turned from a temporality of crisis to a preoccupation with building enduring foundations.

Racial arbitrage is useful in thinking through the ways that in a (constantly transforming and dynamic) racially segregated society, certain agents are well positioned to traverse the gaps between racial factions and to create value from their unique interpretive capacities. Cedric Robinson uses the concept of "racial regimes" to draw our attention to the "maintenance" of racialized power and systems of representation, particularly in moments of necessarily periodic crisis. "Racial regimes" can help us understand the role racial arbitrageurs play in stabilizing an education system facing a crisis of authority by seemingly restoring naturalized notions of racial leadership at the same time that they represent new configurations of racial orders (Myers 2021, Robinson 2007). Black professionals and middle-class reformers have always played key roles in the administration and distribution of public goods in the post-Reconstruction United States, whether under the sign of uplift; race relations; or diversity, equity, and inclusion (DEI).[4] The case of post-Katrina New Orleans is no different. The massive and sudden wave of charter school reforms catalyzed a transformation in the structure and character of the city and created new opportunities for Black agents who were positioned to interface with and adapt to a new ecology of public, private, and nonprofit organizations in the education sphere. Situated between white dominated interests, an influx of credentialed white outsiders and various factions of Black community life, these Black professionals sat at a crossroads that offered them a privileged epistemic vantage for mediating shifting relations between public schools and Black communities. This capacity to cross the veil is "double consciousness" as professional practice.[5]

I witnessed Darryl put reformers in a room with community members and leaders who hadn't been willing to meet before either because the latter hadn't trusted the reformers enough to talk to them or because the reformers didn't know the community members were important and influential. Sometimes this meant that administrators, nonprofit directors, and charter school teachers got dressed down for extended periods of time listening to withering criticism both of their specific organizations and ventures and the broader reform climate. Part of Darryl's influence came from the illumination reformers experienced in these settings; they were humbled. Darryl's organization used a different term for this role. They said, "We are BRIDGERS. We synthesize, collaborate, and build upon the strengths of others."

While it could be easy to dismiss this language as multiculturalist pablum, my experience in New Orleans indicated that bridging was a crucial site of racialized knowledge production and racial expertise, though an unstable and always developing one. By providing community and leadership factions an interface with reformers, by fostering affective states of humility in the latter, and by articulating a strategic and provisional engagement with charter schools and education reform, arbitrageurs like Darryl capitalized on the void created by reformers' disruptions of the racialized power structures and hierarchies of public education.

Darryl represented one of three faces of racial arbitrage that I foreground in this chapter—the negotiation of the shifting relations between individual and community under neoliberalism. As narratives of education and reform proliferated, there opened up a space for actors who could claim to help others navigate the sea of stories. This guidance was valued not only for its ability to pare down the quantity of perspectives at play but also for its adeptness at assuring schools, nonprofits, and entrepreneurs about who in the community number among the deserving and about which tales are to be trusted and conferred credibility. Darryl is one among many examples of (mostly) Black folks working within or alongside reform-oriented organizations and movements who attempted to guide both local and transplanted, whites, Blacks, and others in unsettled times. While not architects of the reform system, racial arbitrageurs are key to maintaining the vitality of the agenda in the face of breakdowns, disappointments, and unforeseen challenges.

This attentiveness to the role of maintenance work also serves to better make sense of the fundamentally racialized character of neoliberalism, a term that is frequently used to characterize the privatization of New Orleans' school system. Critics of education reform have rightly criticized the neoliberal character of a process in which school governance was transformed through privatization as well as the ethos and pedagogical models of the new schools. However, it is critical to recognize that neoliberalism is not a transcendent ideology that descended upon New Orleans fully formed from the summit of Mont Pelerin. One of the key flaws of the imposing model of neoliberalism, besides its methodological idealism, is that it often ascribes to a particular set of ideologues from the mid-twentieth century the power of creating historical tendencies that predate their influence, and it does so in a way that ignores or misunderstands the centrality of racism and antiblackness to so-called neoliberal maneuvers. Black Southerners have negotiated attenuated forms of market-oriented citizenship and forces of responsibilization since the Reconstruction period, highlighting the racial crucible in which many of the features of neoliberalism were anticipated.[6] Recognizing the longer genealogies of certain features of neoliberalism allows us to see education reform in New Orleans as part of ongoing histories of racial capital. Doing so centers race in the neoliberal story and reorders its temporal boundaries. Rather than see the antidemocratic and individuating expert cultures of neoliberalism as an imposition from without, we should regard the reform project as the reconfiguration of national, regional, and local struggles over racial capitalism.

As part of a labor ethnography, this chapter focuses on the ways that ongoing transformations in the social contract and in labor and property regimes change how Black educators as workers navigate their interventions and reproduce racialized orders. Racial orders in the United States emerged through practices of domination such as slavery, apartheid, and segregation. New Orleans is a particularly important place to reckon with the production of the "illusion of race" (Fields and Fields 2012). A central site in the American slave trade, it also served as a location in which race was woven into institutions touching on labor (Arnesen 1994), learning (Devore and Logsdon 1991), and inheritance (Dominguez 1986). The dramatic and unprecedented privatization of the New Orleans school system has put New Orleans back at the center of conversations about race and inequality in the United States where the city is paradoxically both an exception and an exemplar.

Racial arbitrage is an important element in the construction, maintenance, and deconstruction of racial orders, one without specific moral or political imperatives. Creole and Black elites have used their positions among and between different racial, class, and political communities to the benefit and detriment of themselves as well as poor and working-class Black people, often at the same time. Their leadership has been lauded as a kind of radicalism (Hirsch and Logsdon 1992) as well as criticized as the self-serving doings of a professional managerial class willing to administrate the marginalized to their own limited advantage in the name of racial representation (Reed 1999).[7] Racial arbitrageurs are neither fully dominated puppets nor actors venally pursuing their own self-interest. Their agendas are worth examining on their own terms and scrutinizing according to their ideological and strategic objectives in the context of specific historical and institutional locations. These activities and agendas are constrained by circumstances, but that is true of all politics.

We should think of racial arbitrage as a kind of techno-social expertise closely associated with the social organization of work in the United States.[8] If we think of labor as a culturally and historically specific mode of social organization rather than a universal, then we can appreciate how work in the United States has generally relied on racialized modes of expertise and arbitrage, from the overseer to the union boss to the human capital manager. DEI initiatives have come under great scrutiny from the left and right in recent years; even when this criticism is unfair, it underscores the inadequacies of liberal multiculturalism and the politics of recognition. What gets overlooked, however, is how these efforts are organized as work, as professional endeavors, and how the professionalization of DEI and racialized expertise has transformed these efforts. The professionalization of racialized expertise is a key stabilizing force in New Orleans education reform and is a key venue in which formerly public and communitarian impulses towards equality have been channeled in entrepreneurial and privatized directions.

While there are examples in the nineteenth and early twentieth centuries, it is after the victories of the mid-twentieth-century civil rights movement that we see racial arbitrage by Black people incorporated into governance on a mass level, and these people do not just act as subjects to white patrons. As in many cities across the nation, New Orleans saw the proliferation of Black actors in government positions and state-dependent social service agencies and organizations (Germany 2007). This growth came in the context of Lyndon Johnson's War on Poverty but persisted as much from the mass organization of Black communities and elites as from federal directives. These positions were fertile grounds for the development of racial and class expertise. It is no accident that charter schools have been more prevalent in urban cores and "chocolate cities"—a term that denotes a particular racialized political economy rather than the simple fact that city is majority Black.[9]

However, public employment and public services in general as specific sites of racial brokering proved to be fragile spoils in the fight for justice and equality. Over the course of the late twentieth century, social services, public agencies, and publicly supported community programs came under severe attack, both programmatic and ideological, and, when they survived, were subject to new forms of punitive accountability (Wacquant 2009). While many popular accounts of post-Katrina education reforms depicted the storm itself as the catalyst for sweeping privatization, the ground was laid years before the storm. A small group of policymakers, including a number of Black political leaders, supported and passed laws in the few years before Katrina that enabled the state takeover and rapid conversion to charter schools (Lay 2022). The space for maneuver seized upon after Katrina accelerated many of these efforts. In the subsequent years, most of the public housing in the city was destroyed—at times in the name of "the community," with officially recognized community leaders serving as voices in support of demolishing public housing and replacing it with mixed income developments (Arena 2011). Again, even if we consider the destruction of public housing to be a form of structural violence, the point shouldn't be to decry these "community voices" as fools or cowards. Rather, I would ask us to take note of how essential the production of such a perspective has become to the operations of municipal politics.[10] Public solutions were disregarded and discredited during reconstruction and recovery efforts as well. Volunteers, religious organizations, and private contractors were relied on for reconstruction efforts, resulting in the inefficient provision of assistance as well as the reorientation of subjects of aid in neoliberal molds (Adams 2013). Most germane to our conversation here, the state government, with the support of foundations, the federal government, and various elite factions, seized control of 90 percent of the city's public schools; fired nearly 8,000 unionized, mostly Black educators and school employees; and turned the schools over to forty plus private management organizations over the course of nine years.

How does the reorganization of public services, and schools in particular, under private management with narrow and punitive state accountability alter the terms of racial arbitrage as a form of labor and knowledge production? This question is by no means settled. Racial arbitrage in New Orleans education reform is experimental. What kind of racial expertise is developed and experimented upon when the kinds of people who may have worked as a unionized teacher or for city government instead work for nonprofits and private organizations? What is the tension between the strategic interests of various stakeholders in the emergence of these new forms of racial arbitrage? How do Black figures operating within reform infrastructures accommodate and challenge the demands of their white colleagues and managers or become compromised and alienated from their values? How do the politics of multicultural recognition (Povinelli 2002) become refigured when racial arbitrage is privatized? These questions matter because, to date, the role of racial arbitrage and the actors who deploy it as a form of racialized expertise have slipped between the cracks of dominant narratives about post-Katrina reform.

Prevailing narratives cast reformers as white interlopers fresh off the plane from the Ivy League, and local Black New Orleanians are cast as either supporting and consuming or resisting and criticizing reform. My examination of these actors is not meant to affirm or exalt them nor to criticize them as a class, easy as that may be. As a Black person of the professional and managerial classes and a former Teach for America corps member, I have quite a lot in common with these folks, affinities that proved to be no small advantage in building ethnographic rapport. I'm less concerned with the fact that these individuals are unrecognized than I am with showing how the work they do is undertheorized as a mode of racialized knowledge production increasingly necessary for the functioning of reform efforts. My use of the term racialized expertise here does more than denote the content of these arbitrageurs' labors. Rather, it brings together theories of neoliberalism, with a focus on epistemology and subjectification; theories of capitalism as a knowledge and information economy; and theories of racial capitalism.

Any attempt to understand and transform the charter school regime in New Orleans requires a more layered and subtle understanding of Black political agency than is present in dominant narratives, one that understands Black politics as historical and diverse and operating in the wake of decades of power-bloc competition among racialized leadership and community factions.[11] In the following, I discuss a person and an organization whose work exemplifies two other key aspects of racialized arbitrage. I explore care work and regime maintenance in the story of a teacher-development manager and the efforts of a Black-dominated education reform nonprofit to use school choice to achieve collective freedom. The first is Morgan, a Black transplant who worked with teachers and school leaders; I came to know the Black Organization for Choice through Darcy (a Black transplant) and Roland (a Black national figure who traveled to New Orleans frequently). This organization worked primarily with Black community organizations in order to facilitate their adeptness at shaping reform agendas. I must emphasize that aside from Daryl, each of these arbitrageurs are transplants to New Orleans and represent the re-articulation of Black leadership in New Orleans to national networks and the recomposition of Black elite strata in the city. Through their stories, I seek to attend to this arbitrage as a technical craft, knowledge work, and labor. Each of these subjects does this arbitrage as a significant part or all of their primary work role. The kinds of racial expertise they deploy and develop are not simply contingent and tactical performances but strategic and increasingly formalized techno-social endeavors. Their work resides not only in conversations and relationships but in strategic documents, rubrics, PowerPoint decks, core values statements, contracts, and protocols. Often derided as ineffectual, vapid, or pacifying, this kind of community engagement work is a critical node for understanding the reconstruction of racial orders in the United States. It must be approached critically but also be taken seriously.

MORGAN

Morgan's day-to-day work reflected the geographic and temporal fragmentation of education labor in post-Katrina New Orleans—a great contrast to the relative predictability of unionized school work. I had a hard time pinning Morgan down to shadow her for a day of work. Morgan worked at an education nonprofit as a development manager for new alternatively certified teachers in classrooms. This entailed a highly irregular schedule shaped around the needs of whatever fires needed to be put out at the time. Morgan was responsible for tracking the progress of these teachers; providing on-site evaluation and feedback as needed; and developing group after-school training for members of her portfolio, who were spread over multiple charter schools in different networks. Morgan also communicated with principals and administrators in order to exchange perspectives and information designed to improve the given teacher's performance. Sometimes, when a teacher was performing poorly or was under consideration to be fired or not retained for the coming year, this involved consulting with a principal or dean.

While most accounts depict charter school–oriented reform organizations as relentlessly focused on improving teacher performance in terms of test results, Morgan had been hired to develop teachers' racial expertise. Unlike other development managers, Morgan's portfolio was focused on Culturally Responsive Pedagogy (CRP).[12] Some mistook this designation to mean that Morgan only trained Black corps members, which rankled Morgan. Morgan saw it as her job to deprogram teachers from the "oppressive" and "controlling" pedagogies in practice at many charter schools and was not afraid to contradict school leadership if they disagreed with her approach. Practically, this meant Morgan didn't work in some of the schools more committed to no excuses–style pedagogies—or, as she put it when I'd ask her what she thought about charter school X or network Y, "Man, you know I don't fuck with them" or "That's why I don't mess around with them." Nevertheless, I observed that Morgan had strong relationships with the schools and principals she did fuck with.

Morgan did not fit the typical mold for a teacher or staff member from her organization. But the increasing pushback that education reformers faced in New Orleans prompted charter-friendly reformers to look for ways to defuse the tension. When Morgan decided to leave the classroom after teaching for several years after the storm, the nonprofit's director sought her out for this teacher-development role. Morgan was known as an excellent teacher with "strong data." The director prized Morgan's evidently authentic relationships with her school community. Morgan's nonprofit had been subject to intense scrutiny for recruiting mostly white transplants to teach, and the director was focused on bringing in staff who could serve as bridges to "the community." Thus, while Morgan most directly instructed her teaching portfolio in the techniques of CRP, she also served as a model for colleagues and created community-facing programming, such as a summit on leadership, which was planned with high school students. This wasn't always a smooth process. There were times when Morgan wondered about "getting out of here." Sometimes other staff weren't sure which side Morgan was on. Some school leaders had asked that Morgan not work with their teachers at all. Other staff members confused CRP with other approaches to diversity and multiculturalism, betraying a frustrating lack of awareness and attentiveness to Morgan.

While we must situate Morgan's work within the neoliberal audit cultures of the broader education-reform movement, it is just as critical to attend to the frictions and contradictions of that subject position and the ways that workers of all stripes resist and subvert their designated tasks. Morgan was subject to the coercive imperatives of audit cultures but used them as a license to explore more personal goals and projects. While decrying the testing-accountability system, Morgan took pride in the fact that her teachers had some of the highest scores among all her organization's teachers. Meeting this bar allowed Morgan the freedom to pursue CRP with less interference from higher ups. In fact, Morgan argued to her bosses that her teachers meet the "low bar" of test scores *because* they were being trained in CRP. Morgan took advantage of the satisfaction she obtained from hitting testing metrics to expand and develop CRP programming with her teachers and community members. But this was contested terrain. Morgan got into arguments with higher ups at the same time as she relied on her bosses to advocate for her when the utility of CRP was questioned. Morgan's ability to do her work can be read as a sign of the ways that racialized arbitrage can manifest as a fragile compromise resulting from ad hoc strategic maneuvering. This work was a provisional space for Morgan rather than a realization of her ambitions.

Morgan was a different kind of transplant than the white elites and professionals who take up most of the airtime in discussions of post-Katrina New Orleans. Hailing from another regional Southern metropolis, Morgan grew up visiting New Orleans with family. A member of a historically Black sorority and a frequent attendee of church services, Morgan participated in segments of New Orleans Black institutional and cultural life that most other teachers and staff from her organization couldn't or didn't access. Committed to teaching in a Black community, Morgan came to New Orleans as an alternatively certified teacher in the first few years after Katrina. When Morgan first applied for the role, she indicated that she would be willing to go anywhere in the country. However, Morgan told me that after a phone interview, the recruiter she spoke with was convinced Morgan would be perfect for New Orleans. Unlike many other new young teachers, Morgan was placed at one of the schools that remained under veteran Black leadership, and she maintained closer relationships with her school community than with the nonprofit that placed her in the school and in which she worked during my field research. During my time in New Orleans, just when I thought I was getting a handle on the networks and stakeholders, Morgan would say something to me like, "How haven't you talked to Mama Sarah?" or "Do you know Coach?" There was a casual authority to these questions. When Morgan posed them to me, it wasn't a challenge or test of my local knowledge. Morgan assumed that of course anyone who knew anything about education in New Orleans would know who Mama Sarah or Coach was. Morgan's sense of community and values were centered in networks removed from the reformers that I had spent much of my time getting to know up to that point. Morgan attempted to make sure that her teachers were just as aware and at ease with these alternative mappings.

While accounts of neoliberalism in post-Katrina New Orleans are correct to emphasize the stripping of public goods as a form of racialized dispossession (Klein 2007), they tend to fall short in recognizing the ambivalent and contested relationship that Black residents and leadership factions have with the state. Black New Orleanians are more than subjects, wards, or victims of the state; they also have a history of warily appropriating it to their own diverse needs and projects. This is no less true in the aftermath of school privatization than during the Great Society.[13] Appreciating this political complexity in an unromantic and sober fashion is critical to understanding how racial arbitrage structures the political compromises that have emerged over the nearly two decades since Hurricane Katrina. Morgan was intimately familiar with a skeptical and practical attitude towards state projects. Morgan's father was affiliated with the Nation of Islam and was "hardcore into Black development. He was a business owner; he lived his philosophy . . . He dreamed of a world where Black people owned the things in their communities . . . We should have our own . . . He didn't trust the government." Morgan's mother identified as a radical who was "less so now" but had a sustained record of working to improve literacy in Black communities. This commitment to Black communities was the most central principle in Morgan's life. When I asked Morgan if she had considered becoming a teacher in college before she was recruited, she told me, "No . . . I knew I wanted to do something that involved the betterment of Black people, but I didn't know what it would be yet . . . But talking to the recruiter helped me realized how many of my leadership activities in undergrad already involved education in some way." While Morgan's day job was as a teacher-development manager, she saw the position as a provisional step towards improving Black communities and building Black leadership in the form of students who were taught by educators trained in CRP.

In addition to satisfying the requirements of audit cultures and programmatically instituting CRP, much of Morgan's job entailed rendering legible talents and capacities that went unrecognized in the predominantly white work culture of most New Orleans charter schools and education nonprofits. Rather than see this as simply uncovering an abstracted form of talent, we should recognize that arbitrageurs like Morgan were constructing language and expertise for valorizing and recognizing racialized labor. I got to see Morgan do this facet of the job twice. The first time I knew ahead of time, and the second I didn't recognize until later. On the first occasion, I met Morgan at her office in the Central Business District, and we drove around to a couple schools nearby to meet with teachers in her portfolio. It was clear that Morgan had friendly and deep relationships not only with the teachers but with school leadership and office staff as well. At our second stop, I sat in on an interview between Morgan and a judge for a prestigious national teaching award. One of Morgan's teachers was nominated for the award, and the selector was gathering testimony. Much of the conversation was about the teacher's effectiveness as an instructor and their leadership among their peers, but Morgan made sure to emphasize the kinds of "identity work" that this teacher did with their students. Morgan explained how this teacher, even with kindergarten students, took on "issues like slavery," which she later told me was "something people don't take on org-wide." Morgan emphasized that this work was critical throughout schooling, that it wasn't recognized enough, and that, when it was, it was foisted onto Black teachers like her mentee without consideration for the teacher's other responsibilities. Morgan had the double duty of mentoring her teachers in CRP and also fostering the conditions that would allow this work to be recognized by school leadership. In doing so, Morgan helped to renegotiate the line drawn between official responsibilities and unrecognized work.

The second time I went to work with Morgan, I had initially expected a more casual hangout. Super Sunday, the Sunday closest to St. Joseph's Day, is when Mardi Gras Indians parade through the neighborhood, and the largest procession occurs in Central City. Morgan and other educators I knew would be out, and Morgan offered to let me tag along. As we walked through the crowds we constantly encountered friends, colleagues, mentors, and mentees. We came upon a group of Morgan's teachers enjoying the party, drinks in hand. While talking with the teachers, several of Morgan's former high school students approached. They were filming a rap video and a couple of Morgan's teachers (all Black) were more than happy to join in, waving a bottle of liquor casually. After the scene was shot, we returned to more mundane conversation. Morgan connected one of her students who did hair with a teacher in need of said services. I stood back from the group as I realized that they were all the same age, save Morgan (who was only a few years older at that). They would have all passed each other by if not for her. The kinds of connections present here were also part of Morgan's work. However, at the same time that Morgan rendered these two groups of young Black folks visible to each other, she also illuminated for me (a lifelong observer of class stratification within Black communities) a subtle distinction. Morgan's students, while sharing much with these Black teachers, were not the same. They were not marked by the distinction of elite college educations or sponsorship by nonprofits. On the surface, the teachers and students shared a racial identity, but one should not exaggerate the thickness of attachment that identity involves (nor underestimate it). At the same time that the education reform movement worked to recognize and valorize students like these students and teachers like these teachers, they also constructed fine-grained mechanisms for sifting among them to separate the deserving from the undeserving. Morgan's work could be appropriated for this purpose, but it was also more than that—it was a strategy for making community in shifting sands.

These new and talented teachers were valorized in such a way that, even when they shared the same birth years as relatively recent local graduates, they were ascribed an air of maturity and competence that exceeded their age. The youthfulness of being a young teacher is different from the youthfulness of being a recent public school graduate. In the field I would talk about this scene and somewhat provocatively ask school leaders when they would start hiring their own and Morgan's former students at the same frequency as they hired transplants. After all, ten plus years into reform, their organizations had taught all the local young twenty-somethings. I was used to their posturing about diversity-recruitment efforts, but most leaders were more sincere and somber about the idea of hiring their own students in the future. They did not think their students were ready. As pleasant as that rap video—and the moment of connection it created—was, in the eyes of the leadership, there was still a vast gulf between Morgan's students and Morgan's portfolio of teachers. I'm reasonably sure that if Morgan ran a school, she would have no reservations about hiring her former students. But as much as Morgan worked to render their talents and capacities legible to reformers and their audit cultures, there were limits to what was possible in the conjuncture. Morgan worked in a space of maneuver not transcendence.

As the reform movement evolved over the course of the 2010s, it became increasingly clear that the political transformation represented by the charter school movement had led to a reconstruction rather than liquidation of Black leadership factions within the city. The class composition and national and regional articulations of these factions had changed, but they had by no means been eliminated. The charter school movement faced declining philanthropic interest from national sources as well as the challenge of maintaining "flexibility and autonomy" as schools began to return to local control after the expiration of the emergency charter mandates. This crisis required a reconceptualization of the terms of legitimacy for what had been seen as an exceptional measure. While this maintenance work can be perceived as a cold reproduction of structures of domination, it also entails forms of care work in spite of these structures. Black educators have long been forced to persist within schooling systems designed to subordinate their communities (Givens 2021, Payne 2008). While many of the Black educators working within the charter regime may not have agreed with privatization, they often felt some kind of duty to engage and transform the system in accord with various forms of indigenous Black political agendas. Morgan left her role as a development manager a few years after my time living in New Orleans, a common fate for Black women doing community engagement and cultural change work in liberal multicultural organizations. Having pushed the envelope too far, she found other opportunities in the education nonprofit sector and her expertise was lost while her work continued to legitimize the organization. She continues to live and work in New Orleans but looks back at her time working in white-dominated organizations with some regret. She had imagined that she could both transform education reform from within and inform her connections within the broader community of their activities. Reflecting on the long arc of nearly two decades of reform, she was less sanguine, saying that white reformers were "playing us from the start." The privileged epistemic vantage of the racial arbitrageur does not ultimately confer control over the value of their intellectual property, their unique perspective is still alienable, and they remain disposable when strategic priorities shift alignment.

DARCY, ROLAND, AND THE BLACK ORGANIZATION FOR CHOICE

There is a long history of professionalized "race relations" in the United States going back to the late nineteenth century (West 2006). Insurgent during the abolitionist era, it became professionalized and was articulated to national patronage networks after emancipation. While Darryl and Morgan worked within white-dominated organizations, there were also Black organizations that attempted to play the reform landscape to their own advantage. The core group of reformers had sidelined these organizations in the first few years after Katrina, but before the storm there was a significant amount of support for elements of the reform agenda from the Black professional classes and political leadership. Rather than view Black participation in reform agendas as merely catering to or participating within white neoliberal agendas, we have to understand this engagement on its own terms.

Darcy was not from the South. As a graduate of an HBCU law school and college, Darcy moved to New Orleans for the opportunity to "make an impact on our community." Unlike the other kinds of racial arbitrageurs discussed so far, Darcy did not work for a white-dominated organization, but for the Black Organization for Choice (BOC), a national group for which Darcy served as a New Orleans coordinator in 2013–14 (he has since moved to another role in local education politics). While Darcy communicated with white-dominated nonprofits and charter management organizations, on the day-to-day level, you were more likely to find him collaborating with Black organizations like the Urban League and Xavier University. Darcy's focus was primarily on building and articulating an autonomous Black reform/prochoice agenda. When I asked Darcy why he worked for BOC instead of other predominately white organizations, which had greater resources, he told me, "There are only a few orgs that have the lens I am working in, which is about helping Black low-income families, about being unapologetic, about being able to take a stance." The priorities and strategies of BOC were different from other nonprofits, but it nonetheless favored charter schools, private management, and parent choice. Darcy put it this way: "Working with BOC is really about not limiting the options children have for receiving a good education."

Black politics and racial arbitrage are too often imagined as peripheral to white-dominated political interests instead of seen as necessary and dynamic components of a larger racialized political infrastructure. White reaction and counterrevolution against Black political agency is but one moment rather than the sole mover in histories of racial conflict and dispossession. When Darryl invoked powerful white interests, he correctly underscored the ways that white-dominated political formations really did seize control of the formal levers of power in the New Orleans education system after Katrina. However, as opposed to imagining that the educational powers and authority of the Black professional and managerial classes as well as of community organizations were erased by the physical and political aftermath of Hurricane Katrina, it would be more accurate to regard them as displaced, dislocated, and dis-organized. Through

Darcy, I was able to appreciate specifically how members of Black professional and managerial classes might reconstitute and reorganize their influence and authority in a charter school–based, privately managed system. One of Darcy's frequently deployed techniques of racial arbitrage—one Darryl used as well—was putting white reformers into rooms where they were vastly outnumbered by Black educators, politicians, businessmen, activists, and community members—that is, where, contrary to spaces in most reform-oriented organizations, they were not only not the majority, they were also not the center of attention. Such occasions served to remind the temporarily minoritized reformer and also remind the reader that Black people are not only objects of administration and incorporation, but, as the founder of BOC puts it, there are "unapologetically Black" political factions with autonomous agendas.

I sat in one of these rooms at a famous Creole restaurant in Treme.[14] Reed has warned that narratives of disaster capitalism and clean-slate metaphors in New Orleans underestimate the degree to which segments of what he calls the Black professional managerial class have survived and re-articulated themselves to new agendas (2011). Just because public housing and public schools have been decimated, it doesn't mean that all those who administered them disappeared into the ether—though many were excluded from new systems of governance. The faces in the room served as proof of this continuity and adaptation. Local Black politicians, veteran educators, and community activists sat around tables in a private section of the restaurant. And spaced one or two to each of these tables were white reformers in an unfamiliar situation. An education entrepreneur sat at table three. The head of one of the charter school networks I was conducting fieldwork in was smiling and nodding at table seven. Ivory, a white local of New Orleans and the CEO of a large education nonprofit arrived late and asked if anyone was sitting next to me. (I was happy to move my bag, as I'd been meaning to email Ivory for months). The polarity of authority in this room *felt* different. We only talked about the BOC agenda, upcoming events, and ways to support the organization. These good intentions could have all dissolved when everyone drove away, but the unsettledness of this reversal was notable for the mere fact that all those white reformers felt it important to attend this event in the middle of a school- and workday.

Organizations like BOC scramble the typical left-right coordinates that are often used to assess American politics. BOC combined relatively conservative Black nationalist impulses and philosophies of self-reliance with strategic alliances with powerful white interests. When white-dominated reform organizations invoke Black wisdom and authority, they often refer to one of the founders of BOC, someone I call Roland. BOC's annual national conference happened to be in New Orleans during my field year, and I got to see Roland's powers on full display. Roland was a skilled orator, but perhaps his most effective tool as an arbitrageur was his ability to stitch histories and discourses of Black radical and nationalist politics together with a school-choice agenda. In the course of a keynote speech, Roland invoked Paolo Freire, Harriet Tubman, John Walton, guerilla fighters from Angola, his "good friend Walter Rodney," charter schools, and the Black Panthers. For Roland, charter schools were an as yet unrealized vehicle for Black self-determination. In one of Roland's most effective rhetorical turns, he used shame to motivate Black people for not taking advantage of school choice due to their fears of white money and influence: "There are white people I would go in a foxhole with before some of these handkerchief head negroes." The latter was used to signify the excessive subservience to white interests Roland perceived among certain Black educators. I imagine that many in the room were targeted by that comment and did not conceive of themselves as such.

Much has been written about the ways that neoliberal ideologues, from intellectuals and entrepreneurs to politicians, have transformed the definition of freedom from a positive social good to a negative freedom rooted in the individual right to be free from political restraint (Brown 2015, Mirowski and Plehwe 2015). A theory of neoliberalism that fully accounts for the racialized and antiblack character of the phenomena must also tarry with the genealogies of freedom cultivated by Black nationalist formations.[15] This political tradition too has a theory of freedom at odds with welfare liberalism, but it is not merely a tool or derivative of neoliberalism. Instead, Black nationalists have adapted to the neoliberal moment in ways that shape the future of and do not merely react to the crises of post-Katrina privatizations. Darcy, Roland, and BOC serve to show that racial arbitrage and racial expertise aren't merely accommodationist tactics within white-dominated infrastructures but are also used by autonomous Black political factions to further their own ends. Roland and the BOC represent a conservative cultural nationalist paradigm, as Manning Marable (2015) might put it, in which Black unity and control of political and economic institutions are the primary goal. This is the paradigm Morgan grew up with and it is an underappreciated factor in understanding Black support for charter schools. Speaking at another venue, I watched Roland give a speech in which he articulated the goals and philosophy of BOC: "How do we better enable our people to make freedom actualized? . . . We don't build institutional power by making great schools led by white people . . . We don't have a concept of collective liberation, just individual advancement." Roland framed education as a collective mission of a unified people, and he insisted that the pursuit of this vision would result in a kind of collective self-realization. For Roland and the BOC, education reform was just another tool in a long-term nation-building project.

Given this vision of collectivity, Roland was willing to play a kind of diplomatic realpolitik with other racialized community factions. When not quoting Frantz Fanon, Roland would talk about being in the room with powerful white influencers, dropping names from time to time. Within the nation-building rather than multiculturalist paradigm, these communities and interests are separate bodies to be negotiated with and played for strategic interest. Roland scolded other Black folks who thought they were interfacing with white elites on a level playing field; instead, he explained, "You are going to other people and asking them to fund your revolution. When you have to do that you are in a very difficult position. . . . It's hard to be a race of beggars." Roland was clear-eyed about the relative power between Black educators and white interests, saying, "I had a funder say to me, and I won't tell you who it is, this white man said to me, 'I'm old and I'm white. But this is my god damn money and I'll give it to whoever I want,' and I really appreciated that because there was no attempt to be politically correct. That is just a statement of fact." Roland's perspective differs markedly from someone like Morgan's. Morgan is Black centered but still believes in the utility of transforming the perspectives of white people through tools like CRP. Roland has a more inward-facing philosophy that looks to gain resources for Black leadership. He wasn't naive about the challenges of doing so, however. Roland, like Morgan, had to challenge prevailing standards and render legible and recognizable the capacities of Black educators. Roland puts this dilemma in colorful language when discussing a meeting with white foundation officers, saying, "I don't want to hear that you're only going to give money to people with a proven track record, because y'all have given millions of dollars to young white people who have never proven a damn thing. . . . Don't say you're only going to fund based on what's proven. You know it's not true; I know it's not true." This assertion not only formed part of an argument for the recognition of Black quality, it also calls out the culturally arbitrary standard of quality that "young white people" are judged by and calls out these white funders by suggesting they know they are playing a rigged game at some level. According to Roland, these funders were aware of the dissonance but played along anyway. Whereas Darryl and Morgan tried to work within and transform white dominated organizations, Darcy and Roland show us that racial arbitrage also takes the form of asserting a kind of independent Black education politics. The expertise they crafted was one that at times sought to ally with or manipulate white elites not to transform or integrate with them.

The racial arbitrageurs in this chapter exemplify three faces of neoliberalism that are often conceived of as originating in the late twentieth century; Darryl represented the shifting role between individual and community, Morgan the reconfiguration of care and responsibility, and the BOC the contradictions of freedom. Notions and refractions of self-improvement and human capital can be seen applied to Black people going back to Reconstruction (Hartman 1997). Recognizing the longer genealogies of certain features of neoliberalism allows us to see how education reform in New Orleans is part of ongoing histories of racial capital. Doing so centers race in the neoliberal story and reorders the latter's temporal boundaries. Rather than see neoliberalism as an imposition from without, we should regard the reform project as the re-articulation of national, regional, and local struggles over racial capitalism.

To say that neoliberalism is a fundamentally racialized phenomenon within racial capitalism is not to make an ontological claim but one about historical tendencies and social practices. While dominant currents gather the most attention, the actions and interventions of Black educators as arbitrageurs of racialized expertise are just as central to understanding racialized neoliberalism. Each of the people I've highlighted in this chapter have characterized themselves as unapologetically Black and at the same time as unflinchingly committed to finding ways to improve education for Black children and Black communities within the reform landscape. While it is true that white outsiders initiated many of the reforms, these stories show that Black agents have had a bigger role in crafting and legitimizing reform than dominant and critical narratives have given them credit for. At this time, Black leaders have taken over organizations that were headed up by white people when I was conducting my early field research in the 2010s. I don't underscore this in a spirit of celebration or to validate charter school–based reforms. When I talked to Morgan years after my field research, she told me how tired she was. She told me how tired Roland was after shutting down BOC. As much as I had originally wanted to dismiss someone who talked about a Black revolutionary like Walter Rodney and a white billionaire like John Walton in the same breath, this fact made me see Roland in a more tragic vein. Miyazaki (2013) reminds us that arbitrage has a "self-canceling tendency." The interventions and opportunities that racial arbitrageurs exploit are fragile and the contributions they make are no guarantee of ongoing relevance or professional stability—a most neoliberal precarity.

I remember Roland looking out over a room of mostly Black educators and saying, "There is not one free Negro in this room." Neoliberal fantasies like choice can be so enticing because they promise a taste of freedom, because one can see in them a twisted continuation of Black freedom struggles for both bourgeois and radical liberation and self-determination. Neoliberalism as a political project is so dangerous because it is a devourer of dreams, a colonizer of Black ambition, a sunken place from which one watches oneself act in accordance with an alien will. The challenge for us is to do better than scoff as we recognize its grip on our counterparts; instead we should look at each other and ask how we reconstruct the Black futures compromised by its hold.

CHAPTER FOUR

Pitching Race

What happens when transients become transplants, when they dig in for the long(er) haul and try to become what they perceive to be more authentically engaged with New Orleans culture and with New Orleans's communities? Certainly, much of the talent brought in after Act 35 has washed in and out of town, but significant players remained, had children, bought homes, and changed roles within education. While so many of these folks were transient, we also have to ask ourselves, What happens when they stay? What kinds of roots do transplants set down? What are the techniques of translation and articulation that facilitate transitions from inauthentic outsiders to something more anxious and ambiguous, if not quite local? New Orleans is a fruitful place for exploring these questions as its purportedly unique cultural qualities do not derive from mystical native essences but, in no small part, from its role as a port city and center of trade and from its histories of absorbing outsiders into the local fabric. If charter-based reforms do endure, it will not be because they ignore or destroy local customs, but because they engage, recognize, master, and transform the markers of what it means for schools to be connected to New Orleans communities.[1]

This chapter highlights one particular evolution in New Orleans reform models—an embrace of "design thinking"—which began with a nonprofit founded in 2010 by a former leader of the charter school movement in the city. Design thinking is a set of principles and protocols for activities popularized by the design firm IDEO (among others) over the past three decades. While design thinking discourse took on an insurgent connotation among New Orleans education reformers, anthropologists have shown how IDEO and other "innovation consultants" have worked with business schools, companies, and organizations to create in practice highly routinized cultures and procedures of innovation (Wilf 2019). Their interventions generally entail an iterative set of qualitative encounters, experiments, and reflections with an emphasis on "centering the user" or, in some instances, the "human." The approach privileges the perspective of this subject and the unique kinds of data (quantitative and qualitative) that can be generated and reflected upon from the user's perspective. Design thinking is not only a set of tools for making things but also a subject-making political project that resonates with modes of "entrepreneurial citizenship," which was cultivated in the ruins of the US welfare state after decades of assault by both libertarian Republicans and market-oriented Democrats (Geismer 2022, Irani 2019). In response, this chapter explores how design thinking came to be seen by a select group of disaffected reformers as an ideal method for cohering the fragmented constituencies of a radically transformed public education system into a common humanity, an inclusionary gesture that, in fact, had subtly fettering qualities for the people of New Orleans.

In attempting to break free of a post-Katrina stasis of "recovery," in 2010 these education entrepreneurs founded a group (drawing heavily on IDEO and Silicon Valley entrepreneurial models) I call Incubator in order to promote design thinking, user-centered design, and lean start-up methodologies as paradigms for "building the future of schools" while overcoming racial inequality in New Orleans and the broader United States.[2] Members of this group freely admitted that, while the post-Katrina transformation of school governance into a private model was radical, design models of teaching and learning inside school buildings were not particularly innovative. Madison, the founder and CEO of the organization Incubator, was an affluent white non-local Southerner who had spent much of his adult life evangelizing for this model of schooling. Prior to founding Incubator, he helped to open and expand charter schools and networks across the United States. In 2006 he moved to New Orleans and was a key leader in the recruitment and authorization of charter school networks in the city. No mere talent recruiter, he was one of the central architects of a new human capital infrastructure based in racialized neoliberal ideals.

After spending months in charter school classrooms observing teachers, the disciplinary cultures and aesthetic conformity of no excuses schools had begun to wear on me. Having arranged to meet with Madison at the Incubator office in the Central Business District, I was at first refreshed by the bright and open space. But then a creeping sense of familiarity set in. As I sat in the office of the ed-tech start-up waiting for Madison to arrive, I was reminded of my hometown of San Francisco, or at least of what so much of it had become. The bicycles tucked neatly in the storage room, the fridge stocked with Bud Light and bottled water, the open offices and varied meeting spaces, the glass panes connoting a culture of transparency, the white people, the Black person, the walls covered in dry erase paint and marker, the reading nook, the laptops leisurely resting upon couch cushions and desks, the brief smiles and head nods, the big flat screen with the video camera, the flyers and sign-up sheets, the dorm-like comfort, the plaid shirts and smart blazers, the mottos emblazoned on arms in black and white portraits—"don't suck less"!—they all felt out of place and familiar at the same time. That this time-space disjuncture could be conjured in New Orleans is a testament to the hegemony of the Bay Area start-up aesthetic despite its pretension to bespoke novelty.

My chat with Madison surprised me. I was expecting a programmatic chat about school models and cultures of innovation. But what did Madison think was the most important thing to talk to me about? Kids. Not the discursive "our kids" whom "it's all about" for those working in education, but Madison's literal progeny, born years after he had begun working to create charter schools for other people's children. Madison confidently asserted, "Look, Christien, the most important thing happening in education reform in New Orleans right now is what happens when all these reformers have kids." He told me that when his children became school-aged, his "whole worldview changed" and that he faced a "moral crisis." He realized how "arrogant" he had been "acting as if I knew what was good for other people's kids. . . . If I'm a user, I'm acting differently." Madison then mentioned one of his colleagues at Incubator, who told Madison that once he had his own children, he too realized that some of the models he had been trumpeting for most of his life were not flexible enough for his kids. This colleague decided to create a school that provided that flexibility, that adhered to progressive pedagogies, and that self-consciously attempted to serve a racially diverse student body. This was the first school Incubator developed. Madison and his colleague's crisis-inspired revelations imply that the prospect of their own children entering the kinds of schools they had been responsible for, with strict discipline and extreme racial and class segregation, had become unthinkable.

This frank mea culpa seemed bracingly honest early in my fieldwork, but I would soon realize that I wasn't a privileged confidant. As sincere as Madison may have been, he was also participating in a coordinated messaging strategy. In a public statement he reflected, "I spent the first half of my career mistakenly thinking I knew exactly how to improve schools . . ." In subsequent months, other informants also told me some version of the "reformers with kids" stories. It turned out that what at first sounded like the tune of honest reflection was instead the clink of affective currency. The emotional precision of this narrative pivot was so sharp it could have been honed in a political focus group. It was seductive and familiar—yet nevertheless evoked long histories of possessive investment and monopolization of affect and kinship. Madison betrays the fact that his political transformation came through reflection on his own self-interest. This performs an empathetic erasure rendered ironic by the fact that "empathy principles" are part of the foundation of design thinking. Hartman (1997) has warned us to be wary of the line between "witness and spectator" because of the inversions and erasures that can occur under projects of empathy. According to Hartman, the white abolitionists' attempt to use storytelling to empathize with the enslaved leads them to substitute themselves and their own affect for the subjectivity of the enslaved. A similar dynamic unfolds around the empathy principles of design thinking. Elizabeth Chin (2015) sees design empathy as a mechanism for the capitalization of affect—adding new layers and frontiers to capitalist exploitation. Design thinking's vision of empathy encourages the designer to see things from the perspective of the user. As critical design scholars have cautioned, this user is often a universalized projection of a very particular kind of normative subject—distorting the very real humans before them.

Madison's conversion to design happened when he imagined himself as a member of the Black communities he had served. It is damning that this empathetic epiphany had not occurred before. That this erasure is articulated through his children underscores how education reform participates in a centuries-long delegitimization and deprivation of Black kinship (Spillers 1987). While Madison imagined the user as a role that could bind him and his kin in a tapestry of shared destiny with Black New Orleanians, it is critical that we recognize the all-too-easy flattening of difference and the privatization of affect and narrative entailed in this particular embrace of design and design thinking.[3] As much as design offers an opportunity for making different and better schools and for fashioning new solidarities, it is also here a mechanism by which regret over racialized patronage facilitates a self-interested rehumanization of the designer.

In what follows I examine how a group of education entrepreneurs[4] in post-Katrina New Orleans established design communities through ritualized three-to-five minute "pitches" and training protocols. While the "human-centered design" methods at the core of their work were intended in part to restore the democratic ethos of public schooling, their efforts in effect represent an attempt to do so by using design methods to "humanize" the Black subjects of the New Orleans school system. It is critical that the discipline of anthropology continue to "question the human at the center" of these deceptively egalitarian designs (Hargraves and Jafarinaimi 2012). These reformers rely on forms of empathetic erasure rooted in narratives of spectacular violence and universalist assumptions about the motivations, behaviors, and capacities of so-called users and so-called designers. While it may be easy to laud design thinking for taking seriously the perspective and experience of its racialized users through "empathy principles,"[5] this chapter shares antiblackness theorists' skepticism of liberal humanization projects and is concerned with the burdens that the relationship between designers and users entails. What is the human at the center of design? Humanity here is not a shared essence, nor an egalitarian relation, but the mark of a process through which surplus affect and the spectacle of blackness is instrumentalized and transmuted into racial capital.

DESIGNING THE FUTURE OF SCHOOL

The discovery and interpretation phases of a design thinking protocol involved in-depth quasi-ethnographic research into the problem faced by the designer first by using participant observation to gather data and then storytelling to share and reflect. For example, one participant in the summer training program I observed in 2014, Mackenzie, was a teacher and a Black transplant who wanted to leverage parents to improve student reading levels. In the sessions and in her pitches she described how she realized, after talking to parents and looking at studies, that low-income parents spent a great deal of time reading to their children but did not use pedagogically effective strategies for consolidating learning outcomes. Each one of the stages of design thinking contains its own feedback loops as these observations are influenced by sharing with colleagues and other parents. This ethnographic data was used as the foundation for the design of small-scale prototypes, which were tested with users, or "the community." McKenzie came up with the idea of including packets paired with books that included pedagogical instructions for how parents could reinforce learning objectives. User and designer feedback was then reviewed and incorporated into future prototypes until a satisfactory solution was arrived at. McKenzie's pilot was well received by parents and colleagues at Incubator, requiring less drastic adjustments than other pilots. The idea had an elegant simplicity to it and only required minor alterations to the content packets before McKenzie began to draw interest in funding the idea at pitch nights.

McKenzie's pilot illustrated not only how the design process could work to solve a straightforward learning problem but also how design thinking was supposed to mitigate the racialized marginalization of contemporary schooling. When McKenzie narrated the genesis of her idea, she talked about one student in particular who struggled with reading. McKenzie attempted to talk to this student's parents about reading to them at night and the parents became frustrated, saying, "We do practice reading! We say our ABC's every night!" There was always a pause after this quote, as the educators in the room implicitly understood this to be a tragic marker of the inadequacy of the parents' pedagogical know-how in contrast to their enthusiasm. The key here is to understand how McKenzie used this story to emphasize how the design process led her to consider the parents as a source of intelligence for student learning in ways she and by extension other educators had not considered. The mostly Black and low-income students McKenzie served were assumed to have parents that were not as involved in supplementary academic activities, but the design protocol revealed through collaboration that they were ostensibly ineffective and unknowledgeable not uncommitted or unenthused. The design process could in theory not only generate solutions but create the kinds of racialized solidarities that had been suppressed by dominant modes of education reform.

Madison's educational philosophy changed once he and his closest colleagues started thinking like *users*. This particular word was commonly used by folks at Incubator and should be distinguished from other subjective engagements with schools and schooling. A user is not the same as a constituent, a community member, a consumer, a parent, a voter, a citizen, or any other subject position that people occupy when engaging with education systems. Scholars of design have noted that while the user is often assumed to be a natural subject position, it should instead be recognized as a particular historically shaped relation and concept (Akama 2017). The user is as much a viewpoint and a vehicle for the designer's empathy as it is an individual person. It is an interface between subject, product, and information flows. As such, it can facilitate a view from nowhere, a perspective evacuated from history and situatedness (Akama et al. 2019).[6]

As Madison stepped into the position of the user and reflected on his choices for schooling his children, he decided that the sameness among all the school choices on offer was a problem. The reform agenda had become too sclerotic and bureaucratic; so, he started Incubator to create an infrastructure for producing "innovators" and "innovation." At each of the pitch night events I observed in New Orleans and New York City where budding entrepreneurs would present their ideas for new school models, services, and technologies to potential funders, community members, and educators, Madison would discuss at length the critical need for educators to be more "user-centered," using a chart titled "Status Quo Structure."

At a training session for entrepreneurs conducted by Incubator, I heard an early version of Madison's take on the status quo in education. Madison started by asking the entrepreneurs gathered in the office who the constituents of public education were. Inscribing the names of disparate communities on the dry erase wall, he worked his way from students and parents to educators to policymakers all the way up to the "global community." Madison asked for any additions to the chart, and the entrepreneurs in training offered subjects like "artists" and "makers." Madison asked the group, "What do we notice about the status quo?" The group ventured several responses as Madison led them to what seemed to be the desired insight: "Look at how top heavy this chart is!" "See how buried students and parents are underneath the sprawling institutional labyrinth above!" Madison aggressively drew circles around the word student, saying, "This is where we focus our energies at Incubator. The user is at the center of our strategy."

Madison's turn towards a new vision of education reform hinged upon his reconceptualization of the relationship between students and schools under the sign of the user. Madison experienced a kind of haunted regret as he realized the kinds of schools he had created for poor Black children were not good enough for his own. He resolved that education reformers needed to have a different way of relating to the students and their communities. Unlike the authoritarian implementation of charter school models in the first few years after the storm (Buras 2015), Madison saw in design a means of rendering the majority Black constituencies of New Orleans public schools legible and incorporable into a vision of education adequate to an information-based economy. While market-reform-oriented politicians characterized the problem of New Orleans public schools as essentially managerial in 2005, Incubator posed design and engineering as the key problem five to ten years later. Incubator drew its inspiration from

Silicon Valley start-up culture as well as a budding start-up scene in New Orleans itself; they claimed that "design thinking" and "empathy principles" provided a counterpoint to the institutional cultures of contemporary New Orleans charters. Incubator and other start-ups tried to create education entrepreneurs who were user-centered, who were not afraid of failure, and could "prototype" their ideas quickly and cheaply and "iterate" based on feedback from users and peers. But circumscribing long-ignored communities under the category of the user ultimately obscures difference and limits agency. Unlike the participant, the user is an agent who is in the last instance subject to the authority of the designer, and the distinction between the two must be overcome (Suchman 2007, 2011). Under the design thinking models used at Incubator, the distinction between the user and the designer ends up both mystified and reinforced.

Madison and Incubator trained several cohorts of educators a year with short- and long-term modules meant to inculcate the entrepreneurial prowess to intervene in education at multiple scales, from reading programs to entire schools. Many of the participants at Incubator were current and former teachers looking to augment their ability to teach in classrooms or to offer school-based products and services. Some were looking to design and found new charter schools. Whether or not they identified strictly as entrepreneurs, design thinking–inflected entrepreneurialism was a tool and identity that could be harmonized with their education objectives. Learning the tools and *the style* of design thinking was as much the goal as the specific end product. The standard design thinking protocol taught at Incubator contained five steps. The steps of "Discovery, Interpretation, Ideation, Experimentation, and Evolution" were typically discussed in value neutral terms that played up the technical utility of design thinking for educators. In my daily observations, I also saw design thinking protocols as a means of assimilating racialized affect and narrative into an information economy. These protocols were a highly technical way of framing the racial and class schisms that emerged amongst changes in post-Katrina school governance. Incubator wouldn't shy away from discussing the racialized character of this rift between management, design, and user, but the reliance on design thinking posed the problem as ultimately about the allocation and circulation of information, transforming a political problem into a technical one. However, this shouldn't be written off as the usual story of "rendering technical," which anthropologists of design are familiar with in both educational and design settings (Sims 2017). This racialized information economy is perhaps "something worse"—the harbinger of an evolving political economy based on the control of information flows rather than capital by a nascent "vectoralist" class (Wark 2019). Design contributes to this epochal shift by drawing empathy, collaboration, and pseudo-democratic participation into not just structures of commodification, but circulations of data and information. As I will illustrate in the following section focusing on a particular pitch, design thinking not only sets out structures for making things but calls for communal rituals that capture and organize surplus affects and narratives towards design ends.

The crucial difference between Incubator and other educators in New Orleans wasn't that they respected students, it was that they believed them to be collaborative knowledge producers in the first place. The user was a category of knowledge production. Whereas no excuses schools primarily saw the data generated by students in the form of test scores and regular assessments as a passive outcome of academic preparation, design thinkers saw users as reflective and dynamic generators of qualitative and quantitative data. In principle and in execution, design thinking posed that quasi-anthropological knowledge production was a fundamental step in designing better products and systems. Furthermore, this knowledge production is not solely focused on generating qualitative data but a cycle of iterative encounters, hence the focus on collaboration together with human/user-centeredness. While the typical charter school remained focused on quantitative outcomes such as test scores, graduation rates, and "life chances," human-centered design was fundamentally concerned with process, ritual, and relationships. The iterative and ritualistic nature of design-thinking communities is key to the humanizing function of their experimental cultures. Nevertheless, the elevation of process and relationships did not diminish the technocratic orientation of design thinkers. While particular products were constantly revised and discarded, the process of design thinking cemented the idea that there was some technical fix for education problems—and that the iterative encounter is ultimately a tool for arriving at it.

While the design thinking wing of New Orleans education reform may share a technocratic and market orientation with the managerial and governance (or no excuses) wing, their efforts are a critical reframing of the political economy of reform. By admitting to the shortcomings and racial cleavages of the top-down governance changes to schools and positing a theory of entrepreneurial and ethnographic innovation, they shifted the terrain from one of entrenched political interests towards one of information flow. The recognition of "community perspectives" and "user needs" became indistinguishable inputs in a design process. This incorporation of racialized conflict and constituencies into an information economy has the potential to selectively include in ways that cut across hardened battle lines. There is some superficial promise in this commitment to collaboration and self-critique. However, there are also fundamental limits to Incubator's call for a new experimental culture.

Madison harshly criticized risk aversion in education reform as an impediment to innovation. Madison didn't blame administrators and teachers for being conservative and focusing on "what works." The stakes were very high and urgent. For Madison, the problem with post-Katrina education reform was perhaps that it was too large scale, too expansive, and took on too much responsibility in trying to wipe the slate clean, which did not allow for lower stakes engagements with students. After all, the original idea for charter schools was for teachers to run small-scale pedagogical experiments that would filter out to other schools not for them to run the entire system (Kahlenberg and Potter 2014). Madison believed that charter schools strayed from that mission due to structural pressures: "When you look around the country at the charter sector, they've been pretty absent from the conversation about innovative school design. . . . Charter leaders are more likely to ask, 'Is the authorizer going to punish me if this model doesn't work?'" This is one of the reasons that Incubator focused on fostering micro-schools in which school leaders tested out their school models with first-year cohorts of fifteen students or less. Madison's critique of the conservative tendencies of education reform at a system level would never change the fact that the New Orleans veteran teaching corps was decimated and fired after Hurricane Katrina, nor would it return the majority of schools to local democratic control. However, the traction that Incubator gained to conduct small-scale education experiments with new school models and entrepreneurial ventures did attempt to add new ways for educators and communities to actively participate in the reform project.

Madison and Incubator were intensely focused on providing an infrastructure for educators to make "small bets" in order to promote experimentation and innovation. Madison wanted to know, "How can we make as many smart $10, $100, $1,000 and $10,000 bets on promising ideas and promising entrepreneurs as we can? How can investors help push the idea forward when it is tiny, when the leader isn't sure yet if it will work? What do people need at this stage? . . . In focusing on smaller experiments, we reduce the costs of failure and speed the feedback process so we can get smarter about what works and what doesn't. And we get students and families more involved in the process." Madison founded Incubator in part to provide the institutional framework for educators and entrepreneurs to "de-risk" and scale down their experiments. However, lower risk and smaller scale don't themselves facilitate the kind of learning and innovation Madison hopes to reap from small bets. While conducting design thinking boot camps for budding entrepreneurs and innovators, Incubator had to work to inculcate new scalar mindsets through games and challenges. Participants were asked to brainstorm and share their ideas for improving education. Sometimes participants related these in the form of questions like, "What if parents had packets paired with their children's books that guided them on how to effectively read with their children?" or, "What if teachers had an app that allowed them to track student performance and communicate with parents all in one place?" Typically, Madison or another facilitator would then ask what the participant needed to test out this idea and get feedback. Participants would offer an estimate of materials, support, or dollars, and invariably they would be asked, "Can you do it with less? Can you do it smaller?" They would then be challenged to test out their idea on a shoestring budget of, say, $50 or $100. These challenges were meant to get participants to think like designers as much as they were geared towards generating meaningful feedback on the specific project. Small bets were certainly a means for lowering risk in any given experiment, but they were also a means of creating a "rapid feedback cycle" whereby the lessons of small failures were able to be integrated ever more quickly into an iterative feedback loop. Indeed, most ventures coming out of these training modules failed. That's the point though. Incubator was focused on creating innovators and entrepreneurs, not innovations and ventures, or as one of the facilitator's told me, "It's not about having the answer, it's about having a process that will get you closer to the answer."

Yet, the stakes for users are never quite lowered in the same way. Yes, participating in a focus group to test a new idea for a school model or an education product may seem low stakes for a student or parent but only in the immediate sense. They still carry the prevailing risks of membership in marginalized groups and of constituents of inadequate public education. When students and parents sign up to be in a fifteen-person pilot for a micro-school model for a whole school year, for example, they are assuming a level of risk that is much higher than the risk taken on by Incubator design entrepreneurs. Staying in their current schools certainly came with risks as well, illustrating a baseline risk that the design thinking protocol doesn't necessarily account for.[7] Risk-taking and experimentation is meant to not only signal innovation but a sense of stakes for the design thinker. Incubator preached the virtues of small failures as learning encounters. But when the bets fail, who calls in the debt?

Inclusion without accountability is a farce. Design thinking protocols mimic intimacy and engagement without addressing the structural fact that by virtue of their professional standing and the pervasiveness of racialized class hierarchy, designers can never be truly accountable to their constituents. While design thinking protocols take place in semiprivate zones of experimentation, design outcomes and aspirations are also quite elaborately staged for public audiences. In the next section I turn to how Incubator organizes the public presentation of its entrepreneurial pitch nights, where spectacular violence and the spectacle of blackness betray the liberating promise of design and further cement the racial orders they desire to disrupt.

RILEY'S MOTIVATION

"MY BROTHA!" I grew to expect Riley's affable greeting over the course of my time at Incubator. I step in, cock my right arm at an angle, meet Riley's hand, bring it in for the chest bump and the double tap on the back. Whether I was at Incubator, a bar, or Riley's classroom, the greeting was the same. I got along easy with Riley. Even before I knew we were both from California and fans of Tupac Shakur, we had a repertoire of gestures, rituals, and sartorial cues that smoothed the rapport building. Riley had been teaching for several years when I came to visit his classroom, and his relaxed authority and clear sense of purpose was the kind of thing I hoped my classroom looked like when I was teaching at a charter school in Harlem. Riley's classroom practices focused both on academic rigor and the theme of "WAR," which was a metaphor for the forces of oppression and domination that held back low-income Black students who made up the vast majority of the room. Students recited Tupac's poem "The Rose that Grew From Concrete" from memory and if you looked on the wall you could see written statements from every student starting with the phrase, "I declare war . . ." naming all the forces in their lives that might keep them from reaching their goals. Riley was under consideration for national teaching awards and was pointed to as a model for culturally responsive teaching.

I was surprised when I learned how much Riley struggled as a first-year teacher. Not in the way that almost all first-year teachers struggle with basic instructional practices and classroom management. Rather, despite being a Black man coming from the same kind of community as his students, Riley struggled to connect to them. In a profile, Riley reflected, "I struggled to relate to the students, even though I looked just like them." The profile stated that, "The students didn't see any evidence that he came from a similar background, regarding him as just another one of the white folks that they read about. He was Childish Gambino to their Lil' Wayne." Riley reflected that he was too focused on enforcing his authority and not focused enough on understanding students' lives. After one student was murdered by another, Riley suffered a crisis of faith and resolved to become a better teacher, more in tune with his students' lives and communities. Riley changed his classroom philosophy, coming up with the war theme and infusing political and cultural messaging into everyday practice.

However, Riley eventually became frustrated with trying to teach this way within the strictures of a no excuses charter school. Riley applied to work with Incubator to start a new school with a new school model. The school would focus on "unlocking career pathways" and build connections to the community by having students spend significant chunks of their learning time interning with tech companies. Students developed projects that worked to solve local problems—for example, they created websites or social media campaigns for local businesses and entrepreneurs. When students weren't learning job skills, they were supposed to pursue self-directed projects using blended learning, with teachers acting more like facilitators and consultants. During my field research, Riley often had a difficult time explaining how this model was different from traditional trade schools, but he believed that the tech orientation was fundamentally distinct.

Because Riley was not developing his school according to "proven" templates from other charter networks, Riley had to demonstrate promise and cultivate investment in various forms. Riley conducted prototypes of classroom modules as a proof of concept, which involved convincing students, families, businesses, and foundations to participate in small scale testing initially before running a yearlong pilot housed within another charter high school with roughly fifteen students. By building a school model that focused on tech-industry training while students were still in high school, Riley had to negotiate relationships between a burgeoning start-up culture based in the Central Business District and students spread across the city. Riley's school model was an argument for community-oriented entrepreneurial-capacity building as social justice. These skills were not merely instrumental for Riley; they were a pillar of freedom and autonomy for his students. Riley's success rested on the ability to direct investment towards students both as "bundles of skills" (Urciuoli 2008) and, as Riley put it in some of his pitches to investors, as "solutions" rather than "problems." Like Morgan from the previous chapter, Riley worked to cultivate the recognition of values and capacities he felt to be underappreciated by schools and reform organizations. Riley's school model argued that students had laboring capacities that could be unlocked by schools in the present and not deferred to college or postcollege life.[8]

Pitch nights are one of the highlights of Incubator's long-term training module. Budding entrepreneurs presented three-to-five-minute statements to sell a crowd of potential investors and community members on their ideas, often competing for small amounts of funding. The cohort I observed and interviewed in 2014 practiced these pitches once a week with each other before presenting to crowds in both New Orleans and New York. While the philosophy of design thinking and experimental culture of Incubator provided an epistemological foundation for humanizing reform, it was in pitch nights where this work was brought before the public and gained momentum. These ritualistic performances were the sites where design thinkers realized themselves as a collective and did the work of building a selectively inclusive community. They were also locations in which spectacles and narratives of Black suffering and inequality could be captured and organized as a design problem, as an input within an informational ecosystem rather than a catalyst for political action or an arresting aporia. Post-Katrina New Orleans was saturated in affectively charged narratives—whether in academia, media, or in communities—of racial inequality. Rather than harnessing this affect for processes of mourning or recovery, the entrepreneurs at Incubator offered design thinking as a means of converting this surplus into action and progress.

Riley thought Incubator would be a promising source of support for this project. He was accepted into an Incubator training program, where I followed the early part of his journey to found a new school and witnessed some of the ways that the design thinking community would challenge and shape his project. Through Riley, we can see how the fungibility of blackness is something that not only is imposed from without but is also often ambivalently, and perhaps tragically, taken up by Black agents in the reform landscape—a compromised and compromising position that demonstrates the class fractures and professional ambitions among Black communities, which are critical to understanding the development and endurance of the charter school movement in New Orleans.

I met Riley in the midst of his discontent with his charter school and got to know him better at various bars and coffee shops frequented by young teachers in gentrifying strips of New Orleans. Still uncertain about whether he would return to his teaching position in the coming year, he invited me to a pitch practice session where his cohort would prepare for an upcoming showcase. I showed up to an initially relaxed and casual affair. "Does anybody want another beer?" one participant asked the two dozen or so current and former educators (mostly under thirty) about an hour into the session. The organizers worked hard to craft the space as one in which both the audience and the cohort felt connected and comfortable enough to push the budding entrepreneurs. Incubator iconography could be found all over, emblazoned on various pieces of swag. The headbands were the most striking, the bright orange incongruous against the plaids and other muted colors most participants wore. The Bud Light and practiced friendliness evoked college and collegiality. The mood shifted with anticipation as Riley (a talented public speaker and dynamic presence in the group) took the stage:

> [*Picture of a smiling student on the PowerPoint deck.*] Morris was a student I taught two years ago. He was reading at a first-grade reading level, but he said every day "I'm going to COLLEGE!" His friends laughed at him because he was very poor. He came from a broken home. In the spring semester of his eighth-grade year, Morris was murdered.

The lightness of the moment was pierced by the morbid image of a body bag on a gurney. The specter haunting so many narratives of school reform was present on screen.

At his funeral, they read the results of his eighth-grade tests, and the results indicated that he was on track to receive TOPS, which in Louisiana is a scholarship, full ride, to a public institution. If Morris had lived, he was on his way to "going to college." On the right, we have Jason [*pulls up picture of another smiling student*]. This was another student at our school who ended up being expelled. A year later, he was found to be the person that murdered Morris.

What often happens is that students like Morris and students like Jason bombard the headlines and they get defined as the problem not as the solution to our city. It's a problem. . . . The issue here is when we don't involve students in being the solution to our city, but instead they are constantly defined as the problem. Reform becomes a thing that happens to them as opposed to a thing where they happen to it.

After Katrina and at the time that Morris was murdered, several foundations—and local ones—came to Nola. There were hundreds of millions of dollars to stop the violence in Nola, like Ceasefire. But what if we allocated those resources to training students to be the agents of change? What if we empower students to be the drivers of innovation and the uplift and rebuilding that needs to happen in this city?

What if we had Horizons?

Riley continued the pitch, wondering how things might have been different if his students had a school like Horizons and selling us on the specific school model. Riley's counterparts and others asked questions and sent in anonymous feedback through their smart phones and computers to a link posted on the wall. Riley's colleagues felt a disjuncture between the pathos of the opening and the solution offered, saying, "I literally started trembling when you told those stories, but they were so long I forgot this was a pitch, get to the point" and, "Your opening was powerful, your solutions should be too." At this practice session, the asymmetries between the structural and personal violence faced by Riley's students and the design-oriented solutions proposed were striking to other Incubator participants. We see here the friction between the affective and narrative surplus of Riley's story and the design thinking imperative to convert it into solutions. On the one hand, Riley was being called upon to sharpen his program and presentation; on the other, its disjointedness revealed the irresolvable tensions between the small-scale solutions proposed by design thinkers and the systemic structural violence faced by their "users."

I got to see many versions of Riley's pitch. Riley was nervous before the final pitch night in New Orleans. Having bonded over mutual recognition of our sartorial investments in the way young brothers do, Riley asked if I thought his collared shirt needed to be ironed before speaking to the crowd. I would normally say you should always iron your shirts, but there was no time and too many nerves. We walked back to the wind tunnel with Pat, a white transplant and member of the cohort, and Riley got ready to practice the pitch a few more times. Madison walked by and tried to distract Riley by moving in and out of his field of vision and dropping objects on the floor. Riley lost concentration and Madison seriously but warmly chided him, "You've got to be ready for distractions!" Downstairs, the floor looked like a glorified science fair. Each of the fellows stood by a board with a description of their project, ready to pitch on a one-to-one scale. Charlie, a Black local and Incubator staff member, introduced me to his family. A reporter from the *New Orleans Times Picayune* was present, taking pictures. The crowd was composed of educators and funders; not many appeared to be students or parents.

Each pitcher walked to the front of the auditorium to deliver their idea for transforming schools. Most focused on concrete technical fixes like reading programs, software for teachers, or coding curricula for students, though others had more ambitious total school designs. The purpose of that evening's pitches in New Orleans were to introduce these entrepreneurs to a community more than anything else. I recognized many of the faces in the room from other venues: educators and administrators from charter school networks, researchers from local think tanks and nonprofits; there were also members of the local media present.

Riley was the first to pitch, and his script had evolved from the practice session. Sadly, my favorite part of the pitch had been cut out. The talk of students being their own solutions was left on the cutting room floor. The new iteration was more programmatic, the details of the students' lives stripped out, the why was more structure, less feeling. I asked Riley why he had dropped this critical reframing of students as generators of solutions. Riley told me, "At the end of the day it became clear that my model, the tag line is all centered around giving kids a compelling why and leveraging that or building that through these different pillars, if you will. So I chose to focus more so on the why in this pitch." I continued to impress upon Riley that the line about students being viewed as solutions rather than problems was important, that it said something critical about the way society views Black youth. I thought that the focus on why individualized the students as meritocratic strivers rather than as collective agents of change. The pitch format demanded that Riley balance an account of the problems facing their users and the solutions they propose to develop. There was an inherent tension in this structure and the solution couldn't seem to go too far beyond the scale of the problem. Riley still framed the presentation around the murder of Morris, and he never lost sight of the acute violence facing his students, but he also recalibrated the scaling between his problem and solution by orienting his hook around providing students with motivations. Quite simply, it was a more conservative framing of the violence facing Riley's students as less structural and more personal. The potentially more radical narrative of the practice pitch came closer to a narrative of capacity building.

The New Orleans pitch night was a more relaxed affair than what occurred in New York City several weeks later. Madison took more time in the beginning of the event to break down the story of Incubator and the evening's agenda. The highlight of this pitch was a more polished presentation of Madison's chart of educational stakeholders. The messiness of all the different constituencies of public schools was supposed to be a monument to the bureaucratic mess that schooling had become. Madison promised to focus on the bottom level, the grassroots: parents, students, and community. That night, while pitching in front of a stunning view of One World Trade Center, real money was on the line. The smaller interventions were more popular with the crowd this time, and I could tell that it was vastly more difficult to pitch a school than a program. Before and after the New York pitch I spoke with Riley about his plans for continuing his school development while remaining a teacher. Riley had spent the past few years teaching in a no excuses charter school and the disconnect between his school and the experimental culture of Incubator was wearying. "I don't know how I can go back," he told me. Riley found the culture of the school too suffocating, and his example shows us how the transience of some educators in New Orleans charters may have been due to the stifling environment of their employers and not to their lack of commitment to the city. Riley seemed to be trying to design a school not only to create a future for students but to escape his own intolerable present. Riley worked at a "successful" school when his student Morris was murdered. Riley was a highly regarded teacher, praised for both his pedagogy and his ability to connect to students through shared racial and socioeconomic backgrounds. Nevertheless, Riley was haunted by the fact that neither the long hours of preparation and relationship building nor the home visits and hip-hop-inspired personal essays on his classroom wall were able to prevent Morris's death in any way.

Riley's diagnosis? Charter schools and education reformers didn't view the almost entirely Black student body as assets but rather as problems to be managed. This rhetorical turn in Riley's pitch could be read as a potent critique of the neoliberal and managerial character of charter-based education reform. As a proponent of charter-based reform, Riley nevertheless posited that one of its central issues was that it treated students as objects of administration rather than as collaborators or initiators of educational and community projects. In making this critique, Riley identified a central cleavage among education reformers that continued to develop over the course of my field work, one between the managerial and administrative focus of the major charter school networks and foundations and the collaborative and entrepreneurial focus of a small but growing group of reformers tied to Incubator.

What Riley laid the foundation for in the preceding excerpt was a recasting of the "problem-space" of education reform in post-Katrina New Orleans, in the sense that David Scott uses the term. Scott defines "problem-space" as a tool for conceptualizing political possibility: "What defines this discursive context are not only the particular problems that get posed as problems as such (the problem of 'race,' say), but the particular questions that seem worth asking and the kinds of answers that seem worth having" (2004, 3). Incubator and its participants like Riley dispute neither the core reformer ideal that schools can be the fundamental lever for resolving racial and socioeconomic inequality nor the central project of remaking and intervening in the New Orleans public schools. Incubator and the entrepreneurial wing of reformers attempted to reframe the problem-space of reform by suggesting not only that new questions be posed about schooling but also that they be posed within a new information economy organized under the rubric of design thinking. These shifts are rooted in both the racialized violence and politics of schooling in New Orleans and the impasse experienced by reformers as their engagements with the city become extended past what was perceived, in the years just after Hurricane Katrina, as a moment of emergency. By posing students like Morris and Jason as solutions, rather than problems, Riley both criticized the managerial and administrative ethos of no excuses–style reform and put forward one of the pillars of design thinking, centering the user (with all the limitations this framing entails). By recasting the problem-space of reform as one of experiment and innovation, design thinkers also rearticulated the material and ritual terrain upon which the racial politics of reform were elaborated and reconstructed.

Pitches are public meetings that constitute and reaffirm new communities (Yang 2010). Even when the products on stage were nothing more than hype and speculation (or, in the words of some of my informants outside the design scene, "bullshit"), these events were incredibly productive in material and discursive terms (Sunder Rajan 2006): they cemented narratives of innovation that spread across the entire charter landscape during my research, and they facilitated relationships between performers and audience members. Nevertheless, we would be mistaken if we simply understood pitching rituals in terms of generic community making. It matters that these pitches are ultimately about the fungibility of blackness in a chocolate city. Like the white abolitionist's public tales, the contemporary ritual of pitching relies on the spectacle of Black death and vulnerability, even when testaments to Black marginality are subtler than images of body bags (as they mostly were). Riley's pitch shows how the affective and narrative surplus of the spectacle can be converted into white humanity through design protocols. Riley's pitch may have been more visceral than most in this setting, but it shows how, ultimately, design communities' humanization of Black users entails using racialized violence as the fuel for the circulation of white affect—mining the pain and dreams of Black subjects for the future-making virtue of design, a primitive accumulation for a digital age. Black Studies scholars have persuasively argued that the spectacle of Black death and the mediated repetition and circulation of this spectacle is an essential element of fashioning white humanity (Hartman 1997, Jackson 2020, Walcott 2021). Whereas Riley wrestled with the irresolvable trauma of his student's murder and was uneasy in the telling, his mostly white listeners seemed to become affectively charged and reassured that they were both empathetic and also solutions-oriented humans. Rather than bind all together in a common humanity, the fungibility of Black suffering here bolsters white humanity. This exchange both elevates Riley and holds him at a remove. I empathize with Riley—I had practiced this pitch with him before—but hearing it told in that room, I too felt diminished.

As much as the ethnographic engagement with and valorization of students, parents, and "diverse" teachers as anthropological fonts of data and knowledge may create opportunities for an ideal of authentic collaboration, these interfaces also contain the seeds of a racialized conscription. The epistemological regime that design thinkers seek to cultivate remains blind to its continuing articulations to structural violence, and it engenders new kinds of exploitation, a "new Jim Code" (Benjamin 2019). While design thinkers can make protocols for observing and collaborating with users, these processes don't erase the relative asymmetries in power and stakes between participants in the design process. What reads as an invitation to egalitarian collaboration on behalf of newly enlightened educators and entrepreneurs can act as a species of compulsion into a kind of focus group or intelligence gathering operation, especially when care isn't taken to create equitable structures of dialogue between lead designers and users. In ascribing new kinds of value to the knowledge produced by students, parents, teachers, and communities under the experimental culture of design thinking, Incubator also generates new demands for that knowledge. This asymmetry poses a serious question for designers: what kinds of formal equality, universal humanisms, and power relations are assumed in design processes and how might the disavowal of the foundational violence shaping design encounters further retrench forms of inequality?

The epistemic culture fostered by Incubator established new material terrain and ritual activity through which the narrative and affective surplus of blackness could be converted into white humanity and instrumentalized as capital. The notes entrepreneurs take on community needs, the feedback users provide on a pilot program, the pitch designers give about the problems facing New Orleans students—these are all the material bases for the quotidian production of new information economies of racializing knowledge in the form of innovation-driving data. Racial capital is reproduced in and through this data. What is not visible in pitch sessions and design thinking manuals is whether or not this participatory assemblage conscripts users into a burdensome apparatus of laborious reportage as well as what afterlives and circulations their data may produce.

While collaboration and participation are articulated with such an affirmative and egalitarian affect in design thinking, we should be wary of getting too swept up in the good feeling. Design thinking may shift the problem-space of reform, but it also might be providing answers to questions posed by everyone except those subjects that have come to be known as users (again betraying the fundamental agential circumscriptions of the concept). When you look at surveys and ask parents about their critiques of post-Katrina education reforms, one of the biggest complaints is the destruction of neighborhood school zones and the inability to have a guaranteed spot at a nearby community school. Indeed, reformers have been vexed as to why parents in the aggregate, given their new "freedom to choose," do not send their children to the "best" schools possible, based on accountability metrics. Why do so many parents refuse to make "optimal choices"?[9] This isn't just a matter of convenience or a yearning for the comfort of a bygone era of community solidarity. The desire for neighborhood schools evokes an enduring political tendency in Black communities that reformers seem to ignore: the desire to be left alone and unbothered. According to Cedric Robinson (2000), this desire is a fundamental element of the Black Radical Tradition—a tradition that first manifested in forms of disengagement and marronage. The neighborhood school represents a longing for the automaticity of being able to send one's children to a local school and not have to think about it too much, to trust that they will be safe and decently educated. This trust in the public is distinct from the onerous responsibilization of market models and parent choice. This impulse reminds us that there are legitimate political alternatives to participating in interventions and institutions, that one could demand more of them and less of themselves, that one can refuse to participate, that one can reframe "entitlement" (Cox 2015) from an epithet to a positive political right.

What kind of education politics would be possible if we rejected the notion that Black students, Black teachers, Black politics, and Black communities were deficient and deviant, that they were in need of improvement, development, and capacity building? What if we refused the idea that the solution to racialized class inequality was the incorporation of Black subjects into a predetermined universal body politic? As Audra Simpson (2007) reminds us, these refusals are neither the ending nor the ends of politics but are claims of authority and generative acts in and of themselves. The question for designers as well as anthropologists is: How might we all learn to see these refusals not as roadblocks but as invitations to be and think otherwise?

Even the most empathetic approaches to intervention into racial inequality, like design thinking, often posit Black people as possessing some kind of lack. "What does it feel like to be a problem?" Indeed. Harney and Moten (2013) ask us to consider the proposition that "there is nothing wrong with blackness." This contention is not a bid for a liberal, universalist equality. Nor is it a rejection of the possibility of relation! Rather, the imperative to recognize that there is nothing wrong with blackness is a call to engage in what Moten (2020) says is the "radical mis-recognition" of solidarity. It runs so counter to the genre of Western man that to embrace this truth (a truth that could only be embraced faithfully in community and through political action and transformation) one must dissociate from the acts of conversion and exchange that facilitate white humanity. When the problem at hand is blackness, the solution for designers is to realize that there is nothing for them to fix at all.

CHAPTER FIVE

Substituting Race

Incubator has helped launch a number of durable ventures in New Orleans since its founding. ConnectED, a gig economy substitute-teaching platform, combines key elements of charter school reform discussed in the previous chapters; by bringing in educators who might not otherwise be hired at charter schools and offering a creative and culturally enriching experience, the company practiced a kind of racial arbitrage in attempting to challenge the racialized human capital regimes and workday practices of typical charters. Furthermore, ConnectED took the ostensible user-centeredness and community mindedness of Incubator and used those principles to find a niche outside of working for particular charter school networks. ConnectED was one of the first businesses to grow out of Incubator, and I first encountered them while attending a meeting of community activists at the Sojourner Truth Community Center in the Treme in 2013. It's no accident that I first met Sidney, a white transplant and the chief operations officer, while he was talking to progressive teachers and education activists. ConnectED drew on a different talent pool than the charter management organizations discussed in chapters 1 and 2; shaped by a different philosophy of human capital, it embraced locality and creativity and the increased availability of locally born educators and artists as a kind of reserve army for teachers in charter schools. Sidney was at the community meeting not only to listen to community perspectives and gather intelligence, but to recruit potential substitute teachers to contract with his company.

No longer unionized at the vast majority of New Orleans charter schools,[1] teachers in New Orleans worked as at-will employees under newly flexible and relatively autonomous administrative regimes. If teachers signed an employment agreement or contract of any kind, it was usually a one- or two-page document stating little more than this fact.[2] In a typical teacher's union contract there are well-defined rules for how much time teachers can take off for personal or sick dates, how much overtime they are paid to cover colleague's classes, and how substitute teachers are to be hired. Without these bargained rules and procedures, charter schools often did not employ substitute teachers, asking staff to cover for each other's absences (often without additional compensation) because they were intensely focused on creating a tightly integrated school culture and were wary of exposing students to adults unfamiliar with school norms and rituals. It is not insignificant that by not being required to pay overtime for coverages, schools saved money by having teachers cover each other instead of hiring substitutes. However, unlike every other American city where charter schools composed a minority in a given district, there was tighter competition for talent between charter schools in New Orleans. With charters nearly the only game in town, administrators had to consider quality of life issues for teachers in ways that New York or California charter schools did not lest they become an unattractive destination for talent. In this labor market context, Robin, the founder and CEO of ConnectED, saw a need and an opportunity.

Working with Incubator over the course of their long-term design-thinking module, Robin reflected on charter schools' problems with substitute teachers and developed a pitch to create a "flexible" staffing model for substitutes more suitable for the no excuses model of school culture and discipline while also enriching the cultural capacities of these schools. Mentored by Madison, a white transplant and the CEO of Incubator, Robin used "lean start-up" methodologies to refine, pitch, and create a business, ConnectED, a digital platform for providing substitutes who were vetted by her trusted judgment; they were trained to be familiar with the work styles and cultures of charters and were able to step in without causing any concern about whether they would be an improper fit. Robin developed many pitches over the course of her training, practicing as often as several times a week. In one of the earlier "quick" pitches, Robin stated, "With ConnectED we are taking on the broken substitute staffing system. Kids have a substitute teacher for an average of six months of their entire school career and that's time that we currently throw away due to a lack of quality and efficient flexible staffing options for schools. We're passionate about enrichment and the need for more community engagement in the school day." In another pitch Robin framed the issue with a more forward and quantitatively defined enthusiasm, "My name is Robin. My company is ConnectED. We are disrupting the $4 billion substitute staffing market, flipping a substitute into something that is awesome, that we can be psyched about. We're matching high-quality subs to schools via a platform efficiently and effectively." In each of these pitches, Robin defined substitute teaching as a "market" that was variously an adversary, an opportunity, large, broken, or in need of "disruption."

These pitches associated quality with flexibility, showing how design thinkers and no excuses reformers shared key tenets of neoliberal theories of human capital despite having a critique of particular market models of charter school reform.

Every pitch was a delicate balance of defining a pressing problem, a sizeable market, and a compelling solution. In different versions of pitches for the same company, you might see each one of these components framed differently, sometimes drastically so. While earlier quick pitches framed the staffing platform as the innovation, at other times it was the talent itself that was pitched as ConnectED's real contribution. An article on ConnectED states,

> Take 30 seconds and stare at the photo above of a [no excuses] classroom in New Orleans. Question: What's the most innovative thing you see? Answer: It's the person sitting at the front of the class. . . . You see, she's not the regular teacher. She's what [Robin], the founder of [ConnectED], calls a guest educator. . . . When [ConnectED] guest educators show up in schools that subscribe to [the] service, kids don't watch movies or do busywork, they keep learning. . . . Whatever she [the regular teacher] is doing, her school is able to treat her more like a professional because of [ConnectED].

ConnectED didn't just provide a "flexible" mechanism for providing substitute teachers to charter schools, it also promised that they would be new kinds of laboring subjects, "guest educators." At times the idea of the guest educator could seem like a bonus on top of ConnectED's core business. The primary issue for principals and deans was to make sure that they could quickly and easily find a substitute teacher who would be able to control the classroom and provide an adequate amount of instruction. However, as ConnectED continued to grow, the idea of the guest educator became a greater part of their continuously developing pitch to funders and school leaders.

It would be easy to see the article merely as a friendly piece of promotion for ConnectED, but it was also part of a broader pitching process. In the comments section, Robin continued to pitch her company as she responded to questions from readers about the appeal of diverse teachers: "Love your thoughts and completely agree with the opportunity to flip the 'off hour' into an 'ConnectED hour' by bringing in diverse community talent. It's been special to see slam poetry champions and public health workers come in and inspire kids at our partner sites during the sub day;" and about certification: "We take quality seriously and are always working to improve our screening processes and partner with groups that provide professional development and certification options. . . . For partners that require specific certifications, we have a wide range of folks in our network—including retired teachers, teaching artists, former administrators—with a broad range of licenses and experiences;" finally, she emphasized the professionalizing force of ConnectED's model: "The requirements vary across school models and states, but in general the standard is quite low—so we're looking to 1) elevate the expectation 2) use what we're learning to shift how we think about staffing and the role of a teacher-as-specialist more broadly." These responses highlighted that the guest educators themselves were a kind of labor innovation. ConnectED's primary innovation was the cultivation of the guest educator as a flexible, creative, and diverse subject. It would be a mistake to think that these subjects are merely "out there" just waiting for the right "flexible staffing platform" to plug them into substitute teaching opportunities at charter schools. To do so would buy into the notion that either "low standards" or a naturalized deep pool of local and creative talent creates the labor availability and subjects that ConnectED needs. Rather, ConnectED works to shape guest educators from a pool of unemployed and underemployed educators, artists, and "creatives" made possible by policy and politics both specific to New Orleans and operating at national and global scales.

Despite the generally liberal and multiculturalist politics of most New Orleans charter school operators, the value of the guest educator as a culturally enriching and creative subject was not self-evident to school leaders. Sidney spent more of his working time as the chief operations officer directly in contact with principals and deans to both understand their needs and cultivate a sense of the value of guest educators. In interviews, Sidney was more assertive about ConnectED educators reflecting local identities and talents that had been marginalized and effaced under charter management organizations' definitions of talent and human capital, telling me that "the culture piece is what excites me more. My background is not in pedagogy. . . . Part of the problem is that veteran educators are not valued by current school runners." He went on to explain, "I came in to town, young and white, with no clue about New Orleans, but I was being treated as high quality talent that the city needed. . . . I hope we can contribute to changing mindsets." ConnectED focused on hiring local artists, entrepreneurs, and former teachers. The goal was to provide flexible and desirable work for both the substitutes and school leaders while also infiltrating and reshaping leadership's sensibilities regarding the cultural underpinnings of talent and human capital. According to Sidney, school leaders don't necessarily see the value veteran and local educators can provide and ConnectED creates an opportunity and an encounter whereby this value becomes legible and manifest.

Robin and Sidney worked hard to build a brand for ConnectED whereby school leaders could trust that a ConnectED guest educator would not just fill a teacher's seat for the day but would fit in and contribute positively to the classroom and school community. Robin and Sidney used workshops and hired former charter school teachers to make sure that they sent in people who were familiar with the school culture of the larger charter networks that made up the bulk of their clients. While ConnectED framed this familiarity and resulting trust in terms of student engagement, the practical means by which their guest educators seamlessly fit in was by knowing and adapting to the classroom management systems of the school, both those that use positive reinforcement and punishment. School leaders I've spoken to were first and foremost concerned about whether or not a ConnectED educator could "hold down the room." Robin and Sidney typically sent a strong fit to a school when building a relationship, such as someone who used to work in a KIPP school but was only looking for part time work while they attended grad school, for example. Such moves helped them demonstrate their ability to provide stability for school leaders facing anything from a typical sick day to more specialized needs such as department retreats or teachers resigning mid-year. While a great deal of interest from school leaders came from this baseline ability to assist in the normal functioning of the school day, Robin and Sidney saw in their satisfaction an opportunity for cultivating the other values of the guest educator. School leaders were looking for stability, and ConnectED developed and utilized various forms of flexibility to meet that need.

FLEXIBLE WORKERS

According to Sidney, school leaders had a certain vision of what they wanted in a teacher, but at times that vision was too restrictive and excluded a broader range of educators and educational experiences from entering charter schools in the city. Sidney focused on using the ConnectED talent pool to push on school leader's visions of talent and human capital through "transformative" classroom experiences. Unlike the staff demographics of most charter schools they contracted with, the majority of ConnectED educators were Black and local to New Orleans. Many of them were also artists, singers, poets, authors, architects, and so on. These guest educators were ostensibly providing value by serving as more engaging than usual substitutes as well as affording opportunities for live interactions with models of aspirational futures. Sidney framed their approach to me in this way: "Our theory of change, it's a complicated value proposition. We believe that students having teachers like them is important. . . . We want school to be a place where students want to be. . . . Having teachers of color that share their background is vital. They have to know that they have options. That they are not just doing it for themselves but for the community." The time that students spent with a ConnectED guest educator was supposed to be culturally enriching and affirming rather than merely adequate to the standards of their regular teachers.

ConnectED drew on a talent pool of marginalized educators and tried to find ways for them to fit in to the charter school landscape. The problem may be that this very fitting in could be as much a process of further marginalization as it could be an opportunity for inclusion and new forms of community. When I interviewed Robin near the end of my fieldwork, she was somewhat embarrassed by the ambition of her early pitches while also admiring the clarity of her vision. Having just finished a year of operation, the day-to-day exigencies of running a business were taking up more of her mindshare than did the ideals she had been pitching. Robin reflected,

> Sometimes I look at people pitching, and I don't mean this in a conde-
> scending way . . . I have moments where I'm like . . . I don't know how
> we're going to make payroll; we don't have dollars; all of my credit
> cards are maxed out; all my things are overdrawn; I've already bor-
> rowed money from more people than I can borrow money from. . . .
> Like, oh shit . . . that level of how do I get to the next week, get to the
> next day? Maybe it does temper the vision a little bit, or make me
> more cynical . . .

Robin was adamant that running ConnectED as a for-profit business was a better way to remain accountable to the schools and
communities she was looking to serve than using corporate
and philanthropic donors would be. Nevertheless, school leaders
held an outsize influence in this model as the direct customer.

Sidney and Robin both recognized in interviews that their own
status as valued talent was both racialized and unfairly ascribed,
and they hoped to use this privilege to help render the capacities of their teachers acceptable and legible to charter schools.
Sidney was in constant communication with school leaders and
teachers and worked to translate and smooth over misunder-
standings, often articulated around the temporal expectations
of the working day. Sidney described to me in an interview how
he had to advocate for a teacher working as a regular substitute.
The teacher had to leave at a certain time of day to pick up their
kids and this rigid quit time (compared to the mostly childless
staff who stay later into the evening) was interpreted as a lack
of commitment by the principal. Sidney tried to communicate to
the principal the other ways this guest educator showed commitment to the school that weren't obvious, such as participation in
community events on weekends and evenings. Sidney reflected
on this interaction by stating, "The way people demonstrate commitment is also cultural; commitment to one of my teachers is

having kids over, volunteering, they're a committed person who has other commitments as well." Sidney also worked to get more permanent employment for subs when possible. Emory, after gaining full-time employment at a school where he had substituted throughout the year, expressed to me his deep appreciation for ConnectED's support and great pride in the recognition of a permanent position. The ConnectED business model was highly dependent on Robin and Sidney's abilities to vouch for, translate for, and legitimate guest educators who were typically not let into charter schools. Robin and Sidney functioned to mitigate the risks schools take by working with "unproven" or non-credible talent, a key link in a speculative chain.

These three values (pedagogical stability, local Black culture, and white professional social capital) coexisted unevenly in the ConnectED business model. Robin and Sidney hoped they combined in a way that used the flexibility of the charter school environment to expand the horizons of learning for students, tying them closer to the community in the classroom and providing school leaders and local educators a means to recognize and connect with each other. As much as Sidney hoped to use the ConnectED platform to enrich student experiences and provide opportunities for marginalized educators, they admitted that the "pedagogical thing" came first for school leaders. Robin was even more forthright about these priorities, saying,

> It's bridging, a hidden value. If I'm being self-critical, we're not transparent about that, like not explicit about saying, 'What I'm doing is translating and communicating between people in charter schools and people who want to be engaged with kids but don't feel like they have or have access to positions, or jobs'. . . . It's a lot of reading someone right away, giving them a sense of who they are. Why do they want to do this? Why haven't they been able to do it so far?

How can I position them in this existing system? That's our role, like a generative in-between space. . . . But I don't tell people that's what we're doing . . . Pushing mindsets is hard. Schools are our customers, so I can only push so much. They tell me what they need.

Robin and Sidney tried to foster a culture of flexibility among teachers during their training sessions. One of the amusing idiosyncrasies of Incubator was the extent to which they embraced improv comedy as a training tool, and ConnectED was no exception to this tendency. As discussed in the previous chapter, Incubator worked with many clients whose experiences in high-stakes charter schools and audit cultures with punitive accountability had led them to operate in risk averse and individualistic ways, only seeking to replicate proven methods of success. In order to transform these subjects into education entrepreneurs who know how to learn from failure and operate socially, Incubator has to find ways to loosen them up and found improv comedy exercises to be an effective tool. During the summer of 2014, I attended ConnectED's summer orientation for new guest educators, and at each session, the group played improv games at the beginning of the day.

Before introducing the facilitator, Robin told the group that she liked to use improv because it taught her flexibility as an entrepreneur and increased her willingness to fail. The facilitator for these improv sessions was also a guest educator for ConnectED and an experienced improv comedian. Before introducing any specific exercises, they explained to the group, "Improv is not just comedy. It's a way to approach comedy, but it's not just comedy . . . It's a way to make your team look better . . . It's a way to learn how to listen." I participated with the group as we played several standard improv games, such as "Yes and . . . ," where participants presented scenarios to each other and then had to build on them without negating anything from their partner. Part of learning to fail here was learning to be OK with looking silly, with telling a bad joke, with having miscommunications—and rolling with them. These improv games were meant to inculcate a flexibility that is a prized attribute of contemporary labor regimes and of education reform in particular. Whereas flexibility for managerial no excuses reform primarily means at-will employment, willingness to work long hours, and positivity and culture fit (as seen in chapter 2), Incubator, ConnectED, and other design thinkers use improv comedy as a tool to cultivate a sense of flexibility that prizes innovation and experimentation, sociality, and risk taking. This contrast shows how the terms of "neoliberal" labor regimes are contested and reconfigured on the ground.

Flexibility also meant different things to the ConnectED contractors and potential guest educators. In one sense, it was a function of their availability in the reserve army.[3] The kinds of local and diverse talent that ConnectED targeted in its business model were flexible in part because they were available and subject to labor precarity in ways that have increased over the course of the twenty-first century. Robin and Sidney would often frame this flexibility in more benign terms, focusing on the ways that retired teachers, grad students, and artists value flexibility in work hours and conditions as a lifestyle choice. They also talked about how a successful ConnectED teacher would allow permanent teachers to rest and recharge, implying that guest educators could be a kind of release valve for the intense work hours and ethics of no excuses charter schools. It is true that many of their guest educators did not want to become full-time teachers, and the idea of part-time teaching work outside of the strictures of no excuses accountability structures could be appealing. But to only consider those desires at face value ignores how they may be shaped by the political economy and labor economy, how people can come to believe themselves to want things that they are in fact forced into by circumstance.

As much as Robin and Sidney liked to frame the ConnectED guest educator as taking up a calling, teaching was still very much a job, and at their summer orientation, they were reminded of this by their potential contractors. While listening to Robin and Sidney talk about community building, playing improv games, and hearing an impromptu speech from Darryl (from chapter 3) about the importance of the work that they were doing, I could sense a certain impatience from members of the group. This impatience expressed itself when potential teachers asked brass-tacks questions about the job during the community building segments. Multiple group members would ask, "When are we going to start working?" or, "When will we be paid?" It was the summer still, so work was very slow at ConnectED and wouldn't pick up until September. At one point, about three quarters into the orientation, the teachers were given a choice to continue practicing teaching techniques or to discuss logistics. The teachers voted overwhelmingly to talk about logistics. They asked again about when there would be more work and at which schools. They asked about opportunities for full-time employment that may grow out of these part-time engagements. They asked about competition from the traditional substitute-teaching company. These questions frayed at the threads of community that Robin and Sidney were trying to stitch together. I told them afterwards that I thought it would be helpful to address these logistical concerns upfront at the next orientation.

Sidney was more in touch with these workaday concerns as he spent the most time communicating with guest educators and principals, waking up by 5:00 a.m. to start a flurry of text messages, confirming with principals how many substitutes they needed, making sure guest educators knew where they were supposed to go and at what time, responding to needs in the classroom as they came up, reassuring school leaders when they had reservations about a contractor. When permanent positions came up at schools contracting with ConnectED, Sidney tried to advocate for guest educators to be hired permanently even if this meant losing a source of value for the company, "We are losing some of our best people, which is not good for our bottom line but good for society." As much as Sidney believed in the work he did, he was aware of its limits, saying, "We could be criticized for just gathering crumbs for local teachers." Sidney tried to balance the mission of the business with the real needs of his talent pool, claiming that teaching was "like a calling for a lot of our educators, they want a good job, benefits, consistency, stability, these are not radical desires for anyone to have." Sidney thought that compared to alternative certification organizations, ConnectED was better placed to bring people into the classroom who "aren't on that track" to start with. Here, ConnectED came to embrace flexibility as a tool of social justice, cutting through the marginalizing tendencies of credentials and social capital in order to bring people into the classroom who are called to teaching but not qualified, at least in the official sense, for teaching.

One of these guest educators, a Black local I call Emory, was eventually hired as a kind of disciplinary dean full time at one of the schools ConnectED frequently worked with. When I interviewed Emory, he expressed an ethic of flexibility that was both a critique of current pedagogical practices at New Orleans charter schools as well as a personal philosophy for navigating dominant institutional settings. Emory had been involved with various mentoring activities and volunteer efforts with children for most of his adult life, including coaching sports teams at different New Orleans schools. Emory came to ConnectED after being referred to Sidney when he applied for a permanent position at another organization. He made sure to emphasize his capability of taking on multiple roles at different schools, noting, "My main job has been as a sports coach, but I also fill in for classes at other schools. . . . Sidney said they would suggest me because of the presence I bring, the adaptability. Sidney put enough trust in me to take on different jobs. They wanted me to do a paraprofessional job, but I didn't have my certification yet, so mainly I do sports and minor assistance in classrooms." Emory took pride in being able to navigate diverse institutional settings, telling me, "I really stress adaptation to your environment in the fullest. . . . I can cover my tattoos with a suit. I can talk so you can't see my gold teeth. I can change how I talk. Just because you see it, don't mean you gotta be it." Emory shows how flexibility can be taken up as a means for subverting dominant hierarchies of cultural capital, even if only in a partial and individualized manner.

Emory was happy to work at the schools he was sent to before securing his permanent position, but he critiqued each of them for a kind of inflexibility that he believed was bad for students. Emory felt that many teachers at these no excuses schools adhered too strictly to official doctrine to the impediment of their teaching abilities, saying, "You can't be a robot, you gotta do what you do. . . . Everyone can't be the same way." He cited classroom management and discipline rules as the arenas where teachers were the most robotic and argued that, as a good teacher, one had to improvise based on the circumstances, "They trusted me to do their thing in sports. . . . But in other settings I was given an agenda, or I would follow a curriculum. . . . Sometimes I would deviate depending on how the students were doing or if they finished early. . . . I wish some teachers would understand that even if you have a curriculum, you have to do how you feel." Emory felt that it was his willingness to go beyond rules, procedures, and expectations that made him a good teacher. Emory's ethic of flexibility licensed him to both adapt to situations and to become more of himself.

As we can see in the operations of ConnectED, flexibility is such a powerful keyword because it operates on so many levels, from subjectivity, to work life, to team building. It is no accident that ConnectED's talent pool is both subject to and engaged with more discourses of flexibility than the mostly white, full-time teachers and administrators at New Orleans charter schools. Black teachers became more flexible in New Orleans and nationally as a result of availability and precarity, both as they faced dwindling job prospects and as Black workers as a whole have been marginalized in the labor market. As rents in New Orleans skyrocketed in the post-Katrina decade, artists and other creative workers were forced to seek more diverse income streams to make ends meet. When Robin pitched flexibility as a key attribute of ConnectED, she did more than sell ease of use. When ConnectED marketed flexibility, it mobilized all of these conditions of possibility into a business model. The ingeniousness of the business model was to weave all these racialized strands of flexibility into a package that was useful and intelligible for both schools and contractors, a feat that required great privilege but also facility with the racial politics of the current reform landscape. The flexibility that created the space for ConnectED to exist also contained the seeds of less liberating possibilities. It was possible, for example, that school leaders' desire for stability and discipline would override the other values in the classroom; that teachers who held down the room would turn out to be more profitable than teachers who excited the students. Rather than infiltrate the schools with alternative models of teaching, guest educators might become increasingly focused on mimicking the preexisting models. Recognition of talent might not lead towards equal appreciation of diverse forms of human capital but a further stratification of it, with local Black educators more welcome in the school but in more contingent and precarious forms of employment.

CLASSROOM MANAGEMENT

While Robin and Sidney articulated their goals through the values of diversity, creativity, and flexibility, guest educators in classrooms were confronted with the need to manage the student population in order to keep their jobs. ConnectED regularly held trainings to help with this difficult feature of teaching, particularly in charter schools with exacting standards of behavior and expectations for control. Sidney invited me to one of these sessions after our first encounter at the community center. As I arrived, I reintroduced myself to Robin. We had met a few years ago at another New Orleans education organization before Robin got the idea to start ConnectED (I was reminded how small this reform world could feel). Robin and Sidney introduced me to the potential recruits attending the professional development session, including an architect and an unemployed veteran teacher, as well as Jay, a Black transplant and a teacher at a no excuses charter school who would conduct the training session. Jay didn't work for ConnectED but had herself worked with Incubator to develop an independent consulting business to help train teachers in the disciplinary and instructional practices favored by New Orleans charter schools. Jay's model focused on the quick repetition of specific scenarios, exercises that would make the execution of classroom authority seem like second nature to the trainees. As we began the training session, Jay modeled the comportment and tone we were supposed to mimic by instructing us to put away our electronics. "Close your laptops," Jay commanded. "A little too aggressive. Let me try again . . . On the count of three, please close your laptops, and fold your hands on your desk. One, two, three. Good job!" Her affect was flatter this time, and she was a bit more positive at the end. "That's how I need you to give directions to students, narrate the steps, and give them no option but to follow your lead. I know it may not come natural to you, but when you practice your lines, your tone, your gaze, your posture, you'll get it."

As I stood in the circle and watched Jay give instructions, dormant muscles from my days as a kindergarten teacher at a charter school started to twitch. I began to remember what it was like to attempt to take command of twenty-five six-year-old children, to demand "100 percent compliance." It didn't come naturally to me, and I struggled my first year teaching to satisfy the classroom management requirements of my school. I and a handful of potential substitute teachers awkwardly attempted to mimic Jay's tone and affect as we practiced our moves. Not everyone here had taught before or taught in this no excuses discipline style. Some were more successful than others. Some resisted more than others. I felt a perverse sense of pride as I quickly shook off the rust from four years away from my charter school classroom, confidently asserted my authority, and gave clear directions in our games and exercises. In retrospect, I can't help but feel that my own discipline in that moment communicated something to Robin, Sidney, and Jay, that my facility with classroom management techniques and their praise for my performance "built rapport" in a way that my descriptions of my field research could not.

At the end of the session, Jay privately told me she wasn't sure she would be able to help this group of potential educators, who were so unfamiliar with charter school discipline, she wasn't sure if it was worth her time. They might need more than Jay could do to fit in and succeed as substitutes in New Orleans charter schools.

I observed a handful of ConnectED guest educators in classrooms at different charter schools over the course of the year.[4] While in school, these educators balanced "holding down the room" with expressions of their artistic talents and local backgrounds. These expressions ranged from minilessons focused on these talents—for example, one guest educator explained book publishing to a class of fifth graders—to explicit statements of their affinity with students ("I grew up just around the corner") and of their exemplar status as models of success. Language was one of the more powerful and immediate techniques of relation, as accents and dialect communicated affinity in ways explicit statements could not. Sometimes discipline and affinity could happen in the same moment. I observed a musician guest educator, who used their stage name, Tiger, freeze the entire room after a student reached out and touched her hair while passing between desks. Tiger gave the student the "teacher death stare" for five seconds before saying a word. In a calm and quiet tone, Tiger asked, "Am I your sister? Am I your friend? Am I your teacher? I am your teacher, and you will not disrespect me like that. I would never touch your hair like that without permission."

On its face, this interaction could take place with any kind of teacher talking to any kind of student. But Tiger was doing some subtle relationship building and boundary setting with her steely gaze and assertive remarks. While any teacher might object to a student touching their hair, Tiger had marked her "do" as off limits earlier in the class session, saying to the students at the beginning, "Let's get to work! I want focus today, so don't ask me about my gigs, don't ask me about my band, and don't ask me about my hair!" Tiger hadn't been introduced yet as a musician, and I noted how this particular announcement of off-limits questions seemed like a brilliant way of creating allure and student investment in her aura, writing in my notebook, *is this just how she talks or is it a strategy? either way its brilliant, she's making herself seem cool and distant at the same time, she's negging the students into wanting to comply with her instruction.* Tiger's hair certainly was alluring, an afro unlike the hair worn by any other teacher I had seen that year. By reaching out to touch Tiger's hair, the student hadn't just crossed a boundary of personal space, they opened a space in which Tiger was able to communicate both affinity and authority, buttressed by the racialized politics of Black women's hair.

Black women, in the academy and popular venues, have noted the frequency with which their hair is politicized in the workplace and among friends and acquaintances; in particular they call attention to the license with which strangers, colleagues, friends, and acquaintances will ask to touch—or will touch unasked—their hair. Tiger's hairstyle, an afro not considered professional in many workplaces (though it was merely unusual in charter schools rather than proscribed), communicated aspects of her identity without saying a word and that particular student seemed unable to resist the tactile compulsion. What I noted about the student, however, is that they themselves had dreadlocks, another Black hairstyle subject to both fascination and marginalization in professional environments. While the student crossed a line by trying to touch Tiger's hair, they were crossing a line of affinity as much as difference. This may be why Tiger asked, "Am I your friend?" and "Am I your sister?" These rhetorical questions had to be posed because students seemed to relate to Tiger as a kind of kin, and Tiger had to communicate her role and authority as a teacher in light of these affinities.

While Tiger was very successful in grabbing students' attention and building relationships, she often needed help from Sidney and Robin to maintain her reputation with the principals at the schools in which she worked as a guest educator. As a musician, Tiger kept an irregular schedule and was often late to teaching jobs or not available during the hours schools needed her. This is where ConnectED became a source of value for the guest educators themselves. Obviously, substitutes are paid for their work. One of the teachers expressed to me that their remuneration and flexibility was favorable compared to their previous teaching work. Key to the functioning of this business was the trust that Robin and Sidney were able to build with school leaders to get teachers in the door who were not typically let into the school building. Sidney explained to me how he had to work with school leaders to make sure they recognized the value of Tiger and others like her:

> We had a situation last week, where one of our more artistic and musical people . . . any school would be lucky to have them . . . We had a situation where the school just needs somebody to manage transitions tightly and be deferential to the staff. . . . Tiger's schedule makes it hard for her to be at a school on time, she lives far away . . . But that communicates to school leader a lack of commitment. It's hard to smooth over this time thing, when they're late multiple times and they aren't deferential. . . . We do honor Tiger and respect them . . . but we need to work with them so that working within the rules and constraints is not demeaning. . . . From the beginning of the year we've shifted from the question of, What do schools need? to, These are our people and they're excellent, and how do we coach schools to see that?

These references to deference demonstrate the ways that teachers in charter schools were expected to take on mindsets and affective stances as part of their laboring subjectivities. As discussed in chapter 2, professional educators are increasingly judged along these axes and not just on the quality of their teaching. Sidney did not disrupt this process when advocating on behalf of Tiger or other teachers whose comportment didn't fit the expectations of school leaders, however. ConnectED merely argued implicitly that a wider range of expression should be considered expectable within these norms.

Given all the ways that New Orleans's no excuses charter schools have been criticized for their whiteness and lack of connection to Black communities, one of the fantastic allures of a ConnectED guest educator was that they could provide a kind of organic transfusion of local cultural content and Blackness. Watching students listen to a slam poet with rapt attention, one might think they were in the presence of an avatar of unmediated authenticity. Of course, the way guest educators expressed their identities and talents were as performative as any other racialized cultural expression. Given all the work that Robin and Sidney did to place and advocate for their educators, it would be easy to think of the ways they tried to fit in to the charter school environment as performative and their cultural and artistic expressions as "natural." I noted to Robin in an interview that I thought ConnectED teachers were called on to perform cultural authenticity as much as they were compelled to try to fit in to the work cultures of charter schools, and Robin admitted that this was something she worried about, reflecting, "I think sometimes, because I'm not from here, because I'm white, because I came through [a national education nonprofit], I think that I encourage acting out that realness instead of saying, 'No, just be real' . . . That's a pretty smart observation, I don't know what to do about it." I elaborated on my concerns as, by this point in our relationship, Robin had interpellated me as a kind of (very minor) consultant or advisor, and I wanted to be clear about my thoughts on the racial politics of this business. I told Robin that I was thinking about the long history of Black people putting on a mask and performing their culture for white audiences in both obvious and subtle ways and that I wondered if there would be times when the perceived value of a guest educator's cultural authenticity would incentivize or push them to put on a show instead of or in addition to being themselves (not that I believed that there was an unmediated or authentic self to be performed). Robin quickly replied, "It gives me major anxiety and makes me sick to my stomach to think I would contribute to that in any way."

Jordan, a Black local, was the first ConnectED guest educator I observed in a classroom setting. When I walked into the classroom, the students' eyes were glued to the screen at the front of the classroom where Jordan had put on a local news clip in which he had been interviewed. Jordan was an author of children's books, and the clip showed him discussing the development and sales of his books. Jordan held himself up as an aspirational image for students, making statements like, "You can be what you want;" "I had to work hard even when I wanted to play . . . You have to grind even when everyone else is sleeping;" and "I make royalties when I'm here talking to you. Sounds like a good life, right?" Jordan struggled to maintain student attention and compliance during most of the class, and Robin, who happened to be on site that day, would pull particular students to the side to help get the class back on track. However, the class listened with rapt attention as Jordan did a live reading of one of his books, clapping at the conclusion. Jordan smiled and noted, "That book took me an hour to write, and I've sold 2,000 copies." For the second part of the lesson, Jordan prepared students to watch a short documentary about death-row inmates and used the post–video discussion to warn students about the dangers of jail, of hanging around with "the wrong crowd."

Jordan's approach to teaching this class was based in aspiration and inspiration, using himself as a model for students to look up to. He assured students that they were like him, pointing out the classroom window toward the larger Gentilly neighborhood as he said, "I'm from this neighborhood. I used to play in this park right here." As the early news clip finished playing, he said to the students, "You notice how I'm speaking correctly? . . . I love to help kids accomplish their dreams." I perceived these messages as a typical kind of Black professional uplift politics and noted how, with the exception of the reading from Jordan's book, the students were relatively unengaged. At one point, Robin interrupted students talking when they were not supposed to be to remind them that ConnectED "brings interesting people to your classroom, so let's give (Jordan) our eyes and make sure our voices are off!" As someone from this neighborhood (though students in this school attend from all over the city) and as a Black successful author who carried themselves with the sartorial and linguistic signs of middle-class respectability, Jordan had all the markers of a potential authentic role model for the students. But something about him left these students lukewarm. He wasn't trained in disciplinary techniques like permanent employees of the school were, but I would later observe other guest educators with similar levels of training who held students' attention for the whole class period. Something about Jordan wasn't connecting with this group.

Months later, I would share these observations about Jordan's lesson with Robin as part of my concerns about the racialized performance politics of ConnectED. I told Robin that I thought Jordan wasn't connecting with kids because he was holding himself above the students as a model of middle-class Black respectability rather than trying to build relationships. Robin took this observation seriously, replying,

> This is really helpful for me. Superficially, it was like a career day talk. This makes me think about Liberty, she's a poet, and as I watched them, they were performing but they weren't putting on a show. That had me thinking like, Jordan is awesome, but there was an inauthenticity to that lesson because it was about them, like I'll say what ConnectED wants me to say. Liberty, she went to a kid who said something rude to them, they had a quiet conversation with the student, like "why would you speak to me like that?" It was more authentic. Maybe that sticks with the student more? If a school does a quick observation, they might be more impressed with Jordan than Liberty because Jordan is putting on a show and Liberty is doing subtler relationship building. They wouldn't be as wowed.

Jordan wasn't misrepresenting himself to students; he did share certain affinities, but he was presenting himself according to a set of dominant standards disconnected from the perspectives of students in the classroom. Jordan was authentic but insincere. Liberty on the other hand was portrayed by Robin as performing the markers of cultural authenticity through poetry but as ultimately being more concerned with holding students accountable to herself.

There was a tension within ConnectED's attempts to bring cultural enrichment to charter schools. The company's vision statement read, "We envision a world where the boundaries between schools and communities are fluid and permeable, where talents of community members are seamlessly integrated into a child's education and where each moment of learning has the potential to surprise, excite, inspire, empower and comfort." Through the examples of Jordan and Liberty, Robin knew that school leaders had different ways of perceiving the success of this vision. Would they go for the show, for easily recognizable markers of cultural authenticity, or would they appreciate the subtle and sincere relationship building that guest educators like Liberty and Tiger do, drawing on affinities at a finer-grained level?

ACCOUNTABILITY

Accountability is one of the crucial keywords for understanding the racial politics of education reform in places like New Orleans. The word came to be explicitly used as a matter of politics and policy in the years since the George W. Bush administration deployed its "No Child Left Behind" policies. The idea behind the program was that schools would be measured by quantitative test scores, that these scores would be judged against school demographics and other factors like year-over-year improvement, and that schools would see funding adjustments and closures as consequences of poor performance. These measures were developed in order to hold public schools accountable for poor performance, particularly in struggling urban districts serving poor students and students of color, districts like New Orleans. But it would be a mistake to think that accountability only belongs to the testing movements of the early twenty-first century. Over twenty years before No Child Left Behind, the Ronald Reagan administration's National Commission on Excellence in Education released a report titled *A Nation at Risk: The Imperative for Educational Reform*. This report tied the fate of the nation to declining public schools and called for new standards for curriculum as well as market sensitive compensation for teachers. This report contributed to narratives suggesting that public schools were in crisis due to their bureaucratic structures at the same time that the Reagan administration was perpetuating the "aggressive neglect" of public schools and other aspects of the public sphere. The framing of public schools as "in crisis" proliferated over the course of the 1980s and '90s through media, academia, and popular culture and functioned as the ideological bedrock for the idea that schools needed to be reformed and held accountable. It is no accident that Teach for America was founded in the late '80s at the height of this discursive assemblage.

No excuses charter schools in New Orleans embraced test-based accountability and have been held up as an intensification of audit cultures in public education. The idea of the charter is that a private operator will contract with a state government–empowered authorizer to run one or more schools on the condition that they meet certain performance targets defined by the state. In exchange for promising to meet these targets, the charter management organizations are free from the kinds of regular oversight that traditional public schools are subject to, such as direct supervision and administration by district superintendents and centralized budgeting provisions from the district office. The meanings of accountability proliferate beyond test scores, budgets, and school closure, however. As discussed in chapter 2, accountability structures the daily working life of teachers in charter schools such that it recalibrates solidarity between teachers and relationships with management. In chapter 4, we saw how Incubator used design thinking to create experimental and epistemic mechanisms for accountability to community through an emphasis on user-centered design. ConnectED itself also brought new faces to accountability in education reform both through its formation as a for-profit venture and through the space it opened up for guest educators to pursue their own agendas at charter schools.

One of the first questions I asked Robin in our early interviews was why she decided to form ConnectED as a for-profit business rather than as a nonprofit organization. I was surprised when Robin replied by framing the decision as a matter of accountability. Robin told me she was "sick of the nonprofit world" after having worked as an administrator in one of New Orleans's growing number of education nonprofits after Hurricane Katrina. Robin's position in particular put her close to fundraising, so she had an intimate sense of the kinds of demands and responsibilities required of a nonprofit-organization head to cultivate donors. Robin insisted that by relying on schools as customers (and seed capital from investors) for funding streams, she would be more accountable to schools and students: "The for-profit model is more accountable and efficient. . . . I thought I could do more as a self-sustaining organization . . . As a nonprofit, you rely on donors instead of your own decision-making. At the end of the day, everyone wants to make money . . . If you don't have the money to pay for staff, space, et cetera, it doesn't matter what your intentions are." One of the arguments levied against "school privatization" and "market-based reform" is that they create structures of accountability that are unresponsive to community needs and democratic norms, something that can only be properly done in a healthy and robust public sphere. Robin argued that the for-profit and private model could be more responsive and accountable because of its reliance on customer business. This argument shows that the distinctions between public and private don't have predefined relationships to keywords like accountability but rather that the distinctions between public and private are precisely where the meanings of these keywords are worked out (Gal 2002).

Just because ConnectED guest educators were hired to do a particular job didn't mean that job was the only thing that happened when they were on campus. In interviews with Emory and Mandy, a Black transplant and poet, it became clear that they took their presence in school as an opportunity to disrupt school disciplinary and cultural systems with their own notions of accountability. As discussed in chapter 2, the charter school classroom was a heavily surveilled space as a direct result of the audit and accountability cultures favored by education reformers. ConnectED guest educators were often subject to this kind of oversight, particularly when first starting out at a particular school. For example, during Jordan's lesson, discussed earlier in the chapter, the other adults in the room included myself, Robin, and one or two teachers and administrators from the school who would check in from time to time. However, depending on the specific job and class, the capacities of the school administrators that day, and their trust in the specific guest educator, teachers like Emory and Mandy were often left alone with little supervision. Since they weren't responsible for testing the students, they were left to their own devices so long as students were perceived to be well behaved and nondisruptive. Emory and Mandy used this relative freedom as a space of "fugitivity" in Fred Moten's sense of the term—a space in which Black subjects pursue their own political projects under the radar while inhabiting dominant institutions (Harney and Moten 2013).

Emory characterized his role with ConnectED as being a kind of advocate or liaison for kids, interceding when he felt that school disciplinary cultures were damaging to students from his community. Emory told me,

> A school might want to take a disciplinary action against a student and I try to intervene so they don't get kicked out or suspended. I see if I can intercept that so they're [the student] in school. . . . I said, 'You have to understand the environment they come from' . . . Basically,

the smallest things they would suspend a child for, and I tried to figure out what's really going on . . . They had a bad problem with suspensions, and I had a problem with that . . . They were sending kids home on public transit if parents couldn't pick them up."

Rather than treating his role as a guest educator as a precarious and fragile one, Emory embraced the power of liminality to communicate to schools when their disciplinary policies were harmful and out of sync with the lived realities of Black low-income students. Emory was hired as someone who schools felt could keep students in line according to prevailing discipline structures, but his arrival was also an opening for the partial transformation of these systems.

Whereas Emory criticized school discipline systems because they didn't make sense or were blind to the situational specificities of school populations, Mandy displayed a far more irreverent attitude towards classroom management at the school in which she was placed as a guest educator. After asking Mandy if there were a lot of rules at her placement school, Mandy replied,

> Yeah, and I'm like, Fuck that. There were a lot of rules like walking silently in the halls and on lines . . . My main goal was not to be a tyrannical educator. I'm teaching poetry, I can't tell them what to do. We use story circles, techniques from the Free Southern Theater . . . I told students I wouldn't make them follow all the rules, but they need to be aware of how other teachers would. Let the kids be kids but let them know they are operating in a certain structure and that's fucked up also, and we would talk about that also. In our class we read about discipline . . .

Even more explicitly than Emory, Mandy treated her classroom as a space of fugitivity. We should be under no illusions that the space that Emory and Mandy and other teachers make within the disciplinary confines of charter schools as contracted and precarious educators was a revolutionary remaking of the reform system. However, such infrapolitical openings show accountability to be a field of uneven contestation rather than uniform domination. If the entrepreneurial model of ConnectED can be used to extract value from the flexibility and authenticity of its talent pool, it can also create a space in which these same educators call the customers to account for these racialized disciplinary cultures.

New Orleans is often depicted as an exceptional cultural sphere within the United States, in part due to its unique mixture of cultural influences. By thinking of attempts by education reformers to build community relations under the rubric of creolization, we can see them as part of historical patterns of the production of new social worlds in New Orleans.[5] Attempts at increasing staff diversity or better understanding particular ideas of community and history were not necessarily cynical manipulations of multiculturalist logic; they could also be viewed as sincere renegotiations of the frontier between insider and outsider. These efforts were never fully successful and could lead to unexpected outcomes. However, outsiders don't necessarily stay outsiders, at least in the same way; nor do locals remain unshaped by colonial encounters. While it is important to attend to the ways that outside interventions have displaced and harmed local interests, it is just as vital to examine the ways in which the dividing lines between the two are shifted, blurred, and displaced as emergency measures extend into more permanent engagements.

ConnectED was but one example of a growing scene of educational entrepreneurs in New Orleans. While on its face this company is trying to fill a niche for charter school–savvy substitute teachers, the means by which they conducted this business was through the entrepreneurialization, recognition, and regulation of racialized identity. This process happened openly through the mobilization of local Black culture as a value for schools and an employment asset for guest teachers but also less explicitly through Robin and Sidney's mobilization of race and class privilege to gain entrée into their desired markets. Guest educators functioned both as aspirational and as risks, and they were meant to cement new forms of community with schools in ways that are not yet certain. The story of ConnectED is instructive insofar as it shows how sophisticated productions of racialized and localized identities aren't necessarily alien to reform efforts and may indeed be the key to their persistence. The way charters and reformers can become recognized as belonging to New Orleans may become increasingly subject to the authority and recognition of brokers with the social capital and connections to translate and navigate between disparate social strata. These efforts can certainly create the appearance of diversity, engagement with community, and tradition. However, without fundamentally altering the power structures and material basis of school control, this recognition could instead serve to relocate the loci of cultural production into more regulated forms.

ConnectED's brokering was marked not by cynicism but by sincerity. They may not have connected schools with communities of marginalized educators in a politically contentious manner or shifted the overall hiring patterns and incentives of charter networks, but they were creating new and real forms of community and new terms for recognizing community. Danger arises when these forms of brokered interaction crowd out and displace other visions and actors. There are significant limits to the kinds of recognition in play here. Guest educators were called on to simultaneously be authentic to themselves and their communities and authentic to the disciplinary cultures of charter schools, a task that may be impossible. These competing authenticities are not even, with the fidelity to charter school cultures paying for limited latitude with self-expression. While Sidney and Robin hoped that a track record of success would give their flexible employees more freedom to be themselves in the classroom and transform schools' conceptions of who might be a good teacher, the possibility remains that their interventions between school leaders and local guests will have to be a more enduring feature of their business model. At the same time that they advocate on behalf of marginalized educators, they also help to define the limits of their participation in the charter school environment.

Epilogue

What Do You Believe In?

In the final months of my primary field research in the summer of 2014, I attended beginning-of-the-year professional development sessions at the two charter schools I had followed most closely over the course of the previous academic period. Like many charter school networks, these two schools required teachers to begin their academic working year weeks before students arrived, much earlier than most traditional public schools. I experienced this myself as I reported to work in 2008 three weeks before my fellow Teach for America corps members who were employed in NYC Department of Education schools. As committed as teachers in charter schools claimed to be, the dog days of summer have a way of sapping the energy of even the most zealous. Zadie, a white local and the principal at one of my primary field sites, needed a way to inspire her teachers and she turned to a medium often used by managers of all stripes—the inspirational YouTube video. Clicking through her professional development powerpoint deck to a slide that read, "Do you believe?" Zadie began playing a recording of a speech by fifth grader Dalton Sherman, delivered in 2008 to a gathering of thousands of Dallas Public School teachers. Sherman begins,

> I believe in me. Do you believe in me? Do you believe I can stand up here, fearless, and talk to all 20,000 of you? . . . Because here's the deal: I can do anything, be anything, create anything, dream anything, become anything—because you believe in me. And it rubs off on me. Let me ask you a question. . . . Do you believe in my classmates? Do you believe that every single one of us can graduate ready for college or the workplace?
>
> You better. Because next week, we're all showing up in your schools—all 157,000 of us—and what we need from you is to believe that we can reach our highest potential. No matter where we come from . . . you better not give up on us. No, you better not.
>
> Because, as you know, in some cases, you're all we've got. You're the ones who feed us, who wipe our tears, who hold our hands or hug us when we need it. You're the ones who love us when sometimes it feels like no else does—and when we need it the most. Don't give up on my classmates.
>
> Do you believe in your colleagues? I hope so. They came to your school because they wanted to make a difference, too. Believe in them, trust them, and lean on them when times get tough—and we all know, we kids can sometimes make it tough.
>
> So, whether you're a counselor or a librarian, a teacher assistant, or work in the front office, whether you serve up meals in the cafeteria or keep the halls clean, or whether you're a teacher or a principal, we need you! Please, believe in your colleagues, and they'll believe in you.
>
> Do you believe in yourself? Do you believe that what you're doing is shaping not just my generation, but that of my children—and my children's children? There's probably easier ways to make a living, but I want to tell you, on behalf of all of the students in Dallas, we need you. We need you now more than ever. Believe in yourself.
>
> Finally, do you believe that every child in Dallas needs to be ready for college or the workplace? Do you believe that Dallas students can achieve? We need you, ladies and gentlemen. We need you

to know that what you are doing is the most important job in the city today. We need you to believe in us, in your colleagues, in yourselves and in our goals. If you don't believe—well, I'm not going there. I want to thank you for what you do—for me and for so many others.

Do you believe in me? Because I believe in me. And you helped me get to where I am today.

I noticed that not all the teachers in the room seemed particularly enthralled or engaged while the video was playing. At the end of the playback, Zadie said to the room, "That video always gets me choked up, particularly at the point where he bows and you realize the power of words." Zadie asked the gathered staff to spend the next five minutes filling in the box on their professional development worksheet for that day titled, "What do you believe in?" When the teachers shared, they talked about believing in hard work, believing in themselves, and most of all believing in "our kids."

Charter school teachers have often been depicted as fundamentally different kinds of workers and education professionals. But Sherman's speech wasn't given to a group of charter school teachers; it was given to the general body of Dallas public school teachers. Sherman's speech shows what education reformers and teachers in charter schools share with their colleagues in traditional public schools. Educators in both charters and traditional public schools tend to share many of the beliefs evoked in Sherman's speech. As the teachers in Zadie's school emphasized, I would venture that they share with the teachers in Dallas some kind of belief in the potential and capacity of the students they serve, the vast majority of whom are Black and brown and come from low-income families and segregated communities. Above and beyond this common belief in the capabilities and futures of students, these educators shared a stronger, but less explicitly articulated belief that, in a society structured through racialized dominance and class stratification, teachers are ultimately responsible for their students.

The entire logic of contemporary education reform falls apart if students no longer need teachers or, rather, no longer believe they need education in the ways that currently prevail. By posing schools as the sole institution necessary for combating inequality, charter schools betray the belief not only that students need to be improved but also that improvement is the key to incorporation into a universal body politic in which there are no fundamental racialized cleavages. Schools and teachers must refuse this burden. These refusals need not be destructive or internalist.[1] We can see attenuated forms of these kinds of refusals among the "racial arbitrageurs" discussed in chapter 3. When Darcy, Sage, and Morgan put mostly white transplant reformers in rooms with local Black elders and community authorities, there was a subtle game of refusal at play. These arbitrageurs were communicating to these reformers that though they may have seized control of school governance from the "backbone of the Black middle class," the arbitrageurs' authority was not exclusively wrapped up in these institutions; they had a cultural and communal authority that the arbitrageurs displayed not necessarily with the goal of creating mutual understanding. Morgan may have wanted her teachers to connect with students and community elders, but Darcy, Roland, and the BOC sought to reclaim territory for Black leadership that needed not be understood by white reformers, only respected. Refusals can be generative without being progressive or radical.

Unchallenged by proponents of any kind of school is the idea that education should be organized as a form of work. What would it mean to refuse teaching and schooling as work? I can't imagine it, in part because this would require imagining a society without work, a task beyond the horizon of this text. But what kinds of consequences and articulations emerge when we try to think education beyond the work ethic? As discussed in chapter 2, it is crucial to go beyond critiquing the working conditions of teachers in charter schools and apprehend the racial politics of professionalizing education labor as work itself. The fact that refusing work in totality seems so unthinkable speaks to the embeddedness of productivist ethics in both American and capitalist society.[2] In chapter 1, I argued that charter schools' conceptions of talent and human capital atomized teachers as a racial leadership class. In chapter 2, I argued that these schools embraced affective demands and rituals that militated against the endurance of teachers and employees who weren't socially isolated enough to devote extended hours to work. In both chapters, the figure of the veteran teacher (likely Black given the district makeup before Katrina) who asks what time school gets out is used to indicate their unsuitability for the charter school workplace. I prefer to see these limits veterans set on their work as important refusals. In education reform, any limit to work intensity was seen as harmful to children. Rather than view the demands of veteran teachers, of teachers with families, or of teachers who didn't want to work eighty-hour weeks as selfish, we should see these as potentially liberating refusals of work. Supporting these demands could help break the link between work and schooling.

Refusing is not an easy stance to take, however, even when one recognizes its potential. Most education professionals expressed reservations about the project of charter schools. Principals and teachers would complain about the ways that testing warped their pedagogical imperatives, yet they committed long hours to test prep and impressed upon their students the importance of state tests. These educators may have disliked or even hated testing, but they acted as if test-based accountability not only was inevitable but was legitimate. While there are plenty of charter school advocates who will defend strict discipline policies, many teachers I spoke with found it profoundly alienating to enforce silence, march children along taped lines on hallway floors, display zero tolerance for minor infractions, move children's names up and down charts to indicate their behavioral performance for the day, yell at children, call parents about "behavior problems," suspend students, or reward students for "good behavior," to name a few classroom-management techniques. Nevertheless, the vast majority of teachers in these schools proceeded to teach as if these discipline structures were necessary and desirable. I know this from personal experience. "What do you believe in?" can be an insidiously taunting question.

Refusal is one of the great promises of anthropology. At our best, we refuse to take the world for granted and in so doing hold out the possibility that the world could be otherwise. But our powers of demystification can only take us so far. In this book, I have not sought to pull back the curtain on the Wizard of Racialization or to incite shock at the forms of exclusion and inequality perpetuated by the working cultures of charters schools. In each chapter of this work, I have depicted individuals and communities who have deep commitments to public schooling as a mechanism of social justice and biopolitical improvement. As much as I wish to speculate on what it might look like to refuse the linkage between schooling and improvement, what their stories show is why it is so hard to do so and how enthralled we all are to our fantasies of race, education, and work, which are inextricably bound together.

NOTES

INTRODUCTION

1. Thank you to Justin Richland for calling attention to the biblical resonance of the flood in a set of very generous comments on a draft of my master's thesis on teachers in New Orleans.

2. Adams (2013) has probed the ways that faith-based initiatives and neoliberal privatization schemes were intertwined in the post-Katrina "recovery."

3. The RSD was created in 2003.

4. The state of Louisiana was eligible to seize control of schools that were deemed to be "failing," which was determined by whether they met a certain level on their school performance scores, an annual metric composed of student test scores and graduation rates, among other factors. This would have authorized the RSD to take over sixty-eight New Orleans schools. However, in a special session in November 2005, the state legislature made an exception allowing for the state to take control of schools that had school performance scores below average, adding thirty-four additional New Orleans schools to RSD oversight. This exception was only applied to schools in the city of New Orleans itself. Thirteen schools remained under control of the Orleans Parish School Board, as they had achieved

school performance scores above the state average. This measure was opposed by many of the legislators representing Orleans Parish itself (Maggi 2005).

5. Andre Perry (2017) has written powerfully about the ways that this foundational dispossession remains an open wound among factions of New Orleans's Black community and has nevertheless been disavowed and little acknowledged in reform organizations. As I have given more public talks on this matter, I have found myself slowing down and reminding myself to never become numb to this brutal fact and asking the audience for greater reckoning with its effects.

6. Student enrollment in public schools dropped from 65,610 students before the storm to 24,969 the first full year schools were open in 2006–7. In the 2014–15 school year the enrolled population had risen to 43,948. The public-school student population also changed from 93 percent Black before the storm to 87 percent Black afterwards, consistent with the change in the city as whole from 67 percent to 60 percent Black before and after the storm. The youth population has declined relative to the rest of the city, however (Louisiana Department of Education 2016).

7. Cedric Robinson (2007) uses the concept of "racial regime" to call attention to the ways that particular racial orders are maintained and reinvent themselves in the face of crises.

8. Given rates of turnover each year and a reliance on younger teachers, principals have become increasingly focused on hiring people who can "fit" into their school models. After the post-Katrina reforms, the proportion of teachers with five or fewer years of experience increased from 33 percent to 54 percent, and the proportion of teachers with greater than twenty years of experience decreased from 34 percent to 5 percent. Furthermore, teacher turnover per year increased from 7 percent to 18 percent. (Barrett and Harris 2015).

9. My wife was also a Teach for America corps member at a traditional public high school in New York City and later worked for the organization from 2010 to 2018. We began dating during college, and she moved to New Orleans with me for field research. She

worked on a national team within the organization and did not do any local New Orleans work.

10. Over decades of organizing, federal intervention, and white counterrevolution (against busing and suburban-urban district unification), the forms and terms of segregation have changed, but nearly the same percentages of students attend racially isolated schools now as during the time of Jim Crow segregation.

11. Though there are increasing levels of union organizing in charter schools.

12. Lipman (2011) also foregrounds the link between charter school expansion and racialized spatial dispossession in the city of Chicago.

13. Here I agree with Woods (2017) on the centrality of racial domination and white supremacist statecraft in the American South as a model for neoliberal developments.

14. A formulation that is at best paternalistic in how it dismisses the families and communities of students.

15. I am not referring to misbehavior here but to the power and brilliance of students to shape their learning conditions.

CHAPTER ONE. HUMAN CAPITAL

1. Though several charter schools in New Orleans, and many others across the country, in Los Angeles in particular, have had successful unionization drives.

2. I use fantasy here not in a pejorative sense but merely to contrast the certainty of this vision of an educational audit culture with the bounty of research that challenges the idea that identifying, quantifying, and acting upon teacher performance and quality is so clear cut. Fantasy, here, is used anthropologically to indicate a motivating discourse playing on a complex and situational set of social desires.

3. Researchers and reformers in New Orleans still regard teacher quality as the number one "lever" for improving school quality while admitting that this is the arena in which reform has struggled most (Harris et al. 2015).

4. This tendency is a feature of "fragmented centralization" (Monahan 2013) whereby authority is concentrated high up in social hierarchies and accountability is intensified downwards on more vulnerable members of society; the phenomenon can be seen in the restructuring of the US welfare state more broadly—for example, in the increasingly punitive surveillance experienced by welfare recipients (Wacquant 2009).

5. Fields and Fields use the term "racecraft" to describe this quotidian and ritualized naturalization and emphasize that, "distinct from race and racism, racecraft does not refer to groups or to ideas about groups' traits, however odd both may appear in close-up. It refers instead to mental terrain and to pervasive belief" (Fields and Fields 2014).

6. These two exits do not so neatly coincide as popular history might have it (Lassiter 2013). Furthermore, this move cannot be only attributed to antiblack animus, as the class interests of white property owners were bound up in school construction and perceived housing values. New school construction had driven property values in prior decades (Stern 2018), and negative associations with integrated schools could drive them down as well, augmenting incentives for white flight seen nationwide.

7. These perceptions have the quality of what Paul Willis called "partial penetrations"—critical interpretations of the world that stem from "common sense" as Gramsci defined it, which nonetheless contain key misrecognitions and obfuscations (Willis 1981).

8. A 2015 report characterized the state of pre-Katrina schools: "In the 2004–05 school year, Orleans Parish public schools ranked 67th out of 68 districts in mathematics and reading test scores in the Louisiana accountability system. Fully 63 percent of public schools in New Orleans were deemed 'academically unacceptable' by Louisiana accountability standards, compared to just eight percent of public schools across Louisiana. The graduation rate was 54 percent, 10 percentage points below the state average. And Louisiana consistently ranked 49th out of 50 states on national tests. The next-to-lowest ranked district, in the next-to-lowest ranked state, had nowhere to go but up" (Harris et al. 2015).

9. I assume that Aubrey meant there wasn't one excellent school serving primarily poor and Black students as there are several selective public schools that have been regarded as some of the best in the state.

10. Despite being a relatively poor city, New Orleans has the second highest proportion of students in private school (to San Francisco). At the time of Act 35, the public schools were 94% Black, despite the city population being only about 68% Black (Vaughn et al. 2012).

11. The official status that demarcated a school as failing was called "Academically in Crisis."

12. As noted before, schools have been historically linked to real estate value and reinvestment in schools can go together with privatized redevelopment of housing (Lipman 2011, Stern 2018). As some leaders of New Orleans school reform stayed long enough to have children ready to enter public schools, they focused on creating diverse schools that could attract middle-class and professional parents (Carr 2013). Without the protection and provision of affordable housing, this attractiveness can contribute to housing pressure for low-income families as public housing is replaced with fewer mixed-income developments and wealthier families move into the city (Arena 2011).

13. According to the Cowen Institute, in 2007, half of the prospective teaching pool failed a newly implemented basic skills exam (Vaughn et al. 2012).

14. In fieldwork conducted after these interviews, I encountered charter schools focusing more on soft skills and community relations, in part due to the lack of success their students were having in college and in part as a response to community pushback against high suspension rates and punitive discipline.

15. "My/our kids" is a particularly frequent phrase among TFA corps members.

16. Again, this shift towards impersonal, standardized, and portable evaluation is a hallmark of audit cultures.

17. Charles Payne (2008) has cautioned against over-romanticizing teachers or attributing to them a particular kind of progressive

politics, claiming that Black (and other) public school teachers are often one of the greatest sources of pathologizing and functionalist accounts of their low-income students.

18. The union estimated that roughly one third of teachers did so after being fired.

19. According to *Mother Jones*, "In Philadelphia and across the country, scores of schools have been closed, radically restructured, or replaced by charter schools. And in the process, the face of the teaching workforce has changed. In one of the most far-reaching consequences of the past decade's wave of education reform, the nation has lost tens of thousands of experienced black teachers and principals . . . the number of black educators has declined sharply in some of the largest urban school districts in the nation. In Philadelphia, the number of black teachers declined by 18.5 percent between 2001 and 2012. In Chicago, the black teacher population dropped by nearly 40 percent. And in New Orleans, there was a 62 percent drop in the number of black teachers. . . . In all, that means 26,000 African American teachers have disappeared from the nation's public schools—even as the overall teaching workforce has increased by 134,000. Countless black principals, coaches, cafeteria workers, nurses, and counselors have also been displaced—all in the name of raising achievement among black students. While white Americans are slowly waking up to the issue of police harassment and violence in black communities, many are unaware of the quiet but broad damage the loss of African American educators inflicts on the same communities" (Rizga 2016).

20. We should think of their firing as part of a class coup against the "Black Urban Regime" (Reed 1999), a power bloc ascendant during the period after the civil rights movement in which Black politicians and civil servants gained control of the levers of local government in select cites across the United States. This does not mean that individuals within the Black professional managerial class cannot re-articulate themselves to new structures of power as we have seen in public housing and the political domains (Reed 2011).

21. This is not to say that CMOs never engage parents in other modes. However, these efforts are uneven and haphazard "participatory technologies" (McQuarrie 2013) as opposed to instances of systematic democratic participation in school governance.

22. In *The Garden Path*, a novel on post-Katrina school reform by former charter CEO and education professor Andre Perry, a veteran Black teacher working at a charter school noticed the longer work hours of younger white colleagues and "worried that Crescent City students would mistake work hours with work ethic" (Perry 2011).

23. While there were memories of specific "bad" teachers, in New Orleans, the "bad teacher" attached to raced, classed, and gendered specters. Patricia Hill Collins (2000) calls these characters of the welfare recipient, the mammy, and the matriarch "controlling images" that help to justify the oppression of Black women. Melissa Harris Perry (2011) cites the work of political scientist Martin Gilens (2000) and feminist theorist Ange-Marie Hancock (2004) to make the point that white attitudes about welfare policy are influenced by stereotypes about the work ethic and the sexuality of Black women and their inability to control Black children. These attitudes and images have been exploited by politicians and intellectuals as part of an effort to dismantle the welfare state (Macek 2006). Adolph Reed echoes these observations when discussing myths of the underclass. The bad teacher stereotype articulates to these controlling images by setting up veteran Black educators as both victims and perpetrators of black pathology. This is significant because a class that was in part responsible for the management of deviance has been cast as deviant themselves. Under the rubric of ethics, results, or talent, veteran teachers were derided for not conforming to changing professional norms.

24. John Hartigan (2000) argues that white people are constantly conducting indeterminate "interpretive labor" with regards to race and racialization.

25. Andre Perry examines these teachers in a chapter titled "Haunted Schools" (Perry 2010, 184). The students in the novel describe the white teachers who stay on campus through the night

hours as "ghosts" haunting the school. Their principal, described as a Wall Street type from Harvard, "wanted a different type of teacher" and claimed that "the quickest, most efficient way to turn around a failing school is to exchange the human capital."

CHAPTER TWO. PROFESSIONALISM

1. The average teacher working day near the period of field research was ten hours and forty minutes according to the Gates Foundation (2012). The United Federation of Teachers New Orleans also post limits to the working day in its "Know Your Rights" section of its website, but such limits are frequently skirted in practice.

2. See Freeman (2014) on "emotional labor regimes."

3. In chapter 10 of *Capital*, volume 1, Marx ([1867] 1990) famously emphasized that the working day was both an economic and political battleground.

4. For Marx ([1867] 1990), "the working day is . . . capable of being determined, but in and for itself indeterminate."

5. They are "an antinomy, of right against right, both equally bearing the seal of the law of exchange. Between equal rights, force decides. Hence, in the history of capitalist production, the establishment of a norm for the working day presents itself as a struggle over the limits of that day, a struggle between collective capital, i.e. the class of capitalists, and collective labour, i.e. the working class" (Marx [1867] 1990).

6. "The pretensions of capital in its embryonic state, in its state of becoming, when it cannot yet use the sheer force of economic relations to secure its right to absorb a sufficient quantity of surplus labour, but must be aided by the power of the state" (Marx [1867] 1990).

7. Marx ([1867] 1990) describes the naturalization of the working day in this way: "The history of the regulation of the working day in certain branches of production, and the struggle still going on in others over this regulation, prove conclusively that the isolated worker, the worker as 'free' seller of his labour-power, succumbs without resistance once capitalist production has reached a

certain stage of maturity. The establishment of a normal working day is therefore the product of a protracted and more or less concealed civil war between the capitalist class and the working class."

8. This brings to mind Marx's ([1867] 1990) example of blacksmithing: "The occupation, instinctive almost as a portion of human art, unobjectionable as a branch of human industry, is made by mere excess of work the destroyer of the man."

9. Marx ([1867] 1990) notes that, "by extending the working day, therefore, capitalist production, which is essentially the production of surplus-value, the absorption of surplus labour, not only produces a deterioration of human labour-power by robbing it of its normal moral and physical conditions of development and activity, but also produces the premature exhaustion and death of this labour-power itself. It extends the worker's production-time within a given period by shortening his life."

10. A hypothetical exaggeration. At least I hope it was.

11. Per Buras (2015), by 2011, Black teachers composed 50 percent of teachers in charters, down from 75 percent, and white teachers were 46 percent of the workforce, up from 24 percent. Forty percent of teachers had three years or less experience.

12. Kathi Weeks wants us to question these deeply held attachments to work. Weeks (2011) contends that by naturalizing work as mode of activity and subjectivity, we have depoliticized it as a terrain of struggle and narrowed our conception of the levels upon which social life work operates. For Weeks, work is not just an economic practice, but also a "social convention and disciplinary apparatus" that people engage in out of more than economic necessity. Weeks reminds us that in Max Weber's theorization of the work ethic, it is at its core deeply irrational. As Moishe Postone's asserts, "On a deep, systemic level, production is not for the sake of consumption" (1996, 161 quoted in Weeks 2011). Work "produces not just economic goods and services but also social and political subjects.... Exploitable subjects are not just found; they are, as Michael Burawoy famously argues, made at the point of production." Echoing the work of Salzinger (2003) and Freeman (2000), Weeks reminds us that gender is not something one merely brings into

the workplace, but that subjects become "gendered in and through work." This formulation holds for racialization and other forms of social differentiation as well, and Weeks states that the work ethic has been a powerful locus for making claims upon the worthiness of racialized subjects in American history. Given the racialized discourse of teacher quality discussed in chapter 1, this point should not be lost on us. Weeks (2011) helps us to realize that work doesn't just make things, it makes subjects.

13. Weeks claims that to be properly critical of work, "We have to challenge both production and productivism" (Weeks 2011). Weeks again invokes Postone to claim that "the ensuing analysis intends not to advance a 'critique of capitalism from the standpoint of labor,' but to pursue a 'critique of labor in capitalism'" (ibid.). Weeks criticizes not only the ways in which work is exploitative, i.e., extracts surplus value from workers, but the way "work dominates our lives." Work itself is a political problem and Weeks asserts that even many Marxist and leftist critiques of capitalism still carry a productivist philosophy at their core. This is why Weeks finds the autonomist Marxist tradition particularly useful: "The autonomous Marxist tradition is thus useful . . . insofar as it simultaneously centers its analytical apparatus on work and disavows its traditional ethics. Central to that tradition is not only the analytical primacy accorded to the imposition of work as fundamental to the capitalist mode of production, but also the political priority of the refusal of work—a priority recorded in the call not for a liberation of work but a liberation from work" (ibid.).

14. A 2016 American Federation of Teachers resolution titled "Advancing Our Professionalism," stated, "WHEREAS, our work and its importance to the well-being of our country and communities is diminished by those who would starve the public sector, hold wages hostage (as happened in the Detroit Public Schools district), devalue professional experience and public employees, and turn to outside 'experts' who may be dangerously ignorant of our work, all of which deprofessionalizes our jobs and erodes the vital services we provide; and WHEREAS, the devaluation and

deprofessionalization of our members' work and the work of our communities is deeply rooted in the racism, sexism, classism and other institutional forces affecting those we serve; and WHEREAS, the AFT was founded 100 years ago as a 'consciously feminist' movement that challenged administrators to give teachers more control over their working conditions, secure professional salaries and win academic freedom: RESOLVED, that the American Federation of Teachers and our affiliates will fulfill our mission as unions of professionals by advocating for the professional needs of our members with the same intensity we advocate for other terms and conditions of employments, such as compensation and wages" (AFT 2016).

15. Lisa's reflection gives form to Weeks's claim that "professionalization . . . is more about style, affect, and attitude than about the content of the work" (Weeks 2011).

16. One of the points that Marx makes and Postone reiterates is that capital and the wage labor relation make prostheses of workers and capitalists in principal. The capitalist is "capital personified," and the worker is dominated by the wage labor relation, forced to sell their labor power to reproduce themselves.

17. Looking at the expanding service sector of the American economy in the late twentieth century, Robin Leidner (1993) theorized this phenomenon as the "routinization of service work." Leidner posed that as the service sector expanded dramatically over the course of the twentieth century, corporations began to demand greater routinization and standardization of worker interactions with customers. Relations that had previously been left to the personal discretion and charisma of individual service workers had become subject to systematic and scientific management, entailing a new relationship between workers and their "selves": "The selves of service workers are bound up with their work in ways quite different from those of workers who interact with objects or data rather than people." Self-transformation became an integral part of success in the workplace, opening up new terrains of management, as Leidner explains, "Nevertheless, the standardization of

human interactions does encroach on social space not previously dominated by economic rationality."

18. Crucially, these skills are not concrete specializations in specific arenas but aptitudes and expertise that can be flexibly mobilized in diverse settings. This brings to mind charter CEO Kerry's claim in chapter 1 that he hires teaching talent based on mindsets because specific teaching skills can be "coached up." The charter school teacher is called upon to market their skills and attitudes in ways that veteran public school teachers have traditionally not. Weeks sees this greater encroachment of work into the sociality of workers as an intensification of the domination of work. A key element of this social authority is the collapse of distinctions between "skills and attitudes." Urciuoli has discussed the ways that neoliberalism encourages workers to think of themselves as collections of skills (Urciuoli 2008).

19. Carla Freeman's (2014) term "emotional labor regimes" is meant to capture not only how middle-class Barbadian women were compelled to conduct affective labor in their professional endeavors but also how the subjectivities entailed in this work expand into other dimensions of their lives.

20. Weeks (2011) reminds us that the work ethic has played this role for a long time, writing, "Over the course of US history, there is a continuous calling into question of the work commitments and habits of different immigrant and racialized populations. Whether it was the panic about the inability of US corporations to compete with a more vigorous Japanese work culture or the ongoing debates regarding the supposed inadequacies of the work orientations of 'inner city residents,' 'the underclass,' 'welfare mothers,' or 'illegal aliens,' the work ethic is a deep discursive reservoir on which to draw to obscure and legitimate processes and logics of racial, gender, and nationalist formations past and present. In particular, as the history of racialized welfare discourse demonstrates, the work ethic continues to serve as a respectable vehicle for what would otherwise be exposed as publicly unacceptable claims about racial difference."

CHAPTER THREE. RACIAL ARBITRAGE

1. Though as Dixson et al. (2015) and Lay (2022) emphasize, there were key Black politicians and constituencies that supported charter school laws and reforms before the storm and continuing on.

2. In many ways, Darryl was right. While, by 2019, all New Orleans public schools had been returned to "local control" under the school board, they all remained or were converted into charter schools.

3. See Buras (2015) and Flaherty (2010) for further discussion on the proliferation of nonprofits and civic activity in the years after the levee failures.

4. This dynamic is not unlike how imperial projects have long relied on and interfaced with various kinds of local experts, elites, and hierarchies at the same time as they have been delimited by the resistance of the broader populations (Fanon 1963, Lowe 2015). Woods (2017) too notes how Black middle-class reformers have long seen their role as preparing the Black masses for inclusion into "civilization" in the post-Reconstruction era. These locals should not be taken for granted as an essential and unchanging element of colonized communities but should be understood as a historically developing class that emerged alongside imperial domination.

5. Adolph Reed (1997) has criticized the overuse of the term to theorize Black people writ large, instead arguing that it reflects the particular concerns and priorities of the Black middle and professional classes and the particular kinds of encounters they have with white people. This is precisely what makes it a useful lens for thinking through the agency and capacities of Black professionals like Darryl in a time of massive neoliberal restructuring of public institutions and social life in post-Katrina New Orleans.

6. Connolly (2018) has criticized the clean time line of a 1970s genesis for neoliberalism as universalizing white experiences of the privatization of citizenship in ways that ignore how Black people in the United States have been negotiating the terms of citizenship through the market for over a century because the public sphere had never been truly available to them.

7. Notably, when Reed critiques Black elites in the post–civil rights era, he does not frame these actors as dupes of a white establishment or as tragic figures. Focusing in particular on the history of Black mayors in major American cities, Reed has questioned the assumption that Black politicians could not do more for poor and working-class Black people because of impositions from white capitalist elites. Reed contends that scrutiny of the records and positions of most of these politicians and elites would reveal that their pro-growth and business-friendly policies are sincere and that these policymakers should not be regarded as organic representatives of Black people as a whole but as semi-autonomous elite fractions.

8. Critical Race Theory as well as recent anthropological work give us rich understandings of race as performance and identity—of its contingent, arbitrary, and historical character (Jackson 2005). These traditions have shown race to be a "social construction" animated by "racial projects" and "controlling images" and operating at social registers that defy "realness" (Collins 2000, Omi and Winant [1994] 2014). Targeting other domains, studies of race science, from eugenics to more recent work on genetic heritage testing, have considered race as a matter of techno-scientific expertise (Palmié 2007, Roberts 2011). These studies have taken care to both debunk any biological foundation for race while also taking seriously the cultural and political articulations that emerge from racialist science and its public reception. Barbara Fields in particular emphasizes the genesis of regimes of racialization in the crucible of capitalist systems of enslavement (Fields 1990).

9. Adolph Reed (1999) would refer to it as the "black urban regime." Following Hunter and Robinson (2018) we should see "chocolate cities" as an analytic through which to view the aftermath of the second reconstruction as a place-making project, a black geography of its own.

10. McQuarrie (2013) calls these "participatory technologies."

11. Clyde Woods's (1998, 2017) magisterial work on the conflict between plantation power (defined broadly) and what he terms the democratic blues development tradition of Black delta residents is an exemplar of this attentiveness to the full complexity of Black political agency. Woods takes the conflict part of this framing

seriously, emphasizing that the racial capitalist domination of plantation blocs through labor exploitation, carceral sequestration, and geographic segregation exist in dynamic conflict with the freedom dreams and political agendas of various Black community factions.

12. Culturally Relevant Pedagogy is a student-centered approached to teaching and learning that posits that knowledge of student's cultural perspectives and backgrounds can improve classroom practices (Ladson-Billings 2014, 2021). CRP sees students as critical knowledge producers in their own right and insists their cultural capacities should inform and direct school operations in conversation with other forms of recognized expertise.

13. See Germany's (2007) account of the "soft state" that emerged in New Orleans after LBJ's War on Poverty.

14. It might seem trivial or patronizing, but we must take seriously restaurants as sites of socialization and the reconstitution of racial orders in post-Katrina New Orleans. Aside from New Orleans's historical association with food, the fall of storefront retail and the rise of dining out means that eating and drinking establishments have become even more important sites for suturing the ties of emerging class and racial alignments.

15. Slobodian (2018) emphasizes that neoliberalism is a direct response to decolonization and the democratic aspirations of formerly colonized peoples and nations.

CHAPTER FOUR. PITCHING RACE

1. This process would be a continuation rather than a disruption of historical patterns of recognition and patronage in the city (Reed 2011).

2. This approach to overcoming racial inequality is very much a project of multicultural liberal inclusion that seeks to purify an imperfect liberal polity; it is not a revolutionary or abolitionist approach to eradicating the conditions of possibility for racism and racial inequality.

3. Not unlike design-curious anthropologists and their informants and collaborators, Madison saw in design the potential for a new mode of relationality through the empathetic interface

of the user. Madison and his cohort of education entrepreneurs are not unique in looking to design as a method for changing their world; Lucy Suchman (2011, 1) has critiqued the notion that design could bring anthropology itself into the future, cautioning anthropologists to regard design as but one "figure and practice of transformation."

4. By which I mean both businesspeople and current and former educators who sought to apply entrepreneurial "mindsets" to non-business activities.

5. Very simply, the idea that the perspective of the user should be a central consideration in the design process.

6. Ultimately, critical designers have posited that despite the empathetic frame, the user represents a particularly attenuated and instrumental form of agency, one that must be expanded through an embrace of co-design, participation, and community account-ability (Costanza-Chock 2020, Sanders and Stappers 2008, 2014)

7. Subramani (2022) has articulated how in post-Katrina New Orleans formerly incarcerated Black men are encouraged to take up the risk-taking subjectivity of entrepreneurialism at pitching com-petitions while at the same time being undermined in this endeavor by the ways in which they are themselves considered risks.

8. This argument resonates with capacity-building projects around the globe and shows the ways that "neoliberal" modes of self-help and cultivation can be taken up from "below."

9. Aggarwal (2014) elaborates on the ways that parent-choice pol-icies are at odds with the very equalities that they seek to facilitate.

CHAPTER FIVE. SUBSTITUTING RACE

1. A handful of charter schools have unionized since the field-work for this project was conducted though none at no excuses–style schools, which are my focus, and none at schools where ConnectED sends teachers.

2. The CEO of the charter school network I taught for in Harlem from 2008 to 2010 would contrast the thinness of this document to the "1,000 page" UFT union contract as a symbol of unburdened

freedom for us as employees. According to them, the thin contract would not "get between us" as employer and employee.

3. As a *Mother Jones* article on Black teachers notes, the United States has been seeing the number of Black teachers fall drastically in public schools (Rizga 2016). The article explicitly connects this decline to accountability-focused education reform, citing education research: "Chris Emdin, an associate professor of education at Columbia University and the author of *For White Folks Who Teach in the Hood... and the Rest of Y'all Too*, told me that many Black educators leave because they are forced to become the kind of teachers they resented when they went to urban schools. 'They want to teach in urban spaces because they want to undo that damage that they've experienced,' Emdin, a former teacher, told me. 'They say, "I hated school. I want to teach math, English, science in an engaging way." And the minute you try to be more creative, the principal says, "Nope. You gotta do more test prep. You gotta follow the curriculum." At every turn they are being told that they can't do what they know in their spirit and heart and soul is the right thing to do. It's causing teachers to leave, students to fail, and it's making these schools factories of dysfunction'" (ibid.).

4. Sidney asked several times if I was interested in working as a guest teacher as part of my research. I declined, both to keep a certain professional distance and to avoid being entangled again in a school discipline system that I found very stressful when I was a classroom teacher at a New York City charter school from 2008 to 2010.

5. Dawdy's (2008) historical anthropology of French Colonial New Orleans challenges many of the preconceived notions of New Orleans's essential hybridity. I evoke this concept here not to suggest a smooth articulation between colonial-era New Orleans and the present day but to call attention to her analysis of the production of New Orleans as a Creole space in the face of local concerns and imperial interventions. Devore and Logsdon have thoroughly documented the persistence of outside intervention in the creation and historical transformation of New Orleans public schools (Devore and Logsdon 1991). This dynamic is critical to an examination of

conflicts over authenticity in New Orleans public schools. Dawdy develops a definition of the Creole and creolization that emphasizes the creation of new worlds and social systems out of the confluence of social types present in colonial encounters. The Creole is not the hybrid distillation of pure native and foreign influence but a "hybrid of hybrids" created out of the improvisational and unpredictable outcomes of colonial social experiments. If there is something unique about New Orleans cultural heritage, Dawdy singles out the material basis by which New Orleans became fertile ground for the kinds of experimentation that led to creolization.

EPILOGUE: WHAT DO YOU BELIEVE IN?

1. Both Audra Simpson and Carol McGranahan note how refusals are not necessarily the end or ends of politics but can be socially productive stances. McGranahan (2016) claims that refusals of received categories of political belonging can be generative and create new kinds of cultural and political community. Simpson (2016, 328) poses refusal as a "theory of the political" and argues that indigenous refusal to recognize the legitimacy of settler colonial states and disavow the foundational violence of dispossession is a claim to sovereignty, writing, "The people of Kahnawa':ke used every opportunity to remind non-Native people that this is not their land, that there are other political orders and possibilities."

2. Weeks (2011) outlines the stakes of this position: "The crucial point and the essential link to the refusal of work is that work—not private property, the market, the factory, or the alienation of our creative capacities—is understood to be the primary basis of capitalist relations, the glue that holds the system together. Hence, any meaningful transformation of capitalism requires substantial change in the organization and social value of work.... The refusal of work is not in fact a rejection of activity and creativity in general or of production in particular. It is not a renunciation of labor tout court, but rather a refusal of the ideology of work as highest calling and moral duty, a refusal of work as the necessary center of social life and means of access to the rights and claims of citizenship, and a refusal of the necessity of capitalist control of production."

REFERENCES

Adams, Vincanne. 2013. *Markets of Sorrow, Labors of Faith: New Orleans in the Wake of Katrina.* Duke University Press.

Aggarwal, Ujju. 2014. "The Politics of Choice and the Structuring of Citizenship Post–Brown v. Board of Education." *Transforming Anthropology* 22 (2): 92–104.

Agid, Shana, and Elizabeth Chin. 2019. "Making and Negotiating Value: Design and Collaboration with Community Led Groups." *CoDesign* 15 (1): 75–89.

Akama, Yoko. 2017. "'With Great Power Comes Great Responsibility' When We Co-create Futures." *Journal of Marketing Management* 33 (3–4): 272–279.

Akama, Yoko, Penny Hagen, and Desna Whaanga-Schollum. 2019. "Problematizing Replicable Design to Practice Respectful, Reciprocal, and Relational Co-designing with Indigenous People." *Design and Culture* 11 (1): 59–84.

Akama, Yoko, and Ann Light. 2012. "The Human Touch: Participatory Practice and the Role of Facilitation in Designing with Communities." *Proceedings of the 12th Participatory Design Conference: Research Papers.* Vol. 1. ACM.

Alim, H. Samy, John R. Rickford, and Arnetha F. Ball, eds. 2016. *Raciolinguistics: How Language Shapes Our Ideas about Race.* Oxford University Press.

Althusser, Louis. 1994. "Ideology and Ideological State Apparatuses." In *Mapping Ideology*, edited by Slavoj Žižek. Verso.

American Federation of Teachers (AFT). 2016. *Advancing Our Professionalism*. American Federation of Teachers. http://www.aft.org/resolution/advancing-our-professionalism.

Amrute, Sareeta. 2016. *Encoding Race, Encoding Class: Indian IT Workers in Berlin*. Duke University Press.

Anderson, Elizabeth. 2017. "Private Government." In *Private Government*. Princeton University Press.

Ansari, Ahmed. 2019. "Decolonizing Design through the Perspectives of Cosmological Others: Arguing for an Ontological Turn in Design Research and Practice." *XRDS: Crossroads, The ACM Magazine for Students* 26 (2): 16–19.

Apple, Michael. 1986. *Teachers and Texts: A Political Economy of Class and Gender Relations in Education*. Routledge.

Arena, John. 2011. "Black and White, Unite and Fight? Identity Politics and New Orleans's Post-Katrina Public Housing Movement." In *The Neoliberal Deluge: Hurricane Katrina, Late Capitalism, and the Remaking of New Orleans*, edited by Cedric Johnson, 152–186. University of Minnesota Press.

Arnesen, Eric. 1994. *Waterfront Workers of New Orleans: Race, Class, and Politics, 1863–1923*. University of Illinois Press.

Barrett, Nathan and Douglas Harris. 2015. *Significant Changes in the New Orleans Teacher Workforce*. Tulane University. http://educationresearchalliancenola.org/files/publications/ERA-Policy-Brief-Changes-in-the-New-Orleans-Teacher-Workforce.pdf.

Benjamin, Ruha. 2019. *Race after Technology: Abolitionist Tools for the New Jim Code*. Polity Press.

Bhabha, Homi. 1984. "Of Mimicry and Man: The Ambivalence of Colonial Discourse." *October* 28: 125–133.

Bill and Melinda Gates Foundation. 2012. *Primary Sources 2012: America's Teachers on the Teaching Profession*. Bill and Melinda Gates Foundation. http://www.scholastic.com/primarysources/pdfs/Gates2012_full.pdf.

Bonilla, Yarimar, and Marisol LeBrón. 2019. *Aftershocks of Disaster: Puerto Rico before and after the Storm*. Haymarket Books.

Bourdieu, Pierre, and Jean-Claude Passeron. 1990. *Reproduction in Education, Society and Culture.* Sage.

Bowles, Samuel, and Herbert Gintis. 2011. *Schooling in Capitalist America: Educational Reform and the Contradictions of Economic Life.* Haymarket Books.

Brown, Wendy. 2015. *Undoing the Demos: Neoliberalism's Stealth Revolution.* MIT Press.

Bucholtz, Mary. 2002. "Youth and Cultural Practice." *Annual Review of Anthropology* 31 (1): 525–552.

Buras, Kristen L. 2015. *Charter Schools, Race, and Urban Space: Where the Market Meets Grassroots Resistance. The Critical Educator.* Routledge.

Buras, Kristen L., Jim Randels, and Kalamu ya Salaam. 2010. *Pedagogy, Policy, and the Privatized City: Stories of Dispossession and Defiance from New Orleans.* Vol. 44. Teachers College Press.

Burawoy, Michael. 1979. *Manufacturing Consent: Changes in the Labor Process Under Monopoly Capitalism.* University of Chicago Press.

Butler, Judith, Ernesto Laclau, and Slavoj Žižek. 2000. *Contingency, Hegemony, Universality: Contemporary Dialogues on the Left.* Verso.

Carr, Sarah. 2013. *Hope against Hope: Three Schools, One City, and the Struggle to Educate America's Children.* Bloomsbury.

Chait, Jonathan. 2015. "How New Orleans Proved Urban-Education Reform Can Work." *New York Magazine,* August 24, 2015. https:// nymag.com/intelligencer/2015/08/how-new-orleans-proved-edu cation-reform-can-work.html.

Chin, Elizabeth. 2015. "The Laboratory of Speculative Ethnology: Suits of Inquiry." *Caribbean Rasanblaj* 12 (1).

Cohen, Cathy J. 2004. "Deviance as Resistance: A New Research Agenda for the Study of Black Politics." *Du Bois Review: Social Science Research on Race* 1 (1): 27–45.

Collins, Patricia Hill. 2000. *Black Feminist Thought: Knowledge, Consciousness, and the Politics of Empowerment.* Routledge.

Connolly, Nathan Daniel Beau. 2018. "A White Story." *Dissent,* January 22, 2018. https://www.dissentmagazine.org/blog/neoliberalism-forum -ndb-connolly.

———. 2019. *A World More Concrete: Real Estate and the Remaking of Jim Crow South Florida.* University of Chicago Press.

Costanza-Chock, Sasha. 2020. *Design Justice: Community-Led Practices to Build the Worlds We Need*. MIT Press.

Cox, Aimee Meredith. 2015. *Shapeshifters: Black Girls and the Choreography of Citizenship*. Duke University Press.

Dawdy, Shannon Lee. 2008. *Building the Devil's Empire: French Colonial New Orleans*. University of Chicago Press.

———. 2016. *Patina: A Profane Archaeology*. University of Chicago Press.

Dawson, Michael C. 2016. "Hidden in Plain Sight: A Note on Legitimation Crises and the Racial Order." *Critical Historical Studies* 3 (1): 143–161.

Devore, D. E., and J. Logsdon. 1991. *Crescent City Schools: Public Education in New Orleans, 1841–1991*. Center for Louisiana Studies, University of Southwestern Louisiana.

Democracy Now! 2007. "The Privatization of Education: How New Orleans Went from a Public School System to a Charter School City." August 30, 2007.

Dewey, John. 1923. *Democracy and Education: An Introduction to the Philosophy of Education*. Macmillan.

Dilnot, Clive. 1984. "The State of Design History, Part I: Mapping the Field." *Design Issues* 1 (1): 4–23.

Dixson, Adrienne. 2011. "Whose Choice? A Critical Race Perspective on Charter Schools." In *The Neoliberal Deluge Hurricane Katrina, Late Capitalism, and the Remaking of New Orleans*, edited by Cedric Johnson, 130–151. University of Minnesota Press.

Dixson, Adrienne D., Kristen L. Buras, and Elizabeth K. Jeffers. 2015. "The Color of Reform: Race, Education Reform, and Charter Schools in Post-Katrina New Orleans." *Qualitative Inquiry* 21 (3): 288–299.

Dominguez, Virginia R. 1986. *White by Definition: Social Classification in Creole Louisiana*. Rutgers University Press.

Duncan, Arne, Daniel Domenech, Anne Bryant, Dennis Van Roekel, Michael Casserly, Randi Weingarten, George Cohen, and Gene Wilhoit. 2013. "Transforming the Teaching Profession." U.S. Department of Education.

Escobar, Arturo. 2018. *Designs for the Pluriverse: Radical Interdependence, Autonomy, and the Making of Worlds*. Duke University Press.

Fairclough, Adam. (1995) 2008. *Race and Democracy: The Civil Rights Struggle in Louisiana, 1915–1972*. University of Georgia Press.

Fanon, Frantz. 1963. *The Wretched of the Earth*. Translated by Constance Farrington and with a preface by Jean-Paul Sartre. Grove Press.

Fassin, Didier. 2013. *Enforcing Order: An Ethnography of Urban Policing*. Polity.

Fields, Barbara Jeanne. 1990. "Slavery, Race and Ideology in the United States of America." *New Left Review* 181 (1): 95–118.

Fields, Karen E., and Barbara J. Fields. 2014. *Racecraft: The Soul of Inequality in American Life*. Edited by Barbara Jeanne Fields. Verso.

Flaherty, Jordan. 2010. *Floodlines: Community and Resistance from Katrina to the Jena Six*. Haymarket Books.

Foley, Douglas E. 1990. *Learning Capitalist Culture: Deep in the Heart of Tejas*. University of Pennsylvania Press.

Foucault, Michel. 2012. *Discipline and Punish: The Birth of the Prison*. Vintage.

Fraser, Nancy. 2016. "Expropriation and Exploitation in Racialized Capitalism: A Reply to Michael Dawson." *Critical Historical Studies* 3 (1): 163–178.

Freeman, Carla. 2000. *High Tech and High Heels in the Global Economy: Women, Work, and Pink-Collar Identities in the Caribbean*. Duke University Press.

———. 2014. *Entrepreneurial Selves: Neoliberal Respectability and the Making of a Caribbean Middle Class*. Duke University Press.

Gal, Susan. 2002. "A Semiotics of the Public/Private Distinction." *Differences: A Journal of Feminist Cultural Studies* 13 (1): 77–95.

Geismer, Lily. 2022. *Left Behind: The Democrats' Failed Attempt to Solve Inequality*. PublicAffairs.

Germany, Kent B. 2007. *New Orleans after the Promises: Poverty, Citizenship, and the Search for the Great Society*. University of Georgia Press.

Getachew, Adom. 2019. *Worldmaking after Empire: The Rise and Fall of Self-Determination*. Princeton University Press.

Gilens, Martin. 2000. *Why Americans Hate Welfare: Race, Media, and the Politics of Antipoverty Policy*. University of Chicago Press.

Giroux, Henry A. 2006. *Stormy Weather: Katrina and the Politics of Disposability*. Paradigm Publishers.

Givens, Jarvis R. 2021. *Fugitive Pedagogy: Carter G. Woodson and the Art of Black Teaching*. Harvard University Press.

Guggenheim, Davis, Billy Kimball, Lesley Chilcott, Bill Strickland, Geoffrey Canada, Michelle Rhee, Randi Weingarten, Christophe Beck, and John Legend. 2010. *Waiting for "Superman."* Paramount Home Entertainment.

Gunewardena, Nandinia, and Alexander De Waal. 2008. *Capitalizing on Catastrophe: Neoliberal Strategies in Disaster Reconstruction.* Rowman Altamira.

Hale, Charles R. 2005. "Neoliberal Multiculturalism: The Remaking of Cultural Rights and Racial Dominance in Central America." *PoLAR* 28: 10.

Hall, Stuart. 1986. "Gramsci's Relevance for the Study of Race and Ethnicity." *Journal of Communication Inquiry* 10 (2): 5–27.

Hancock, Ange-Marie. 2004. *The Politics of Disgust: The Public Identity of the Welfare Queen.* New York University Press.

Hargraves, Ian, and Nassim Jafarinaimi. 2012. "Questioning the Center of Human-Centered Design." *Zoontechnica: The Journal of Redirective Design* 2.

Harney, Stefano, and Fred Moten. 2013. *The Undercommons: Fugitive Planning and Black Study.* Minor Compositions.

Harris, Cheryl I. 1993. "Whiteness as Property." *Harvard Law Review*: 1707–1791.

Harris, Douglas. 2013. *The Post-Katrina New Orleans School Reforms: Implications for National School Reform and the Role of Government.* New Orleans Education Research Alliance.

———. 2020. *Charter School City: What the End of Traditional Public Schools Means for American Education.* University of Chicago Press.

Harris, Douglas, Andre Perry, Christian Buerger, and Vicki Mack. 2015. *The Transformation of New Orleans Public Schools: Addressing System-Level Problems without a System.* The Data Center. http://www .datacenterresearch.org/reports_analysis/school-transformation/.

Harris-Perry, Melissa V. 2011. *Sister Citizen: Shame, Stereotypes, and Black Women in America.* Yale University Press.

Hartigan, John. 2000. "Object Lessons in Whiteness." *Identities* 7 (3): 373.

Hartigan, John, Jr. 2005. *Odd Tribes: Toward a Cultural Analysis of White People.* Duke University Press.

Hartman, Saidiya. 1997. *Scenes of Subjection: Terror, Slavery, and Self-Making in Nineteenth Century America*. Oxford University Press.

Hirsch, Arnold R., and Joseph Logsdon. 1992. *Creole New Orleans: Race and Americanization*. Louisiana State University Press.

Ho, Karen Zouwen. 2009. *Liquidated: An Ethnography of Wall Street*. Duke University Press.

Hunter, Marcus Anthony, and Zandria F. Robinson. 2018. *Chocolate Cities*. University of California Press.

Irani, Lilly. 2019. *Chasing Innovation: Making Entrepreneurial Citizens in Modern India*. Princeton University Press.

Jackson, John L. 2005. *Real Black: Adventures in Racial Sincerity*. University of Chicago Press.

Jackson, Zakiyyah Iman. 2020. *Becoming Human: Matter and Meaning in an Antiblack World*. New York University Press.

Jaffe, Sarah. 2021. *Work Won't Love You Back: How Devotion to Our Jobs Keeps Us Exploited, Exhausted, and Alone*. Bold Type Books.

Jeffers, Elizabeth K., and Adrienne D. Dixson. 2023. "The Plantation 'All Charter' Model and the Long Durée of Resistance for Black Public High Schools in New Orleans." *Educational Evaluation and Policy Analysis*: 01623737231182751.

Jenkins, Destin. 2021. "The Bonds of Inequality." In *The Bonds of Inequality*. University of Chicago Press.

Johnson, Cedric, ed. 2011. *The Neoliberal Deluge: Hurricane Katrina, Late Capitalism, and the Remaking of New Orleans*. University of Minnesota Press.

Johnson, Gaye Theresa, and Alex Lubin. 2017. *Futures of Black Radicalism*. Verso.

Kahlenberg, Richard, and Halley Potter. 2014. "The Original Charter School Vision." *New York Times*, August 13, 2014.

Kelley, Robin D. G. 2002. *Freedom Dreams: The Black Radical Imagination*. Beacon Press.

Klein, Joel I., and Condoleezza Rice. 2014. *US Education Reform and National Security*. Vol. 68. Council on Foreign Relations.

Klein, Naomi. 2007. *The Shock Doctrine: The Rise of Disaster Capitalism*. Macmillan.

Ladson-Billings, Gloria. 2006. "Now They're Wet: Hurricane Katrina as Metaphor for Social and Educational Neglect." *Voices in Urban Education* 10.

———. 2014. "Culturally Relevant Pedagogy 2.0: Aka the Remix." *Harvard Educational Review* 84 (1): 74–84.

———. 2021. *Culturally Relevant Pedagogy: Asking a Different Question.* Teachers College Press.

Lassiter, Matthew D. 2007. *The Silent Majority.* Princeton University Press.

Lay, Celeste. 2022. *Public Schools, Private Governance: Education Reform and Democracy in New Orleans.* Temple University Press.

Lee, Spike. 2010. *If God Is Willing and da Creek Don't Rise.* 40 Acres and a Mule Filmworks.

Leidner, Robin. 1993. *Fast Food, Fast Talk: Service Work and the Routinization of Everyday Life.* University of California Press.

Lewis, Pierce. 2003. *New Orleans: The Making of an Urban Landscape.* Center for American Places.

Lipman, Pauline. 2011. *The New Political Economy of Urban Education: Neoliberalism, Race, and the Right to the City.* Critical Social Thought Series. Routledge.

Lipsitz, George. 1988. "Mardi Gras Indians: Carnival and Counter-narrative in Black New Orleans." *Cultural Critique* (10): 99–121.

———. 2006. *The Possessive Investment in Whiteness: How White People Profit from Identity Politics.* Temple University Press.

Louisiana Department of Education. 2016. *Student Enrollment & Demographics.* Louisiana Department of Education. https://www.louisianabelieves.com/docs/default-source/katrina/final-louisana-believes-v5-enrollment-demographics22f9e85b8c9b66d6b292ff0000215f92.pdf?sfvrsn=2.

Lowe, Lisa. 2015. *The Intimacies of Four Continents.* Duke University Press.

Macek, Steve. 2006. *Urban Nightmares: The Media, the Right, and the Moral Panic over the City.* University of Minnesota Press.

Maggi, Laura. 2005. "State to Run Orleans Schools: Local Board Loses Authority over 102." *New Orleans Times Picayune,* November 23, 2005.

http://www.nola.com/education/index.ssf/2005/11/state_to_run _orleans_schools_1.html.

Marable, Manning. 2015. *How Capitalism Underdeveloped Black America: Problems in Race, Political Economy, and Society.* Haymarket Books.

Marx, Karl. (1867) 1990. *Capital: A Critique of Political Economy.* Translated by Ben Fowkes and David Fernbach. With Ernest Mandel. Penguin Publishing Group.

McGranahan, Carole. 2016. "Theorizing Refusal: An Introduction." *Cultural Anthropology* 31 (3): 319–325.

McKittrick, Katherine. 2020. *Dear Science and Other Stories.* Duke University Press.

———. 2021. *Dear Science and Other Stories.* Duke University Press.

McQuarrie, Michael. 2013. "No Contest: Participatory Technologies and the Transformation of Urban Authority." *Public Culture* 25 (1(69)): 143–175.

Michna, Catherine. 2009. "Stories at the Center: Story Circles, Educational Organizing, and the Fate of Neighborhood Public Schools in New Orleans." In *In the Wake of Hurricane Katrina: New Paradigms and Social Visions.* Special issue, *American Quarterly* 61 (3): 529–555.

Mirowski, Philip, and Dieter Plehwe. 2015. *The Road from Mont Pèlerin: The Making of the Neoliberal Thought Collective,* with a new preface. Harvard University Press.

Miyazaki, Hirokazu. 2013. *Arbitraging Japan: Dreams of Capitalism at the End of Finance.* University of California Press.

Monahan, Torin. 2013. *Globalization, Technological Change, and Public Education.* Routledge.

Moten, Fred. 2017. *Black and Blur.* Vol. 1. Duke University Press.

———. 2020. "'Wildcat the Totality': Fred Moten and Stefano Harney Revisit the Undercommons in a Time of Pandemic and Rebellion." Part 1. Podcast interview by *Millennials Are Killing Capitalism.*

Murphy, Keith. 2015. *Swedish Design: An Ethnography.* Cornell University Press.

Myers, Joshua. 2021. *Cedric Robinson: The Time of the Black Radical Tradition.* John Wiley & Sons.

National Alliance for Public Charter Schools. 2012. *Details from the Dashboard: Charter School Race/Ethnicity Demographics.* https://publiccharters.org/news/details-from-the-dashboard-charter-school-race-ethnicity-demographics/.

New York Times. 2011. "Lessons from New Orleans," October 15, 2011.

The New Orleans Imperative. 2011. WBOK 1230 AM, June 27, 2011.

Noble, Safiya. 2018. *Algorithms of Oppression: How Search Engines Reinforce Racism.* New York University Press.

Noguera, Pedro A. 2016. "Race, Education, and the Pursuit of Equity in the Twenty-First Century." In *Race, Equity, and Education*, edited by Pedro Noguera, Jill Pierce, Roey Ahram, 3–23. Springer.

Omi, Michael, and Howard Winant. (1986) 2014. *Racial Formation in the United States*, 3rd ed. Routledge.

Palko, Mark, and Andrew Gelman. 2016. "How Schools That Obsess about Standardized Tests Ruin Them as Measures of Success." *Vox*, August 16, 2016.

Palmié, Stephan. 2007. "Genomics, Divination, Racecraft." *American Ethnologist* 34 (2): 205–222.

Payne, Charles M. 2008. *So Much Reform, So Little Change: The Persistence of Failure in Urban Schools.* Harvard Education Press.

Perry, Andre. 2011. *The Garden Path: The Miseducation of a City.* University of New Orleans Press.

———. 2017. "Building Educational 'Success' on the Backs of Fired Black Teachers." *The Hechinger Report*, May 31, 2017.

Perry, Marc D. 2015. "Who Dat? Race and Its Conspicuous Consumption in Post-Katrina New Orleans." *City & Society* 27 (1): 92–114.

———. 2021. "Black Freedom, Black Markets: Notes on New Orleans Black Masking Indian Tradition." *Journal for the Anthropology of North America* 24 (2): 108–116.

Peterson, Kristin. 2014. *Speculative Markets: Drug Circuits and Derivative Life in Nigeria.* Duke University Press.

Postone, Moishe. 1995. *Time, Labor, and Social Domination: A Reinterpretation of Marx's Critical Theory.* Cambridge University Press.

Povinelli, Elizabeth A. 2002. *The Cunning of Recognition: Indigenous Alterities and the Making of Australian Multiculturalism.* Duke University Press.

Ralph, Michael. 2009. "'It's Hard Out Here for a Pimp . . . with . . . a Whole Lot of Bitches Jumpin' Ship': Navigating Black Politics in the Wake of Katrina." *Public Culture* 21 (2): 341–374.

Ravitch, Diane. 2010. *The Death and Life of the Great American School System: How Testing and Choice Are Undermining Education.* Basic Books.

———. 2013. *Reign of Error: The Hoax of the Privatization Movement and the Danger to America's Public Schools.* Vintage.

Razzouk, Rim, and Valerie Shute. 2012. "What Is Design Thinking and Why Is It Important?" *Review of Educational Research* 82 (3): 330–348.

Reed, Adolph, and Stephen Steinberg. 2006. "Liberal Bad Faith in the Wake of Hurricane Katrina." *The Black Commentator* 182 (4): 1–6.

Reed, Adolph L. 1997. *W. E. B. Du Bois and American Political Thought: Fabianism and the Color Line.* Oxford University Press.

———. 1999. *Stirrings in the Jug: Black Politics in the Post-segregation Era.* University of Minnesota Press.

———. 2011. "Three Tremés." *Nonsite.org,* July 4, 2011.

———. 2014. "The Myth of Authenticity and its Impact on Politics—in New Orleans and Beyond." Keynote Address, New Orleans as Subject: Beyond Exceptionalism and Authenticity, Tulane University, September 16, 2014.

Rizga, Kristina. 2016. "Black Teachers Matter." *Mother Jones,* September/October, 2016. https://www.motherjones.com/politics/2016/09/black-teachers-public-schools-education-system-philadelphia/.

Roberts, Dorothy. 2011. *Fatal Invention: How Science, Politics, and Big Business Re-create Race in the Twenty-First Century.* New Press/ORIM.

Robinson, Cedric J. 2000. *Black Marxism: The Making of the Black Radical Tradition.* University of North Carolina Press.

———. 2007. *Forgeries of Memory and Meaning: Blacks and the Regimes of Race in American Theater and Film before World War II.* University of North Carolina Press.

Rosner, Daniela K. 2018. *Critical Fabulations: Reworking the Methods and Margins of Design.* MIT Press.

Sakakeeny, Matt. 2013. *Roll with It: Brass Bands in the Streets of New Orleans.* Duke University Press.

Salzinger, Leslie. 2003. *Genders in Production: Making Workers in Mexico's Global Factories*. University of California Press.

Saltman, Kenneth J. 2007. *Capitalizing on Disaster: Taking and Breaking Public Schools*. Paradigm Publishers.

Sanders, Elizabeth B-N., and Pieter Jan Stappers. 2008. "Co-creation and the New Landscapes of Design." *Co-design* 4 (1): 5–18.

———. 2014. "From Designing to Co-designing to Collective Dreaming: Three Slices in Time." *Interactions* 21 (6): 24–33.

Schüll, Natasha Dow. 2012. *Addiction by Design*. Princeton University Press.

Scott, David. 2004. *Conscripts of Modernity: The Tragedy of Colonial Enlightenment*. Duke University Press.

———. 2014. *Omens of Adversity: Tragedy, Time, Memory, Justice*. Duke University Press.

Shange, Savannah. 2019. *Progressive Dystopia: Abolition, Antiblackness, and Schooling in San Francisco*. Duke University Press.

Shapin, Steven, and Simon Schaffer. 2011. *Leviathan and the Air-Pump: Hobbes, Boyle, and the Experimental Life*. Princeton University Press.

Sharpe, Christina. 2016. *In the Wake: On Blackness and Being*. Duke University Press.

Simpson, Audra. 2016 "Consent's revenge." Cultural anthropology 31 (3): 326–333.

Sims, Christo. 2017. *Disruptive Fixation: School Reform and the Pitfalls of Techno-idealism*. Princeton Studies in Culture and Technology. Princeton University Press.

Slobodian, Quinn. 2018. *Globalists: The End of Empire and the Birth of Neoliberalism*. Harvard University Press.

Sondel, Beth. 2015. "Raising Citizens or Raising Test Scores? Teach for America, 'No Excuses' Charters, and the Development of the Neoliberal Citizen." *Theory & Research in Social Education* 43 (3): 289–313.

Spillers, Hortense J. 1987. "Mama's Baby, Papa's Maybe: An American Grammar Book." *Diacritics* 17 (2): 65–81.

Spring, Joel. 2018. *The American School: From the Puritans to the Trump Era*. Routledge.

Stern, Walter. 2018. *Race and Education in New Orleans: Creating the Segregated City, 1764–1960*. Louisiana State University Press.

Subramani, Shreya. 2022. "The Entrepreneurial Catch: Toward an Analytic of Racial Responsibilization." *Current Anthropology* 63 (4): 367–85.

Suchman, Lucy. 2007. *Human-Machine Reconfigurations: Plans and Situated Actions.* Cambridge University Press.

———. 2011. "Anthropological Relocations and the Limits of Design." *Annual Review of Anthropology* 40: 1–18.

Summers, Brandi Thompson. 2019. *Black in Place: The Spatial Aesthetics of Race in a Post-chocolate City.* University of North Carolina Press.

Sunder Rajan, Kaushik. 2006. *Biocapital: The Constitution of Postgenomic Life.* Duke University Press.

Taylor, Keeanga-Yamahtta. 2019. *Race for Profit: How Banks and the Real Estate Industry Undermined Black Homeownership.* University of North Carolina Press.

Summers, Brandi Thompson. 2021. *Black in Place: The Spatial Aesthetics of Race in a Post-Chocolate City.* The University of North Carolina Press.

Tokumitsu, Miya. 2015. *Do What You Love: And Other Lies about Success and Happiness.* Simon and Schuster.

Trouillot, Michel Rolph. 2003. "Anthropology and the Savage Slot: The Poetics and Politics of Otherness." In *Global Transformations.* Palgrave Macmillan.

United Teachers of New Orleans. 2007. *"No Experience Necessary: How the New Orleans School Takeover Experiment Devalues Experienced Teachers."*

Urciuoli, Bonnie. 2008. "Skills and Selves in the New Workplace." *American Ethnologist* 35 (2): 211–228.

Vaughn, Debra, Laura Mogg, Jill Zimmerman, and Tara O'Neill. 2012. *Transforming Public Education in New Orleans: The Recovery School District, 2003–2011.* Cowen Institute for Public Education Initiatives.

Von Schnitzler, Antina. 2016. *Democracy's Infrastructure: Techno-politics and Protest after Apartheid.* Princeton University Press.

Wacquant, Loïc. 2009. *Punishing the Poor: The Neoliberal Government of Social Insecurity.* Duke University Press.

Walcott, Rinaldo. 2021. *The Long Emancipation.* Duke University Press.

Wark, McKenzie. 2019. *Capital Is Dead.* Verso.

Weber, Max. 1958. *The Protestant Ethic and the Spirit of Capitalism.* Scribner.

Weeks, Kathie. 2011. *The Problem with Work.* De Gruyter.

Weheliye, Alexander. 2014. *Habeas Viscus: Racializing Assemblages, Biopolitics, and Black Feminist Theories of the Human.* Duke University Press.

West, Michael Rudolph. 2006. *The Education of Booker T. Washington: American Democracy and the Idea of Race Relations.* Columbia University Press.

Wilf, Eitan Y. 2019. *Creativity on Demand: The Dilemmas of Innovation in an Accelerated Age.* University of Chicago Press.

Williams, Lauren. 2019. "The Co-Constitutive Nature of Neoliberalism, Design, and Racism." *Design and Culture* 11 (3): 301–21.

Willis, Paul E. 1981. *Learning to Labour: How Working Class Kids Get Working Class Jobs.* Columbia University Press.

Woods, Clyde. 1998. *Development Arrested: The Cotton and Blues Empire of the Mississippi Delta.* Verso.

———. 2017. *Development Drowned and Reborn: The Blues and Bourbon Restorations in Post-Katrina New Orleans.* University of Georgia Press.

Wynter, Sylvia. 2003. "Unsettling the Coloniality of Being/Power/Truth/Freedom: Towards the Human, after Man, Its Overrepresentation—An Argument." *New Centennial Review* 3 (3): 257–338.

Yang, K. Wayne. 2010. "Rites to Reform: The Cultural Production of the Reformer in Urban Schools." *Anthropology & Education Quarterly* 41 (2): 144–160.

Zuboff, Shoshana. 2019. *Surveillance Capitalism and the Challenge of Collective Action.* Profile Books.

I N D E X

Founded in 1893,
UNIVERSITY OF CALIFORNIA PRESS
publishes bold, progressive books and journals
on topics in the arts, humanities, social sciences,
and natural sciences—with a focus on social
justice issues—that inspire thought and action
among readers worldwide.

The UC PRESS FOUNDATION
raises funds to uphold the press's vital role
as an independent, nonprofit publisher, and
receives philanthropic support from a wide
range of individuals and institutions—and from
committed readers like you. To learn more, visit
ucpress.edu/supportus.

9 780520 400948